Media Management Review

Media Management Review

Edited by
Charles Warner
University of Missouri–Columbia

LAWRENCE ERLBAUM ASSOCIATES, PUBLISHERS
1997 Mahwah, New Jersey   London

Lawrence Erlbaum Associates, Inc., Publishers
10 Industrial Avenue
Mahwah, NJ 07430

Cover design by Gail Silverman

Library of Congress Cataloging-in-Publication Data

ISBN: 0-8058-1787-5 (cloth: alk paper) — 0-8058-1788-
3 (paper: alk paper)

ISSN: 1090-0969

Books published by Lawrence Erlbaum Associates are printed
on acid-free paper, and their bindings are chosen for strength
and durability.

Printed in the United States of America
10 9 8 7 6 5 4 3 2 1

Media Management Review is dedicated to the hard-working professionals who make up the AEJMC Management and Economics Division and the BEA Management and Sales Division.

We hope that this publication becomes an important resource that expands our knowledge of the complexities of media management.

Contents

Preface

Media Management Review fills a void in the growing field of media management. More and more, colleges and universities are teaching media management courses, mostly in response to students' needs and requests.

In this florishing field, there were no refereed periodicals in which media management scholars could regularly get published and that provided information on the latest media management theories and practices. This volume was designed to solve these problems.

Media Management Review is designed for working professionals. Therefore, its style is not scholarly in tone. If the articles are based on research, the research is deemphasized and the results are written in an understandable and applicable style—applicability being the main focus of this volume. The *Harvard Business Review* served as our model not only for applicability, but also usefulness, readability, and being on the cutting edge of ideas.

We believe we have partially achieved our goal with this volume. There are chapters about television and newspapers, legal issues and mergers, and sexual harassment that any organization will find useful in policy making. There is a case study accompanied by comments from four experts in the field and a research brief that summarizes some interesting and relevant research.

The idea for this volume was born in a Broadcast Education Association (BEA) meeting of the management and sales division. Later that same year, I presented our concept at a meeting of the Association for Education in Journalism and Mass Communication (AEJMC) to the management and economics division, whose members enthusiastically endorsed the idea of *Media Management Review.*

I coordinated an effort to get nominations for editorial board members and editors from these two associations. Top nominees for the editorial board and editor were put on a ballot and sent to the same group as before. I was elected editor, and many of the most distinguished and respected scholars in the field were elected to serve on the editorial board—the list of board members could serve as a "Who's Who" of the top scholars in the field of media management in academia. One member of the board left her university to become a media manager, which emphasizes the board's strength and credibility.

I recruited several top scholars and media industry leaders to serve as advisors giving the publication overall guidance, purpose, and focus. A call-for-papers brochure was sent out to all BEA and AEJMC members and to the deans of business schools across the country. All submitted papers were reviewed by at least two members of the Editorial Board. Those selected for publication by the reviewers were included in *Media Management Review*, with the editor making the final decision.

Acknowledgments

The first bouquet thrown in any tribute to people who made *Media Management Review* happen must be tossed to the contributing authors. Many contributors made extensive changes in their articles, but none complained or argued. Most editors would die for such cooperative and intelligent authors.

I would like to thank my editorial board; without their help, this publication would not have gotten off the ground. Their reviews were finished on deadline, and all reviews were thorough, intelligent, and kept to a high standard for inclusion in the publication.

I would also like to thank Lawrence Erlbaum Associates for agreeing to publish *Media Management Review*; without their help, the review would not exist. Praise must also be handed out to our editor Kathleen M. O'Malley, who expertly guided us the through the complex formatting and production problems.

Finally, this publication is less mine than it is Tom Weir's, my assistant. For the last 3 months of editing, formatting, and organizing the publication, I was in the hospital. It was Tom who did all the work. Thanks, Tom.

Chapter 1

Case Study: The Helicopter Wars

Prepared by Charles Warner
University of Missouri

This unusual case study is included in this first chapter of the *Media Management Review* because it deals with a current issue in broadcast that has significant management implications. As in all good case studies, there is a lot more going on than is read in print. The case consists of a single newspaper story that appeared in *The Kansas City Star* on August 22, 1993, concerning the decision of a local television station to put up a news helicopter. The article is a fairly straightforward and objective report of events, both past and present. We invite you to probe more deeply into what is not specifically stated here. There are tremendous implications for the station and the market, as well as a good many details that led to the decision that deserve to be considered. At the end of the case, there are comments by some leading professionals concerning the wisdom of putting up the helicopter, but the opinion that really counts is yours. As you read, ask yourself: Was this a good management decision or not?

HELICOPTER WARS

"'Agreement' Can't Keep Copters Away From K.C."

—*THE KANSAS CITY STAR*, August 22, 1993, by Barry Garron

News wars on Kansas City TV are going sky high. When WDAF announced 10 days ago that it's going to cover news and traffic with a helicopter, it became a call to arms at competing stations.

Adding to the fire was a suggestion last week by the general manager of WDAF, supported by others, that news helicopters had been kept out of Kansas City by a tacit agreement among the TV stations not to engage in that form of competition. Lease expenses are estimated to be at least a quarter of a million dollars a year.

"There are those who have told me that there were back-room deals done in Kansas City that prevented this service from taking place," said Edward J. Piette, who has led WDAF since October 1991. "I believe that to be the truth."

The general managers of KCTV and KMBC deny such an agreement.

"I find that to be a little ludicrous," KMBC's Dino Dinovitz said of the alleged agreement. Dinovitz declined to disclose his plans for aerial news coverage, but representatives of two helicopter leasing firms said they were bargaining with the ABC station.

Independent station KSHB has no plans for a helicopter, said Mark Olinger, news director.

"I don't want one," Olinger said. "They're very expensive. I've lost two friends now in helicopter crashes. I think you can cover the news in Kansas City pretty darn well without one." KCTV, however, is meeting WDAF's challenge. The CBS affiliate began running promotional spots about its own helicopter last week despite not having signed a lease for one.

"We're not going to let anybody—whether it's WDAF or any other station—out-equip us," said John Rose, adding that the station will have its own helicopter by the end of the month.

Piette's contention that an agreement had existed is supported by employees of aviation companies, including the man who will fly WDAF's helicopter.

"The skinny on the street all the way from camera people at the TV stations to higher-ups was that, 'If you don't do one, I won't do one.' And 'I don't want the expense if you don't,'" said Johnny Rowlands, who operates Airborne Traffic Network. "There's no other reason for one not to be here."

Lee Sixta of Air Associates Inc. added: "We've been working on this for six years. Of course, the three TV stations, the word on the street was they all had a silent pact ... The word on the street was that none of them would get a helicopter and they kind of had a pact. That was always the word I had. I don't know whether it's the truth."

Piette comes from St. Louis, where the stations competed with helicopters because they recognized their value in news coverage.

"I was surprised and amazed that a helicopter service didn't exist from a journalistic standpoint when I arrived," said Piette, who managed KSDK immediately before coming here.

News directors say helicopters are necessary in cities such as Denver, which is surrounded by mountains, and Los Angeles, where the metropolitan area sprawls for large distances. They also agree that some stories, including brushfires, sinking ships, missing persons and the massive flooding this summer, are best covered from the air.

Including traffic, Piette said, there are enough such stories in Kansas City to justify the routine use of a helicopter in news coverage.

Don North, KCTV news director, also said the regular use of helicopters will improve TV news.

"A lot of what television does well is video," he said. "There is no question that we can get certain types of stories covered better from the air."

Others are skeptical. Dinovitz said leasing a helicopter is "ridiculous" because the cost does not justify the benefit. "I'm not saying it is a bad tool," he said. "It has its purpose when necessary but are we talking marketing or are we talking news coverage? I think, in WDAF's case, specifically, you're talking about marketing primarily."

In Milwaukee, a market similar in size to Kansas City, two television stations used helicopters in the early 1980s but stopped after a few years.

"They're good and they're useful and they're very expensive," said Jill Geisler, news director of WITI, the CBS affiliate in Milwaukee.

"When we had ours, it became a wonderful aerial camera platform and a very expensive taxi service."

"It was great fun while we had it, but we really couldn't justify it in the budget," she said.

The last time the station used the helicopter before the lease ended was to drop plastic Easter eggs over a camp for developmentally disabled adults.

"Somehow, it seemed like a fitting demise for the helicopter," Geisler said.

COMMENTS ON "HELICOPTER WARS" CASE FROM THE INDUSTRY

Neil E. Derrough, President and General Manager, KNSD, San Diego, California

It seems that the first question that needs to be answered regards the questions that should have been asked by the general manager.

Is the market big enough to support regular use of a helicopter?
Can the station afford it?
Can the station sustain it?
Does the strategy have full management support?
Market geography—is it vast?
Is the helicopter use a news or marketing strategy?
Is the strategy likely to substantially improve the news ratings?
If another station follows the WDAF strategy, is the advantage lost?

If the helicopter use is felt to be both a news and marketing strategy, the station could be locked into a long-term, expensive process. It is unlikely that adding regular helicopter use will dramatically increase the station's news ratings. However, if a news organization is positioned as a dominant news player in the market, a helicopter can solidify that position. If a station is hard charging, with a well-financed and aggressive news organization, a helicopter can help enhance that position.

After pointing out some of the advantages of regular helicopter use, I must advance a word of caution. Regular helicopter use is a costly venture. To be a competitive advantage, the helicopter use should be part of the station's regular news presentation. Ample promotion of the helicopter should be part of the station's promotion strategy. If this helicopter strategy is eliminated for any reason, there is the potential for viewer resentment.

Most news organizations use aerial coverage on a limited basis. When a story justifies it, most stations provide some kind of aerial coverage. This competitive advantage at this point is essentially nullified. However, if the regular helicopter user's have properly promoted their superiority in this area, ongoing helicopter use should be to their advantage.

Because helicopter use cannot be exclusive to a station, promotional devices can be employed to blunt the advantage that the regular user's desire. This technique has been used to discourage stations striving to create an advantage. There are cases where a helicopter strategy may be right for a station. However, in most cases, I do not feel the expense justifies regular helicopter use.

If WDAF-TV was in that group of stations that can correctly feel positive about the strategy after answering the questions I raise, then they did the right thing. However, my instincts tell me they were not in that group.

To summarize, if a station is to use a helicopter on a regular basis, it must be part of a well thought-out strategy that fits the station positioning. It must be supported by the senior levels of the station ownership. The market revenue must offer economic rewards for employing the strategy. The market geography should be vast enough to justify the helicopter as a necessary news tool.

It is the old story of newsrooms being "bottomless pits." Where do you stop adding on the expense? Any justification of the helicopter strategy that is not economically driven to get a return on the investment is not smart management. To add on the costs that a helicopter will produce, it must be done for the right reasons and should produce results that can be clearly substantiated.

John Kueneke, Senior Vice President,
Pucitzer Broadcasting, St. Louis, Missouri

Before moving back to St. Louis, I was general manager of KCRA in Sacramento—a station with a high profile in the use of helicopters. Because of the huge geographic area we covered (San Francisco to Lake Tahoe, Red Bluff to Fresno), a helicopter was a valuable tool in covering breaking news situations. We used the helicopter extensively for forest fires in the fall, flooding in the spring, and, of course, an occasional earthquake. The chopper was the highest profile news-gathering tool the station used, and our helicopter pilot at the time, Dan Shively, was one of the market's most recognizable on-air people. KCRA owned the helicopter and used it primarily for breaking news. However, although we owned the chopper, we still were never able to justify using it on a daily basis to cover morning traffic.

In St. Louis, all stations lease helicopters from Helicopters, Inc.; in return for a minimum quarterly commitment of air time, each station's helicopter is painted with their logo and channel number. Again, we use the chopper primarily for breaking news coverage. It was invaluable during the 1993 and 1994 floods. Not only did the chopper deliver the best pictures of the flooding, but at times it was the only way to bring back live pictures. Our pilot, Allen Barklage, and reporter Jean Jackson were able to capture live both a levee break and the subsequent loss of a farm house. Again, as in Sacramento, we are unable to justify the cost of flying the chopper for traffic coverage. However, we have arranged an innovative trade agreement with Metro Traffic for morning traffic service. Allen Barklage, flying our helicopter, services our station's needs as well as those of a number of radio stations.

KCRA's financial commitment to its helicopter was high, yet appropriate for the market. By realistically assessing the need for helicopter time, any major market station should be able to match their usage with a cost-effective lease to provide that necessary "big story" coverage. I was surprised no station in Kansas City had regularly used a chopper before WDAF.

Susan Eastman, University of Indiana

WDAF's general manager foolishly sacrificed the long-term budget to get a short-term ratings advantage—an advantage, moreover, that will probably be wiped out in a few days or weeks by the acquisition of helicopters by competitor KCTV and perhaps KMBC.

It is undoubtedly true that helicopters significantly improve news coverage in mountainous cities and huge, spread-out cities where getting around by car is nearly impossible because of enormous distances and impenetrable traffic. But Kansas City is flat and relatively small, and traffic usually moves smoothly. Helicopters also provide stupendous shots of natural disasters like mud slides and wildfires—events common to Los Angeles, but not Kansas City. However, Kansas City does have one potential situation for which helicopter shots would be ideal: floods along the Mississippi River and its tributaries. Yet, an annual cost upward of $250,000 is hardly justified by such an infrequent need.

In an era of handy car phones, distance and traffic jams no longer imperil "getting the story in" by deadline, and microwave trucks can beam TV pictures from nearly anyplace. Helicopters uniquely provide panoramic pictures that may be beautiful, but are rarely essential to high-quality news coverage. Perhaps WDAF should look into a blimp!

Barry L. Sherman, College of Journalism and Mass
Communication, University of Georgia, Athens

It seems to me that WDAF's decision to lease a helicopter is justified on both
journalistic and competitive grounds. On the journalistic side, events of
recent years have changed the "flyover" mentality common to TV
news—the perception that the only events worthy of coverage emanate
from New York, Los Angeles, and a handful of other major markets. From
the flooding of the Mississippi to the terrorist bombing in Oklahoma City,
significant events in broadcast journalism are as likely to happen in smaller
markets like Kansas City as in the traditional "hard news" markets of the
industrialized east and far west. Having a helicopter on hand enhances a
local station's ability to gather and report news, and to make that news
available to its network and other national and international news outlets,
including CNN.

Mr. Piette's decision to lease a chopper is more than defensible on competitive grounds. As Vernon Stone's research for the Radio-Television News
Directors Association (RTNDA) has consistently pointed out, local news is
the most important profit center to many television stations, especially
network affiliates. In the current climate of ownership changes and "affiliate
roulette," enhancing the local news product is critical to sustaining viewership and to promoting station awareness and identity. Today's viewers have
an increasing number of options for news—from regional cable news to
online computer services. As the first (or sole) operator of a helicopter,
WDAF can gain an important competitive edge in its marketplace.

Moreover, to consider Kansas City (ranked 28th) as a "small market"
defies contemporary demographic and marketing trends. Advertisers now
spend more than $100 million annually on television advertising in this
area. The market has moved up one Area of Dominant Influence (ADI)
position in recent years—an indicator of market growth and potential.
Moreover, the character of the city makes it especially attractive to advertisers, with the proportion of lower income households far below those of
many markets above it in ADI rank. Should the helicopter add one or two
points to the station's ratings, additional advertising revenues should more
than offset the operational costs of the venture.

Finally, the "gentleman's agreement" between the three affiliates not to
lease a chopper smacks of the kind of collusive and anticompetitive behavior that marked the television business in an earlier age. Television stations
are no longer a "license to print money," and the price-fixing and other
backdoor deals designed to protect the "cash cow" have outlived their
usefulness. In addition, such schema are ethically questionable and morally
indefensible among organizations purportedly committed to freedom of
expression and to exposing malfeasance in local business and government.

In the final analysis, WDAF's strategy must pass two tests: one internal
and one external. Inside the station, the considerable cost of leasing, main-

taining, and staffing the helicopter must undergo a valid cost–benefit analysis. Do the additional ratings and revenue gains offset (and help amortize) the substantial cost of the service? This is a question the general manager must weigh with the controller. Externally, does the public perceive the chopper to be an important additional source of news, weather, and traffic information, or, like a space-age set and three-dimensional weather graphics, is it little more than additional window dressing on the news? Addressing this question requires a serious study of the next few ratings books, and perhaps a series of interview and focus groups among viewers in the region.

Chapter 2

Response of Newspaper Circulation to Local Economic Changes

F. Dennis Hale
Bowling Green State University

This chapter reviews a study that examined how newspaper circulation responds to changes in the local economy. For example, what happens to circulation when family incomes in a community increase or when the number of poor persons grows? Circulation was measured as household penetration, or the percentage of occupied households in a county that receive the local daily newspaper. Household penetration is critical to a newspaper's success. It influences the total circulation that generates 25% of a paper's revenue, and it determines a newspaper's market dominance, attractiveness to advertisers, ad rates, and ad revenue.

The study analyzed 187 multicounty markets in 40 states in which a newspaper dominated its home county. In every market, the home county and one neighboring county were analyzed. The four measures of newspaper penetration were: (a) presence of the weekday edition in the home county, (b) presence of weekday edition in neighboring county, (c) presence of the Sunday edition in the home county, and (d) presence of Sunday edition in neighboring county. (Eighty percent of the dailies had a Sunday edition.) The four penetration measures were obtained for the U.S. Census years of 1980 and 1990.

The four newspaper penetration measures were compared with 32 economic, social, and media variables in the 187 pairs of home and neighboring counties for 1980 and 1990. The 32 variables included the following:

- Most central to the study were five economic measures of: household income, families below the poverty level, home value, rent, and unemployment.
- Nine sociological variables were: population density, population, households, Caucasians, persons native to state, age, home ownership, high school educated, and college educated.
- Newspaper variables other than penetration were: chain ownership, Sunday edition, morning edition, total daily circulation, total Sunday circulation, subscription cost, advertising rate, and wire services.

- Ten media competition variables were: cable penetration, basic cable charge, radio stations, television stations, and county penetration of six national magazines.

Statistical analysis determined whether newspaper penetration was related to the five local economic measures and to sociological and mass media variables. The analysis compared the percentage change in newspaper penetration from 1980 to 1990 with the percentage change in other variables.

FINDINGS

Changes in the 187 markets between 1980–1990 mirrored national trends. Chain ownership of dailies grew, as did morning and Sunday publications. Weekday circulation dropped while Sunday circulation expanded. Magazine circulation slumped even more than weekday newspaper circulation. Cable penetration and the number of television and radio stations all grew.

One purpose of the study was to examine the impact on newspapers of Reagan/Bush economics of the 1980s and the financial losses of the middle class. Columnist Kevin Phillips reported that during 1977–1990, incomes in the top 1% of families increased 45%, whereas incomes in the top 10% increased 20%. Family incomes in the ninth and eighth deciles increased only 6% and 3%, respectively, whereas families in the seventh decile enjoyed a 0% growth; families in the first through sixth deciles saw incomes drop from 3% to 11%.

How were such economic changes related to newspaper penetration? Two types of economic measures in this study—media characteristics and community demographics—provided some clues. Circulation penetration was unrelated to media economic variables such as newspaper ad rates, newspaper subscription prices, and local cable charges. But penetration was also unrelated to community economic variables. When the four penetration measures were contrasted with the five community economic variables, only 1 of 20 comparisons was significant. Rent charges were negatively associated with local weekday penetration. Thus, when rent charges increased rapidly, per-capita purchases of weekday editions of newspapers decreased in the home county.

Newspaper penetration was unrelated to the other economic variables of family income, home value, unemployment, and poverty level. These are important indicators of local economic health. If a factory moves out of a community, poverty levels and unemployment increase and household income and home values fall. In addition, the community's retail base deteriorates, cutting into a newspaper's major revenue source of advertising. But, according to these findings, a local economic slump does not harm circulation and the circulation side of revenue.

Social demographics were more successful than economic variables in predicting circulation. First, population density and population growth were negatively related to weekday penetration in the home county. Second, even stronger negative associations existed between newspaper penetration and households; associations were significant for all four measures of circulation penetration. Thus, rapid growth in population and households caused circulation penetration to stagnate.

Age and homeownership were also positively associated with local weekday penetration. As persons grow older, or become attached to a community through homeownership, they are more likely to subscribe to a local paper. A surprising finding was the positive association between home-county weekday penetration and cable penetration. Thus, increases in cable subscribing were positively related to increases in newspaper penetration. People apparently were not canceling their newspaper subscriptions to pay for cable.

Because both newspaper and magazine penetration fell during the 1980s, it was expected that the two would be related. However, only 1 of 24 associations among the four newspaper penetration variables and the six magazine circulation measures was significant. Local weekday penetration of newspapers was related to penetration of *Better Homes and Gardens*. The positive relationship indicates that the two were similarly responding to community conditions. Whatever was suppressing newspaper penetration during the decade was also suppressing *Better Homes and Gardens*. But this was not true for *People, Time, Cosmopolitan, National Geographic*, or *Sports Illustrated*.

CONCLUSIONS

This study examined changes in newspaper penetration by analyzing the economic and social characteristics of communities and mass media variables. Thirty-two economic, social, and media variables were used to evaluate weekday and Sunday penetration of papers in their home and neighboring counties. Of a possible 128 relationships, 24 were statistically significant.

Findings underscored the contrast between weekday and Sunday editions of newspapers. The 1980s was unhealthy for weekday penetration; it dropped by 9% in home counties and by 4% in neighboring counties. However, Sunday penetration remained stable, dropping by only 1% in home counties and actually increasing by 2% in neighboring counties.

Sunday and weekday penetration differed in other ways. Sunday exceeded weekday penetration in home and neighboring counties in both 1980 and 1990. But the gap between the two widened over the decade—from 6% and 1% of households to 14% and 7%, respectively. Publishers who are attempting to strengthen weekday circulation need to transfer what is successful for their Sunday paper to their weekday edition. This could succeed if what is appealing about the Sunday paper is not tied exclusively to the extra time available for reading on Sunday.

Variables in this study were unsuccessful in explaining Sunday circulation. Only 3 of the 32 variables were related to Sunday circulation. Growth in households was negatively related to Sunday circulation in both home and neighboring counties; a rapid increase in households depressed Sunday penetration throughout the circulation area.

Change in households was the only variable that was negatively related to all four measures of newspaper penetration. Change in households was responsible for one fourth of the significant relationships with newspaper penetration in the neighboring counties. Altogether, there were only 8 significant relationships among the various variables and Sunday and weekday penetration in neighboring counties. This contrasted with 16 relationships with Sunday and weekday penetration in the home counties.

Thus, circulation in neighboring counties is more fickle and less predictable. This creates a problem for newspaper executives because neighboring circulation is a substantial contributor to total circulation. The neighboring counties in this study averaged 39,000 people, compared with 156,000 in the home counties. Newspaper penetration in neighboring counties in 1990 averaged a hefty 48% on Sunday and 42% on weekdays. But variables other than the ones in this study were related to this circulation in the neighboring counties.

Not surprisingly, total weekday circulation of newspapers was positively related to home and neighboring penetration of the Sunday paper and home penetration of the weekday paper. Household penetration tends to increase with total circulation of papers. Most newspaper characteristics were unrelated to penetration. Subscription and ad rates, chain ownership, and wire services simply did not explain newspaper penetration. If newspaper characteristics make a difference, they involve idiosyncratic factors that were not measured here. These could include color photographs, news hole size, comic selection, aggressiveness in news coverage, circulation sales strategies, or community involvement.

The study was most successful in explaining home weekday penetration—where there were 13 significant associations. Home weekday penetration was negatively associated with households, population density, college educated, and population, and it was positively related to age, homeownership, and Caucasians. These findings indicate the difficulty of maintaining local weekday penetration in the 1990s in a community experiencing rapid growth. In such an environment the variables that were negatively associated with penetration (i.e., density, population, households, and college educated) may be increasing in strength, and the variables that were positively associated with penetration (i.e., age, homeownership, and Caucasians) may be diminishing. That clearly presents a challenge for newspapers because such fixed conditions cannot be manipulated by publishers.

The heart of this study was the economic variables. Local economic conditions were unrelated to newspaper penetration. The economic losses of the poor and middle class in the 1980s, which were documented by columnist Kevin Phillips, were unrelated to changes in newspaper circulation in this study. Newspaper circulation may be independent of the local economy because daily newspapers already have become a class medium that primarily serves groups in higher social and economic strata. Changes in income, unemployment, and poverty largely affect lower economic groups that are weak users of newspapers or nonsubscribers. As newspapers become more of a class than a mass medium, they may have difficulty identifying with the news needs of lower economic groups.

Chapter 3

Assessing the Potential of a Full-Featured Electronic Newspaper for the Young Adult Market

Glen T. Cameron
Barry A. Hollander
Glen J. Nowak
Scott A. Shamp
University of Georgia, Athens

Many academic and industry thinkers believe young adults, particularly those with a college education, are an appealing and potentially profitable market for electronic newspapers. To assess this belief, 84 college students were asked a battery of questions about their computer and media use. A few days later, these subjects used a full-featured electronic newspaper in two separate sessions. Use of the electronic newspaper grounded student opinions in actual experience. Afterward, the media-use questions were re-administered to the subjects, along with a detailed assessment of the electronic newspaper. Results suggest that the electronic newspaper was generally well received, particularly by accomplished computer users. The electronic newspaper was generally viewed as fun, easy, and satisfying to use. Graphics, backchaining to previous issues of the paper, the latest news and weather, and access to the Internet were especially appreciated. Despite of liking the electronic newspaper, students were not particularly inclined to subscribe to an electronic newspaper. The findings shed light on the development of electronic newspaper business models.

INTRODUCTION

Having died in the 1980s in the videotex version, electronic newspapers have regenerated. In 1994, 75 newspapers were online (60 with commercial services and 15 located on the World Wide Web), with more announcing service every month. As reflected in the trade press, optimism runs high (Glaberson, 1993, 1994a, 1994b; Haddad, 1993a, 1993b, 1993c, 1993d; Lail, 1994; Markoff, 1993a, 1993b, 1993c, 1993d, 1993e; & McNaughton, 1993a, 1993b, 1993c). However, videotex, which was based on supply-driven marketing, was greeted with similar enthusiasm. Videotex offerings arose not from the desire to satisfy a consumer need, but as a new combination of existing technologies for which consumer needs would have to be manufactured (Curien & Gensollen, 1987; Hester, 1982; Schneider, Charon, Miles, Thomas, & Vedel, 1991). The need never materialized for videotex.

Unlike the videotext market of the 1980s, a significant portion of the U.S. population has the necessary hardware to go online, with modems rapidly becoming standard equipment in home computers. In 1994, 33% of American households owned computers, with 13% having modems (Resnick, 1994b). A recent Times-Mirror study estimated that about two thirds of the 18 million households equipped with modems were subscribing to online services (Coates, 1995). By 1996, Cameron and Curtin (1995) estimated the welter of unique, multimedia features and specialized content characteristics available online will be retrievable in about one third of America's homes.

Despite the rapid, and apparently ready, acceptance of online offerings, Cameron and Curtin (1995) offered a guarded outlook regarding the new manifestation of electronic news. Because determining and stimulating demand for futuristic products is generally more difficult than acquiring the ability to produce them, they suggested that newspapers need to take a more strategic approach toward electronic news services. Ultimately, the ability to deliver a product is not what determines viability; rather, success is most contingent on consumer interest and actual demand. Presumably, electronic newspaper development today is driven by projected consumer demand, rather than the "panoply of new technologies" (Cameron & Curtin, 1995), but many newspapers appear to be primarily guided by what is technologically possible.

The current chapter attempts to help newspapers avoid the supply-driven marketing mind set: "Consumers should want this nifty new technology because we can provide it." The current study obviates this thinking by assessing the reactions of a market that might be drawn to electronic newspapers of its own accord—the young adult. The chapter also attempts to learn which particular features, if any, of electronic newspapers are appealing to this target market. To do so, this study attempted to avoid the validity problems inherent in surveys of individuals who have limited or no actual experience with a new technology. To ensure that assessments were based on actual experience, study participants used an electronic newspaper called the Protopaper before providing their reactions and evaluations.

ELECTRONIC NEWSPAPERS AND YOUNG ADULTS

Previous research provides at least one strategic direction in looking for promising markets. Unlike videotex, the electronic newspapers of the 1990s provide content and multimedia features that are widely perceived as appealing to young adults (Brooks & Kropp, 1994; Catlett & Brooks, 1994; Cobb-Walgren, 1990; Frieske, 1995; Haddad, 1993c; Hammer & Kennedy, 1993; Thompson, 1993). Electronic newspapers are nonlinear and increasingly multimedia environments that are often most attractive and familiar to young adults. In fact, it is predicted that younger users represent the predominant "e-paper market" (Online, 1994–1995). The "youthanizing of the Net" may be exaggerated; however, research does suggest that younger users prefer computer-driven information delivery (Catlett & Brooks, 1994; Thompson, 1993) and have an affinity for electronic newspapers they do not have for print counterparts (Brooks & Kropp, 1994; Hammer & Kennedy, 1993).

Potentially appealing elements include multimedia delivery of stories and the ability to navigate to previous stories, raw data, and even reporters' notes. Online papers are also sociable, offering young adults electronic places to learn about consumer products and to chat with fellow readers. Other chat areas enable discussion of the news and interaction with reporters and editors about stories or story ideas. In addition, users can jump from the electronic newspaper to the remainder of the network world, including, on some systems, the popular World Wide Web (WWW). Compared with delivery of the print paper, an electronic newspaper is always available to the typically peripatetic young adult, remaining only a computer log-in away. In addition, some analysts project that electronic versions of newspapers will remain subscription-free (Lainson, 1995)—a price point appealing to all consumers, but particularly important to the college-age and younger adult market.

ELECTRONIC NEWSPAPER BUSINESS MODELS

A review of the literature on newspaper readership and discussions with industry experts suggests there are four business models being used to justify investments in electronic newspapers. The current study, although an initial, exploratory examination, provides an opportunity to evaluate their utility for assessing the feasibility of marketing electronic newspapers to young adults.

New Subscriber Model

Given newspapers' drop in market penetration in both the general and young adult markets, many believe that electronic newspapers represent a viable medium for attracting younger readers. According to this model, newspapers should invest in electronic delivery methods to attract a new set of subscribers (i.e., ongoing, electronic subscribers; Bogart, 1989; Fink, 1996; "Virtual Reality," 1994). Such subscribers do not supplant current print subscriptions because this model assumes that young adults are not currently subscribing or intending to subscribe. In this model, an electronic newspaper takes its place in the newspaper stable as a distinct publication with its own readership base. As such, it becomes, with advertising, a self-supporting profit center.

Maturation Model

Another widely used model characterizes electronic newspapers as a way to establish the news-reading habits that provide the basis for later print newspaper reading/subscription. Similar to school-based "newspaper in education" programs, the belief is that if one can get younger people to read (and develop a dependency on) newspapers, they will be more likely to subscribe later on. Thus, the maturation model is based on the premise that newspapers must establish some kind of relationship with young readers until maturity and life responsibilities (e.g., financial, shopping, childrearing demands) compel them to subscribe to a print paper (Bogart, 1989; Fink, 1996). In this model, electronic newspapers are a foot-in-the-door marketing device for printed papers, and may even be a loss leader. Electronic offerings could be marginally unprofitable, yet, because of their net long-term benefit to the newspaper enterprise, represent a justifiable investment.

Multiple Subscriber Model

Research on multiple subscribers (Bogart, 1989; Stephens, 1975; Stamm & Fortini-Campbell, 1981; Wanta, Hu, & Wu, 1995) prompts a third scenario. Under this model, electronic newspapers are positioned as a unique source of news and advertising. As Wanta et al. (1995) found, individuals subscribe to multiple papers or information sources when the additional providers offer something beyond "the typical *news of the day* stories in newspapers" (p. 113). This unique content is usually some form of additional advertising content, but could also include the unique forms and features of editorial content found in electronic newspapers. Advertising examples would be searchable classified ads and regional advertising not available in the local print paper, such as state-wide employment opportunities or display advertising for businesses in major cities near the reader's hometown. Content examples might be news about more than one community of importance to a reader (e.g., a salesperson with a multicity territory) and specialized sports or business coverage.

Economic Efficiency Model

The fourth widely held view justifies electronic newspapers in terms of the economic efficiencies associated with electronic delivery. On the cost side, the efficiencies result from capitalizing on sunk investments in newsroom and production talent. For example, electronic newspapers provide an additional use for the news and information already gathered and produced in the creation of the printed paper. To the extent that electronic newspapers utilize existing newsroom resources for printed newspapers, they have relatively low news-gathering and newsroom costs (Brill & Cook, 1995). Efficiencies also arise on the production side, in that electronic newspapers' manufacturing and distribution costs are lower than those for printed papers (e.g., no paper, ink, or delivery expenses). In addition to cost efficiencies, this model recognizes that electronic newspapers often achieve efficiencies for advertisers as well. For instance, electronic media, typically improve message targeting and customization. With electronic delivery, advertisers can use subscriber profiles to send customized messages to narrowly defined audiences. The profiles can be derived from information volunteered by the user during online registration, as well as from automatic tracking of online activity indicating user interests. Electronic delivery also enables newspapers to do transactional, or direct response, advertising (i.e., advertising that includes the option of ordering items on the spot). This capability provides newspapers with an effective and efficient mechanism to attract advertising dollars that would otherwise be diverted to direct mail and telemarketing providers (Cameron, Nowak, & Krugman, 1993).

In summary, how electronic newspapers are received and what roles they may play in addressing declining daily newspaper market penetration merits study. Some of their characteristics are likely to be more appealing and useful than others, and certain elements may coalesce with content features to win a place in the market (Urban, 1985). An examination of how young adults respond to electronic newspapers can also help newspapers assess the value of the four widely applied business models when it comes to evaluating and marketing electronic ventures.

RESEARCH QUESTIONS

In light of the need for newspapers to increase readership among young adults, this study systematically addressed the following questions: (a) Overall, what do young adults want and need in an electronic newspaper? (b) What do young adults like about a full-featured electronic newspaper after they use one? (c) What are the prospects that young adult users will become regular users or subscribers to electronic newspapers? and (d) Which, if any, of the four business models is most appropriate for the development and marketing of electronic newspapers to young adults?

METHOD

To assess the potential of electronic newspapers in the marketplace, an electronic newspaper called the Protopaper was created. Located on the WWW, the Protopaper included many of the elements associated with commercial electronic newspapers. Specifically, the Protopaper included editorial copy, photos, and graphics from three publications: the student newspaper at a southeastern university, an arts and entertainment paper in the community, and the daily newspaper for the community. Audio news stories were included from three local radio stations.

To test the promise of the young adult market for such an electronic newspaper, student volunteers from an introduction to mass communication course were recruited for the study. Extra credit was offered as an incentive. These students represent members of one of the primary electronic newspaper target markets. Students completed a preliminary questionnaire 1 week before they used the electronic newspaper, which asked about their computer use, comfort with computers, media use, and demographics. Students then participated in two sessions, spaced 1 week apart. After receiving brief instructions about logging on to the computer, students were free to use the electronic newspaper as they saw fit. Sessions lasted about 1 hour, with some subjects using the electronic newspaper for nearly all of the allotted 2 hours. After the two sessions, students were then asked another set of questions about their attitudes about the Protopaper and electronic newspapers in general.

RESULTS

Participants

Eighty-four students participated in the study. The average age of participants was 20 years. Twenty-one percent of the participants were male. The participants were generally advanced users of new communication technologies. Nearly all subscribed to cable TV (91%), with about half (46%) also having premium channels. Ninety percent owned VCRs and 75% owned a personal computer, with 70% of those being IBM compatibles and 20% being Apple machines. About half of the participants (44%) owned modems and one third (33%) owned a CD-ROM for the computer. One in five of the subjects (21%) subscribed to Prodigy, 15% subscribed to America Online, and 14% subscribed to Compuserve. Participants mainly used their computer for school or work-related activities, generally 1–2 hours per day, and for word processing in particular. Relatively little time was spent using computers as an entertainment device, a link to online services, a home budgeting tool, a communication tool, or for electronic mail.

Media and Computer Use of Participants

In general, our subjects viewed computers as essential, useful, enjoyable, and pleasantly challenging. At the same time, student subjects did not perceive themselves as expert computer users. There was greater variance with respect to newspaper use. Nearly half (44%) of the subjects said they did not have time for a daily newspaper and tended to read only selectively in the newspaper. When asked, students did not report that they typically got news from other media. Apparently, the student subjects were simply not heavy news consumers. However, they did spend a great deal of time watching television—from local and national network news to such programs as *Hard Copy*. Newspaper reading was light (about 15 minutes or less daily). When asked to rank sources of news and information, national network news was first, followed by the college daily paper and talking with family and friends.

Assessment of the Protopaper

Students generally found the Protopaper easy, fun, and somewhat satisfying to use. Students favorably rated many of the touted features of electronic newspapers, including graphics, immediacy of news and weather, navigation to the Internet, and ability to access previous articles (i.e., story morgues). Ratings for audio clips in the Protopaper were not particularly high, but many students expressed strong interest for the addition of video clips as part of the electronic newspaper. Moderately favorable ratings were given to personalized papers and story abstracts serving as pointers to complete stories. There was relatively low interest in story pagination. Despite the positive overall rating of the Protopaper, and of specific features comprising the essence of the Protopaper, a print paper was rated marginally higher than the Protopaper.

Few students actually gave neutral ratings. Rather, statistical analysis suggests that using an electronic newspaper generated fairly strong opinions about this new technology. For example, virtually half the subjects (49%) expressed some inclination to subscribe to an electronic newspaper, whereas nearly half (41%) expressed the opposite inclination. Only 10% were ambivalent. The item with the greatest unanimity dealt with the disinclination to pay more for an electronic newspaper than for a print subscription.

Factors Related to Student Assessment
of the Protopaper Experience

A separate analysis was used to reduce the number of survey items in a way that captures the major dimensions of students use experiences. This analysis suggested three factors that could be used to assess the potential market for electronic newspapers: (a) satisfaction with the electronic newspaper, (b) likelihood to use or subscribe to such a service, and (c) appeal of the navigational aspects of the medium. A similar technique was used to identify the most likely predictors of satisfaction with and likelihood to subscribe to the Protopaper: computer use/expertise, interest in local news, interest in entertainment news, interest in general news, time spent online, time working with computers, newspaper reliance, diversity of newspapers used, and reasons for reading or watching the mainstream press.

Analysis found two factors that significantly predicted satisfaction with the electronic newspaper. Computer use/expertise was positively associated with satisfaction, meaning that those most comfortable with computers were most satisfied with the Protopaper. A negative relationship was seen between the diversity of newspapers read and satisfaction, with participants who reported reading multiple newspapers less likely to be satisfied with the electronic medium.

Four factors appeared to play a role in the likelihood to use or subscribe to such a service: computer use/expertise, interest in local news, time spent working with computers, and the importance of entertainment information. Computer expertise and the importance of entertainment information were positively associated with likelihood to subscribe to an electronic newspaper, whereas interest in local news and time spent with computers were negatively associated with subscribing. Interest in local news was the only variable associated with the appeal of the navigational aspects of the electronic newspaper, with that relationship being negative.

Global Evaluations and General Comments

A review of student responses to the seven open-ended questions revealed that nearly all participants offered comments regarding the Protopaper and its features. In general, there were more positive than negative comments. For the most part, students indicated that the electronic paper was easy and relatively fun to use. Interestingly, audio stories received many favorable mentions, despite being given relatively low ratings in the features section. This suggests the real appeal and impact of multimedia depends on its actual execution or content. Relatedly, many students praised the ability to access more topic or subject information—either as a result of the electronic paper's topic search capabilities or the ability to access Internet and WWW resources. Students liked to get "quick story histories." Finally, several participants said they liked it that their "hands stayed clean." Conversely, the primary drawbacks of the Protopaper appeared to be related to structure and speed. Many students noted that they often felt "lost" while using the Protopaper. That is, they were unsure about all that they could do, or where they were, in the online world. Many students also expressed frustration with how long the Protopaper server took to load information to the screen.

DISCUSSION

This study was based on an intentional recruitment of participants from the young adult market—a group that has posed considerable marketing challenges for print newspapers. As is true for all empirical investigations, care should be exercised both in drawing conclusions and generalizing beyond the study. For example, this study involved media from a relatively small market, used students from one university, and involved only two extended electronic newspaper use sessions. Nevertheless, the subjects served the purpose of the study: to assess the role that electronic newspapers might play in delivering news and advertising to young adults who generally possess stronger television, multimedia, and computer habits than newspaper-reading habits.

In line with previous research, our study found participants' television habits were more entrenched than their news-reading habits, with television serving mainly for entertainment, but also ranking favorably as a news source. Computer use and ownership were widespread, with advanced applications like online services being used, although not for extensive amounts of time. The subjects were comfortable with computers and new technologies. They were open to new challenges, like e-clipping, that accompany adoption of a new technology.

Applicability of Business Models

The results suggest that there is potential for electronic newspapers to attract young adults, but the prospects for success are mixed. Students' overall responses indicated they liked and enjoyed using the Protopaper, and many of its specific features were generally favorably rated. However, these high levels of satisfaction did not appear to influence purchase intentions. Even after a generally positive trial experience, most students indicated little intention to subscribe to an electronic newspaper.

To the extent that this group's disinclination to pay for an electronic newspaper, although they liked using it, is indicative of the sentiments of most members of this target market, newspaper management needs to consider the four business models quite carefully before investing in electronic information services. For instance, the results suggest that adoption of the new subscriber model will likely lead to disappointment if significant revenue is expected from young adults paying for the electronic newspaper. The most likely scenario is that such ventures will attain favorable reviews from the target market, but the second half of the equation (i.e., revenues) will not likely be forthcoming.

If a longer term perspective is adopted, the current findings provide some support for the adoption of the maturation model to justify electronic newspaper investments. It appears that attracting and getting young adults to use electronic newspapers is relatively easy, as long as the service is provided at little or no cost. Problems arise when it comes to subscription fees. Although a considerable time frame is needed to fully assess the maturation model, the results do not discourage the notion that electronic papers are a productive way to encourage the news consumption habit and build loyalty until the need for a print paper is formed. However, newspapers that adopt this model, must be financially willing to view electronic papers as "loss leaders," rather than profit centers as well as develop conversion strategies and tactics to ensure that the switch to print takes place.

The disinclination of heavy local news consumers to access a redundant electronic source of local news offers a clear direction regarding the multiple subscriber model. The results from even this limited examination indicate that electronic newspapers must offer advertising and editorial content that is distinctly different from the news of the day available elsewhere in the local media environment. Otherwise, the electronic newspaper will either fail or simply supplant print sources, but will not become an additional news source. These findings, along with increasing online service subscriptions, also suggest that newspapers should consider providing Internet access as an element of this model. Becoming an Internet Service Provider (ISP) may help to differentiate electronic and print offerings.

The structure and focus of this study precludes an examination of the competitive efficiency model. Indirectly, however, the current study sheds some light on one aspect of this model. Findings suggest at least one distinct target market—young adults—does hold some promise for electronic newspapers, thus making this a potentially efficient medium for advertisers targeting products and services to members of that group. Whether customized ads and transactional advertising can work to provide direct response capabilities for the newspaper industry remains to be studied systematically.

Marketing Considerations

The results obtained here suggest that creating the desire and motivation to use an electronic newspaper remains the primary marketing challenge. Even when members of the target audience have relatively high levels of personal computer use and experience, electronic papers need to provide a strong incentive or reason to use them. In many respects, the concept of mechanomorphism appears to be one of the major hurdles. Mechanomorphism is the tendency by a user to apply the attributes of a medium to the content being delivered by the medium (Cameron & Curtin, 1995). This is reflected in this study's finding of a negative relationship between time spent using a computer and likelihood to subscribe to an electronic newspaper. Regular computer users may get their fill of keyboards and monitors during the course of their work assignments. Given that young adults also tend to view newspapers as a chore and a time drain (Cobb-Walgren, 1990), it appears that marketing efforts need to distance electronic information services from computer workstations. Thus, the smart television may be a better appliance for delivering electronic newspapers (Ellis, 1995). Interface software and languages that improve server delivery of games and entertainment may also provide a technological solution to bridging the gap between work and recreational uses.

The absence of any significant differences in response to the Protopaper as a function of gender is also noteworthy from a marketing perspective. Cameron and Curtin (1995) questioned the truism that electronic newspapers will be mainly the domain of men. Current findings reinforce their position that women make up a significant component of the online community and respond to electronic newspapers much like men do. Thus, the current findings offer a strategic direction in addressing another worrisome market for the print newspaper—female readership. Circulation trends indicate a drop in readership by women who are household heads (Bogart, 1989; Fink, 1996), and qualitative evidence suggests that women are often the catalysts for dropping the paper in families (Hawley, 1993). Women are most likely to perceive papers as lacking attractive local content or providing information that builds bridges between members of the community. Women also tend to be most sensitive to the accumulation of unread papers in the household—a problem resolved by canceling the subscription. The chat capability and the paperless form of the electronic newspaper address both bridging/community connection needs and disposal of accumulated newspapers. Contrary to popular opinion, women readers might be an important source of prospects fitting the new subscriber model. Most pointedly, women canceling the print paper may be converted to alternative subscriptions to an electronic version that better meets their needs and household concerns.

A different business model needs to be applied, however, when it comes to persuading strong print readers to use electronic information services. Heavier local news consumers in this study distinguished themselves by an unwillingness to subscribe to the Protopaper. Although they typically liked the amalgam of local print and audio content provided by the Protopaper, it apparently was not distinct enough to be worth payment. This provides more support for the notion that electronic newspapers must strive to avoid duplication of content—in this case local news—that is currently available in print. Although advertising was not assessed in this study, the Wanta et al. (1995) study suggests that additional, more extensive advertising content may be one way for newspapers to add value to existing information. There are likely others, including some that probably will require going beyond the types of news and information routinely gathered and disseminated through printed papers. Regardless, the challenge for newspapers adopting the multiple subscriber model is to find ways to add value, uniqueness, and relevancy to electronically delivered news and information.

However, the Protopaper project also suggests that one way electronic newspapers can implement the multiple subscriber model is to serve as a bridge to information available only on the Internet and WWW. The electronic newspaper, then, becomes an Internet Service Provider (ISP) as a way to attract current print subscribers to become multiple subscribers by taking the electronic paper. Providing online access through the paper also provides a mechanism to charge for the electronic newspaper, even when it primarily serves only as a channel to reach the diverse resources of the online world. In addition to Internet access, electronic newspapers should continue to develop and provide searchable classified ads, regional or national employment services, and specialized content, like ESPNET's SportsZone with late-breaking scores, detailed statistics, and real-time audio/video.

Improving the Electronic Newspaper

Narrative comments suggest that electronic newspapers must be faster at responding to reader requests. Users did not like waiting for the screens to appear. Broadband information delivery through existing cable systems offers one solution (Ellis, 1995). Knight-Ridder proposed an offline version of the electronic newspaper downloaded to a tablet or smart television so that most information is quickly accessed by residing onsite (personal communication, staff at Knight-Ridder Information Design Lab, 1994). These are technological fixes of one sort or another to address a problem clearly enunciated by the current users of the Protopaper: "Don't make me wait."

Some industry thinkers believe the electronic newspaper should emulate the traditional pagination of the print paper ("Virtual Reality," 1994). Pagination would help address this study's limited anecdotal evidence that some users feel lost. However, abstracts and navigation opportunities were favorably rated by most participants.

CONCLUSION

This study offered insights about what young adults might want and like in an electronic newspaper, and whether young adults are a good market for electronic newspapers. The electronic newspaper was generally well received, being viewed as fun, easy, and satisfying to use. Graphics, back-chaining to previous issues of the paper, and access to the Internet were noticeably appreciated. Despite liking the electronic newspaper, students were not particularly inclined to subscribe to an electronic newspaper. These findings shed light on four business models offered for the development of electronic newspapers. Essentially, the new subscriber model shows little promise given the disinclination to pay for the Protopaper. The multiple subscriber model could be effective in attracting young adults, provided the electronic paper avoids duplication of print media and perhaps serves as the ISP for young adults who readily navigate to the Internet and WWW. The maturation model could be supported by the data here, but quite clearly electronic newspapers would be "loss leaders" in terms of subscription revenue for newspapers. Finally, the cost-effectiveness component of the economic efficiency model was beyond the purview of this study, but efficient advertising based on targeting ads to young adults or women shows potential.

REFERENCES

Bogart, L. (1989). *Press and public: Who reads what, when, where, and why in American newspapers.* Hillsdale, NJ: Lawrence Erlbaum Associates.

Brill, A., & Cook, S. (1995). *Digital Missourian online newsroom integration study: Summary of findings.* Manuscript in preparation presented to Online-News Discussion List, April 23.

Brooks, B., & Kropp, J. (1994, August). *Persuading children to read: A test of electronic newspapers.* Paper presented at the meeting of the Association for Educators in Journalism and Mass Communication, Atlanta, GA.

Cameron, G. T., & Curtin, P. A. (1995). Tracing sources of information pollution: A survey and experimental test of print media's labeling policy for feature advertising. *Journalism and Mass Communication Quarterly, 71*(2), 178–189.

Cameron, G. T., Nowak, G. J., & Krugman, D. M. (1993). The competitive position of newspapers in the local/retail market. *Newspaper Research Journal, 14*(3), 70–81.

Catlett, T., & Brooks, B. (1994, August). *The electronic newspaper as a pedagogical tool for the classroom: A means of hooking younger readers?* Paper presented at the meeting of the Association for Educators in Journalism and Mass Communication, Atlanta, GA.

Coates, J. (1995, October 15). Masses resist the internet. In *Chicago Tribune* [Online]. Available: http://www.chicago.tribune.com.

Cobb-Walgren, C. (1990). Why teenagers do not "Read All About It." *Journalism Quarterly, 67*(2), 340–347.

Curien, N., & Gensollen, M. (1987). Determining demand for new telecommunications services. In Organization for Economic Cooperation and Development (Ed.), *Trends of change in telecommunications policy* (pp. 135–143). Paris: Organization for Economic Development.

Ellis, L. (1995, January 2). TCI backs Microsoft Net with 20 percent stake. *Multichannel News,* p. 623.

Fink, C. (1996). *Strategic newspaper management.* Boston: Allyn & Bacon.

Fitzgerald, M. (1988, May 21). Computer "virus" hits first U.S. newspaper. *Editor & Publisher, 121*(21), 22.

Fitzgerald, M. (1994, January 1). Heading for the information highway. *Editor & Publisher, 127*(1), 11–14.

Frieske, D. (1995). *Memory for print and broadcast news in young and old adults: A resource-deficit approach.* Unpublished doctoral dissertation, The University of Georgia, Athens.

Glaberson, W. (1993, December 17). New York Times to begin on-line service. *The New York Times,* p. C15.

Glaberson, W. (1994a, January 17). Newspapers race for outlets in electronic marketplace. *The New York Times,* pp. D1, D6.

Glaberson, W. (1994b, February 7). Earthquake coverage, with electronic extras. *The New York Times,* p. D6.

Haddad, C. (1993a, May 30). Newspapers form unit to deliver electronically. *Atlanta Journal/Constitution*, p. 5.

Haddad, C. (1993b, July 8). More newspapers are adding delivery by computer. *Atlanta Journal/Constitution*, p. 2.

Haddad, C. (1993c, July 11). Cox's electronic newspaper may be the bait needed to get kids hooked. *Atlanta Journal/Constitution*, p. G6.

Haddad, C. (1993d, October 16). Cox cable unit set up to transmit digital data. *Atlanta Journal/Constitution*, p. 3.

Hammer, C., & Kennedy, G. (1993). Digital Missourian involves a new generation. *APME Readership Committee 1993 Report.* New York: Associated Press Managing Editors.

Hawley, M. D. (1993, August). *Dropping the paper: The role of women in local daily subscription cancellations.* Paper presented at the meeting of the Association for Education in Journalism and Mass Communication, Kansas City, MO.

Hester, A. (1982, July). *Electronic newspapers: A preliminary report.* Paper presented at the 4th World Future Society Conference, Washington, DC.

Lail, J. D. (1994, January). Newspapers on-line: Electronic delivery is hot ... again. *Quill, 82*(1), 39–44.

Lainson, S. (1995, October). Online discussion. [Owner-online], Available: news@marketplace.com

Markoff, J. (1993a, May 7). 17 companies in electronic news venture. *The New York Times*, pp. D1, D15.

Markoff, J. (1993b, September 3). A new information mass market. *The New York Times*, pp. 1, 4.

Markoff, J. (1993c, September 5). The Internet. *The New York Times*, p. 7.

Markoff, J. (1993d, November 3). Traffic jams already on the information highway. *The New York Times*, pp. 1, 9.

Markoff, J. (1993e, December 8). A free and simple computer link. *The New York Times*, pp. 1, 5.

McNaughton, D. (1993a, July 8). Cox, Prodigy to offer news by computer. *Atlanta Journal/Constitution*, pp. 1–2.

McNaughton, D. (1993b, July 8). Papers to debut computer edition. *Atlanta Journal/Constitution*, p. 1.

McNaughton, D. (1993c, July 11). Cox plugging into electronic revolution. *Atlanta Journal/Constitution*, pp. 1, 6.

Online discussion (1994–1995). Available: owner-online-news@marketplace.com

Resnick, R. (1994a, July). Newspapers on the net. *Internet World, 5*(5), 68–73.

Resnick, R. (1994b, March). *Online discussion, Re: Interactive publishing alert—March issue now available.* Available: owner-online-news@marketplace.com.

Schneider, V., Charon, J., Miles, I., Thomas, G., & Vedel, T. (1991). The dynamics of videotex development in Britain, France and Germany: A cross-national comparison. *European Journal of Communication, 6,* 187–212.

Stamm, K. R., & Fortini-Campbell, L.(1981). *Community ties and newspaper use* (ANPA News Research Report No. 33). Reston, VA: American Newspaper Publishers Association.

Stephens, L. F. (1975). *The influence of community attachment on newspaper reading habits* (ANPA News Research Report No. 17). Reston, VA: American Newspaper Publishers Association.

Thompson, D. (1993). *Mass communication and the newspaper of the future: Some effects of modality, story type and search experiences on reading time, memory and information location.* Unpublished doctoral dissertation, The University of Texas at Austin.

Urban, C. D. (1985). The competitive advantage of new publishing formats. In M. Greenberger (Ed.), *Electronic publishing plus* (pp. 41–56). White Plains, NY: Knowledge Industry.

Virtual reality: Newspapers and the information superhighway. (1994). Proceedings of the J. Montgomery Curtis Memorial Seminar, American Press Institute.

Wanta, W., Hu, Y., & Wu, Y. (1995). Getting more people to read more newspapers: Factors affecting newspaper reading. *Newspaper Research Journal, 16*(1), 103–115.

Chapter 4

The Structural Determinants of Television Ratings Share: Network Affiliation, Broadcast Band, Cable Penetration, and Market Concentration

Roger Cooper
Texas Christian University

Media managers are constantly searching for new and better ways to understand why viewers choose programs on their channel. In an uncertain broadcast marketplace where the number of competitors steadily grows, television stations currently use a variety of techniques or strategies to maximize (or maintain) viewership. The best and most obvious, of course, is through the purchase of programs that appeal to a large audience. However, this is an inexact science, judging by the high percentage of new programs that fail each year. In addition, television stations attempt to hold viewers from program to program by properly structuring the flow of programs throughout a schedule. Stations also cross-promote programs within and across day parts, as well as through other media (e.g., newspapers, radio, billboards). These techniques (and others) undoubtedly continue to be important tools for television stations, particularly in an ever-expanding, ever-competitive media marketplace.

Yet the audience found on any channel would also logically be mediated, to some degree, by factors external to the influence of any single program. In other words, a station's audience is determined or limited by the presence of structural variables inherent to the station or market. Among these influences are: (a) network affiliation, (b) the broadcast band on which programs air (VHF, UHF, cable), (c) the level of cable penetration within any market, and (d) the degree of market concentration. These structural influences are present in every U.S. television market, yet there is little systematic knowledge of their influence on the ratings of programs or their ability to predict a station's overall share of the audience. Moreover, it is not known how these factors interact to produce these effects.

This chapter focuses on the explanatory power of these structural components. To understand these influences, the chapter focuses on syndicated programs in local markets, in addition, it: (a) compares audience levels for programs along these four components, and (b) tests the ability of these variables to predict a channel's overall audience. These factors are discussed herein to build a rationale for the study.

NETWORK AFFILIATION AND BROADCAST BAND

Two important characteristics of U. S. broadcasting that logically influence viewing on a channel are network affiliation and the broadcast band. Not surprisingly, network-affiliated stations enjoy several competitive advantages over independent stations, which traditionally translates into higher ratings. First, local affiliates might profit (both literally and figuratively) from the advantage of being identified with the network. Through the cross-promotion of local news and syndicated programming during network programs, affiliate stations might develop an image or perceived identity. Second, affiliates hold several economic advantages over competitors in a local market. They receive financial support from the networks for carrying network programs; they are not responsible for scheduling as much of the broadcast day as independents; they carry the most-watched prime-time shows; and they can associate themselves with major specials and sporting events (see Haldi & Eastman, 1993; Rust & Donthu, 1988). Third, local stations—affiliates most particularly—have the ability to project an image of themselves to viewers through local news (and other avenues), which might enhance or boost the ratings of other programs on that station.

Yet what is the actual impact of affiliation on the ratings of programs or on a station's overall share of the audience? It is expected that as a structural influence affiliation will have a significant impact on a program's rating and overall audience. However, the use of syndicated programs (thus removing the direct influence of any network-provided programs) should provide a strong indication of how important network affiliation is to the audience of programs.

The broadcast band involves programs shown on either the VHF or UHF frequency. A channel's placement on either frequency is considered to have a strong impact on the audience of a program, as well as on that channel's market value (see Haldi & Eastman, 1993). Specifically, VHF stations have a higher quality picture and tend to be sampled first because they are positioned lower on the dial. UHF stations have more over-the-air technical problems (e.g., ghosting and interference), and are not sampled as routinely as stations on the VHF frequency (Haldi & Eastman, 1993).

Most independent stations have also traditionally suffered an additional disadvantage because they are more likely than affiliates to be on the UHF frequency (see Aiken & Affe, 1993). However, cable may have reduced the influence of the broadcast band overall and actually helped independent UHF stations for two reasons. First, carriage on cable systems eliminates the technical weaknesses of broadcasting over the air on UHF, and smooths out differences between strong and weak signals. Second, independents (and often their affiliated counterparts) are often repositioned by cable systems to other channels on the dial, and may exist on a more level playing field with more established stations. However, the broadcast band should continue to be a factor in influencing a channel's audience, and it will be interesting to uncover the actual influence of the broadcast band and its interaction effects with network affiliation.

Thus, it is expected that network affiliation and broadcast band will have a significant impact on the viewership of programs on a channel. However, it is expected that strong local news (found more on affiliates than independents), the ability to promote programs in prime time, the ability to purchase programs of higher appeal, and the general association with the network will serve to make network affiliation the most powerful influence on a channel's audience.

MARKET CONCENTRATION AND CABLE PENETRATION

Just as one would not expect any two television markets to be exactly the same, also one would not expect the structure of viewing choices across markets to be identical. For some viewers in some markets, programming alternatives are relatively limited. For other viewers, programming is virtually limitless. These differences would be expected to mediate overall viewership on a channel because differences in program and scheduling elements (e.g., the number of program options and types available) would differ according to the structure of the market.

Logically, the level of competition within a market would influence overall viewership because more competition would infer more choice options and vice versa. In discussing the economic components of competition, Litman (1985) said:

> The essential difference between a competitive and noncompetitive market is in the distribution of power between the market and the firm. In a competitive market, all power resides in the market mechanism; it is the ultimate regulator of conduct. The firm is a slave to the forces of supply and demand ... (T)he firm in a noncompetitive market has considerable control over its economic destiny. It has significant power, as well as flexibility and discretion over price, output, advertising, and research development expenditures. (p. 116)

If considered within the context of television viewership, markets labeled *noncompetitive* would contain a relatively small number of large and powerful stations that control a substantial proportion of the audience share. The proportions of viewer shares among the television stations in the market would be relatively high, and would be concentrated within a small number of firms. In contrast, *competitive* markets would typically have several viable channels competing for viewers. Audience shares would be more dispersed among the stations, and thus would be less concentrated.

Applied directly to factors that might influence the ratings of syndicated programs on local channels, concentrated markets might produce higher ratings, whereas nonconcentrated markets might produce the opposite. The level of cable penetration might also mediate the level of market concentration. Where cable penetration is higher, viewing might be more dispersed among many stations or cable networks, and thus make the market less concentrated. Conversely, in markets where cable penetration is low, viewing might be more concentrated because fewer options may be available to more viewers. Thus, market concentration as a function of the overall dispersion of viewing from market to market could be an effective measure that predicts viewing on a channel.

It is expected that market concentration, measured in this chapter by the Herfindahl-Hirschman Index[1], will be positively related to a station's audience share, and program ratings will be higher in concentrated markets than in unconcentrated markets. This is based on the belief that levels of concentration produce variations in the number of options and program types available. In markets where only one or two stations control a substantial portion of the market share (thus causing it to be more concentrated), it is expected that ratings will be higher because viewers have fewer options from which to choose, therefore increasing the audience for all programs in the market.

Naturally, the presence of cable reduces the overwhelming dominance that affiliate stations once held in most markets. The influence of cable might also imply that the gap between affiliates and independents is closer because those stations exist among several others imported by the local cable system. However, these influences would not be uniform across all markets, nor would viewers abandon local market stations.

Instead, most viewers appear to use local stations as a consistent part of their repertoire of channels and watch far fewer channels than the total number available (Ferguson, 1992; Heeter, 1985, 1988; Heeter & Greenberg, 1985, 1988; Lochte & Warren, 1989). The elements of localism—whether manifest through local news and/or through the ability to specifically

---

[1]The index was calculated by summing the squares of the total day DMA share (Sunday–Saturday, 7a.m.–1a.m.) for each station provided in the "day part" section in each of the 50 Nielsen Station Indexes. This section included all cable networks and broadcast stations in the DMA that maintained an average quarter-hour share of 1 or greater during the broadcast day. DMA is the total geographic area within a market designated by Nielsen for inclusion in its Market-by-Market reports.

promote syndicated programs to local viewers—plus the substantial influence of network programming for affiliates would appear to underpin a level of popularity, although reduced, for local market channels. Yet cable subscription (or penetration) is a more powerful predictor of increased channel repertoire than remote control devices or VCR ownership (Ferguson, 1992), and would seem to mediate this relationship or exert an influence as a structural factor determining the viewership on a channel.

The power of cable penetration (i.e., the percentage of homes in a market that subscribe to a cable service) in a market is expected to be less than measures of market concentration because: (a) most cable subscribers and nonsubscribers keep local market stations as central to their viewing, (b) viewers maintain a relatively small repertoire of channels, and (c) variations in cable penetration are likely to be less than variations in market concentration.

For this study, 50 television markets[2] measured by A.C. Nielsen Media Research in May 1991 were randomly selected for analysis. From the 50 markets, all weekday stripped first-run and off-network syndicated television programs aired between 7a.m. and 1a.m. (excluding prime-time hours[3]) were analyzed. The syndicated program's 4-week average household rating was used to determine statistical differences among network affiliation, broadcast band, market concentration, and cable penetration.

An additional analysis determined how well these four variables explain a channel's overall audience share. Expressed as a percentage of the Designated Market Area (DMA) television households with a set turned on during the average quarter-hour (7a.m.–1a.m., Sunday–Saturday), share data were used because they were a better expression of the relative strength of the stations competing in the market. Each broadcast station coded as airing at least one syndicated television program was included in the analysis.

RESULTS

There were 2,263 syndicated television programs examined from the sample of 50 markets. For the purposes of this study, affiliates of the Fox network were counted as independent stations. This was done because Fox

---

[2]The markets chosen were: Marquette, Tuscaloosa, Bowling Green, Knoxville, Bend (OR), Colorado Springs–Pueblo, Santa Barbara, Columbus–Tupelo–West Point, Eureka, Fling–Saginaw, Ada, Chico–Redding, Birmingham, Columbia–Jefferson City, Jackson (MS), Fairbanks, Tucson, Minneapolis, Cleveland, Fresno, Meridian, West Palm Beach, Hartford–New Haven, Lubbock, Corpus Christi, Yuma, Helena, Davenport, Shreveport, Roanoke–Lynchberg, Duluth, Phoenix, Albany (GA), Erie, Panama City, Dallas, Utica, Mecon, Rapid City, Sioux Falls, Lacross, Lafayette (IN), Casper, Harlengon, Harrisonburg, Denver, Jonesboro, Anniston, and Binghamton.
[3]Prime-time programs were excluded from the analysis because few stripped syndicated programs were aired during that day part.

stations essentially program their schedules as independent stations during non-prime-time hours (see Aiken & Affe, 1993). Slightly more than half of the programs (1,197) came from Fox (704) or independent (493) stations, both of which carried few or no weekday network programs in non-prime-time hours. The distribution of syndicated programs between affiliates of ABC (380), CBS (355), and NBC (315) was approximately the same.[4] The mean ratings for programs on affiliates of ABC, CBS, and NBC were virtually identical (6.2, 6.1, 6.1, respectively), as were the syndicated program ratings between independent and Fox stations (2.1 vs. 2.2). More programs were shown on VHF (53.6%) than UHF stations. However, 77.9% of the programs on affiliates of ABC, CBS, or NBC were shown on VHF stations.

The mean cable penetration rate of 62.4% was close to the national average at that time (60.3%; Nielsen, 1991). Exactly 15% of the programs were shown where cable penetration was above 75% (high penetration) and 15% where penetration was below 50% (low penetration). The average market concentration level was 1,393. Forty of the 50 markets fell into the somewhat concentrated category.[5] There was almost no correlation between a station's market rank and market concentration, and a moderate one between market rank and cable penetration, indicating a tendency for smaller markets to have higher cable penetration.

Ratings Comparisons

Statistics were used to determine differences in ratings for syndicated programs between affiliates and independents/Fox, and between VHF and UHF channels (see Table 4.1). As expected, syndicated programs shown on affiliates of ABC, CBS, and NBC had significantly higher ratings than those on Fox and independent stations. The average overall rating was four points higher on affiliates than independents. These differences were significant across all day parts. Likewise, the expectation that ratings of syndicated programs on VHF stations would be higher than UHF stations was supported, although the differences between UHF and VHF were not as large as by affiliation. An additional analysis revealed that VHF affiliates attained significantly higher ratings than UHF affiliates, although the differences were not as great as in the two previous analyses. The differences here were significant only during the early fringe and prime access day parts.

---

[4]Another 16 syndicated programs were aired by stations affiliated with more than one network (called *combo stations*).

[5]Index measures below 1,000 were coded unconcentrated, measures between 1,000–1,800 as somewhat concentrated, and measures above 1,800 as highly concentrated. These categories follow standard U. S. Department of Justice conventions for considering mergers, and have been used in other media studies of market concentration (see Bates, 1989).

TABLE 4.1
Test of Differences Between Average Ratings by Network Affiliation and Broadcast Band

Variable	Average Rating	Number of Programs
Network affiliation		
Independent/Fox[a]	2.17*	1,197
ABC/CBS/NBC	6.24	1,066
Broadcast band		
UHF	2.73*	1,049
VHF	5.26	1,214

*The differences between these averages are statistically significant.

[a]Fox is counted as an independent here because Fox stations program as independent stations in non-prime-time hours.

TABLE 4.2
Tests of Difference Between Average Ratings by Market Concentration
and Cable Penetration

Variable	Average Rating	Number of Programs
Concentration		
Unconcentrated	2.23*	260
Concentrated	4.55	282
Cable Penetration		
Low	4.26*	359
High	2.65	357

*The differences between these averages are statistically significant.

Tests of ratings were also conducted by high and low cable penetration, and by unconcentrated and concentrated markets (see Table 4.2). The differences in ratings were significant for both. Additional analyses also found significant differences between unconcentrated and somewhat concentrated markets and between somewhat and highly concentrated markets. However, differences were not significant between programs shown where cable penetration was below 50% and between 50%–75%, or between 50%–75% and above 75%.

Predictors of Channel Share

Together, network affiliation, broadcast band, market concentration, and cable penetration explained 48% of the variance in a station's 7a.m.–1a.m. market share. In other words, the combination of these four variables provides approximately half of the explanation for a channel's overall share of the audience. Individually, network affiliation was the strongest predictor, explaining 38% of a channel's share by itself. The broadcast band explained 29%, market concentration 7%, and cable penetration 3%.

A second test determined the explanatory power for one variable when the effects of the other three were controlled. This type of test helps illuminate the unique contribution of each variable. Network affiliation explained 13% of the variance when the other variables were controlled, and broadcast band added 6%. Neither level of market concentration nor cable penetration provided a unique explanatory contribution once network affiliation and broadcast band were controlled.

DISCUSSION

The results of this study extend our understanding of how key structural variables influence a station's viewership. Specifically, channel factors exert considerable influences on a syndicated program's rating and a station's overall share of the audience. Throughout the sample of markets, syndicated programs shown on network-affiliated stations consistently and almost uniformly attained higher ratings than independent or Fox stations. This was also reflected in the affiliation variable being the strongest predictor of a channel's overall share. The implications of these findings are discussed next.

Network Affiliation and Broadcast Band

Network affiliation was more important to the rating of a syndicated program than whether the program was shown on a VHF or UHF station, although broadcast band was certainly an influence. The uniform advantage held by affiliates is an important finding because none of the programs included in the sample was, in fact, a network program. Yet syndicated programs that aired on these stations appeared to benefit from the association with a network. Most likely, the term *network affiliation* carries with it much more than simply the airing of network programs by a local station. Instead, it likely implies that many of these stations: (a) have an established local identity (through news and, possibly, other local programming), (b) have large viewer carryover from program to program, (c) enjoy the benefit of cross-promoting their programs to a larger built-in audience, (d) may have the financial ability to promote their programs in other media, and (e) may have a longer history in the market. Whether a viewer's choice of programs can be directly attributed to some explicit or implicit channel (or affiliation) loyalty remains unclear and cannot be determined from these data. However, the results suggest that, although cable and level of competition in a local market appear to reduce the influence of affiliate stations, these affiliates continue to control a considerable share of the audience.

Ironically, broadcast station executives consider network affiliation to be the weakest factor in the rating of a first-run or off-network syndicated program (Cooper, 1992). This seems to reinforce the multifaceted meaning of network affiliation. However, the combination of network affiliation, broadcast band, concentration, and cable penetration explained only about half of the variance in channel's overall share. Network affiliation is not the sole reason that some stations perform well, although it would certainly seem to help. Within a single market, there was often a wide gap between the number one-ranked station and the number three-ranked station, even if they were both affiliates. The factors mentioned earlier, plus the skill of individual programmers to purchase and schedule the most effective, highest quality combination of programs, would seem to enhance the strength of any station in a market.

Market Concentration and Cable Penetration

Although it is difficult to assess exactly the direction of the relationship, it is logical to assume that high cable penetration would cause viewing to be less concentrated. There was a clear distinction between the level of market concentration and the overall program ratings. Large markets (with more local stations) were only slightly less concentrated than were small markets (with fewer local stations). This is explained by higher cable penetration in smaller markets, and by the fact that affiliates were relatively strong regardless of whether the market was small or large.

Although the correlation between penetration and concentration was moderately strong (-.45), the overall explanatory value of either was considerably less than channel factors, particularly network affiliation. However, the level of market concentration and cable penetration impacted on the absolute rating of local market programs. Most important, this study indicates that the structural variables influencing viewer choice are not uniform for all viewers in all places, and that these variables may be mediated by the amount of competition and cable penetration present in the market. Just as all television viewers are not created with identical needs and uses, neither is the structure of choices from which they have to choose.

REFERENCES

Aiken, E. G., & Affe, R. B. (1993). Independent station programming. In S. T. Eastman (Ed.), *Broadcast/cable programming* (4th ed., pp. 216–241). Belmont, CA: Wadsworth.

Bates, B. J., (1989). *Concentration in local television markets.* Paper presented at the meeting of the Association for Education in Journalism and Mass Communication, Washington, DC.

Cooper, R. (1992, May). *Finding certainty in an uncertain broadcast marketplace: A series of models to predict success in syndication.* Report to the National Association of Broadcasters, Washington, DC.

Ferguson, D. A. (1992). Channel repertoire in the presence of remote control devises, VCRs, and cable television. *Journal of Broadcasting & Electronic Media, 36,* 83–91.

Haldi, J. A., & Eastman, S. T. (1993). Affiliated station programming. In S. T. Eastman (Ed.), *Broadcast/cable programming* (4th ed., pp. 189–215). Belmont, CA: Wadsworth.

Heeter, C. (1985). Program choice with abundance of choice: A process model. *Human Communication Research, 12,* 126–152.

Heeter, C. (1985). The choice process model. In C. Heeter & B. S. Greenberg (Eds.), *Cableviewing* (pp. 11–32). Norwood, NJ: Ablex.

Heeter, C., & Greenberg, B. S. (1988). A theoretical overview of the program choice process. In C. Heeter & B. S. Greenberg (Eds.), *Cableviewing* (pp. 33–50). Norwood, NJ: Ablex.

Litman, B. R. (1985). Economic methods of broadcasting research. In J. R. Dominick & J. B. Fletcher (Eds.), *Broadcast Research Methods* (pp. 107–122). Boston: Allyn & Bacon.

Lochte, R. H., & Warren, J. (1989). A channel repertoire for TVRO satellite viewers. *Journal of Broadcasting & Electronic Media, 33,* 91–95.

Nielsen Station Index (1991). *Report on syndicated programs: May 1991.* Northbrook, IL: Nielsen Media Research.

Rust, R. T., & Donthu, N. (1988). A programming and positioning strategy for cable television networks. *Journal of Advertising, 17,* 6–13.

Chapter 5

Sexual Harassment and Vicarious Liability of Media Organizations

Matthew D. Bunker
University of Alabama, Tuscaloosa

Sexual harassment is a serious problem in many workplaces, including those of media organizations. National reaction to the Tailhook scandal, the Clarence Thomas confirmation proceedings, and the allegations involving Senator Packwood suggests that the problem is both widespread and seemingly intractable. This chapter examines under what conditions businesses can be held responsible—vicariously liable—for monetary damages for sexual harassment committed against their employees. The chapter explores the different types of sexual harassment as defined by law, examines legal cases in which vicarious liability standards have been adjudicated, examines the largely unreported problem of sexual harassment in media organizations, and explores possible steps that media organizations can take to reduce the likelihood of vicarious liability.

INTRODUCTION

Although Anita Hill's testimony in Clarence Thomas' Senate confirmation hearing first brought the issue to the attention of many, sexual harassment in the workplace is a long-standing problem of enormous dimensions. The Thomas allegations, the Tailhook scandal, and charges against Senator Bob Packwood are only the most prominent examples of a pervasive condition in many workplaces. According to a 1992 *Washington Post*–ABC national survey, 32% of women interviewed said they had been harassed on the job. The poll also found that 85% of men and women said sexual harassment was a problem in the workplace.[1]

---

[1] Richard Morin, Harassment Consensus Grows; Poll Finds Greater Awareness of Misconduct, *The Washington Post*, 18 December 1992, at A1.

For media organizations, the problem has not been one simply of reporting harassment that takes place in other organizations. Media organizations
frequently have been the site of sexual harassment allegations. For example,
a survey by the Associated Press Managing Editors Association found that
nearly 40% of women working at 19 newspapers in the United States said
they had been sexually harassed.[2] The problem also exists in the electronic
media[3] and in the public relations and advertising fields.[4]

Obviously, media organizations need to take steps to reduce or eliminate
sexual harassment. But companies cannot control their employees in all
circumstances. As a result, one problem facing executives in media organizations is protecting their companies (as opposed to harassers) from liability for sexual harassment. Under the legal doctrine of vicarious liability, a
company may be liable for the actions of its employees to the extent the
employer knows or should have known about the conduct.

In the sexual harassment context, the threat of vicarious liability requires
organizations to make it clear to all employees that harassment will not be
tolerated, and to provide a mechanism for prompt action if harassment does
take place. Interestingly, the steps that organizations should take to protect
against vicarious liability are also steps that many would argue are the
ethically proper way to deal with sexual harassment in the workplace.

This chapter explores the legal issue of the vicarious liability of media
organizations for sexual harassment by their employees. It examines two
distinct types of sexual harassment and the legal requirements for each. The
legal standards for holding organizations liable for harassment committed
by employees are then examined. Next, it explores media-specific cases in
which allegations of sexual harassment have been made. Finally, it offers
concluding perspectives on how media organizations can best deal with
both the legal and ethical obligations to prevent sexual harassment.

SEXUAL HARASSMENT DEFINED

The federal statutory remedy for sexual harassment derives from Title VII
of the Civil Rights Act of 1964. That statute states that it is "an unlawful

---

[2]Carolyn Weaver, A Secret No More, *Washington Journalism Review*, September 1992, at 24.
See also, Gail Flatow, Sexual Harassment in Indiana Daily Newspapers, 15 *Newspaper Res. J.* 32
(1994); Katherine C. McAdams and Maurine H. Beasley, Sexual Harassment of Washington
Women Journalists, 15 *Newspaper Res. J.* 127 (1994); Kim Walsh-Childers, Jean Chance, & Kristin
Herzog, *Sexual Harassment in U. S. Newsrooms: A Preliminary Report*, a paper presented at the
1994 annual convention of the Association for Education in Journalism and Mass Communication, Atlanta, GA.

[3]Kate Maddox, Sex Harassment in the Media, Electronic Media, 9 December 1991 at 1; Anne
P. Pomerantz, No Film at 11: The Inadequacy of Legal Protection and Relief for Sexually
Harassed Broadcast Journalists, 8 *Cardozo Arts & Ent. L. J.* 137 (1989).

[4]Susan Fry Bovet, Sexual Harassment; What's Happening and How to Deal With It, *Public
Relations Journal*, November 1993, at 26.

employment practice for an employer ... to discriminate against any individual with respect to his compensation, terms, conditions, or privileges of employment, because of such individual's race, color, religion, sex, or national origin."[5] Although the statute does not delineate liability for sexual harassment with any specificity, numerous courts have filled in that gap over the years.

There are two distinct types of harassment. One is the situation in which raises, promotions, or other job benefits are conditioned on agreement to sexual demands. This category is often referred to as *quid pro quo harassment* (literally, something for something) or *tangible job benefit harassment*. Quid pro quo harassment also would include discharge, refusal to hire, or assignment of unpleasant tasks resulting from rejection of sexual demands.

To establish a prima facie case of quid pro quo harassment, a plaintiff must prove that he or she was subjected to unwelcome sexual harassment based on sex, and that "the employee's reaction to the harassment affected tangible aspects of the employee's compensation, terms, conditions or privileges of employment."[6] The employee also must demonstrate that the job benefit or detriment was conditioned on the acceptance or rejection of the harassment, and that the employee was qualified to have received any benefit denied because of his or her rejection of the illegal conduct.

The second category of sexual harassment is *hostile environment harassment*, which includes situations in which there is no direct economic or job status inducement or threat by the harasser. Rather, hostile environment harassment arises from a pattern of conduct in the workplace that might include unwelcome sexual advances, sexual innuendoes, and other sexual conduct that interferes with the victim's ability to perform on the job. The Equal Employment Opportunity Commission (EEOC) defines *hostile environment harassment* as sexual conduct that "has the purpose or effect of unreasonably interfering with an individual's work performance or creating an intimidating, hostile or offensive working environment."[7]

In 1993, the U.S. Supreme Court held that the standard for establishing a hostile environment claim did not require that plaintiffs demonstrate psychological damage in order to recover. In *Harris v. Forklift Systems,*[8] Teresa Harris, an equipment rental manager, alleged that the president of Forklift Systems subjected her to harassing comments throughout her tenure with the company. Harris claimed—and the trial court agreed—that Charles Hardy, the president, insulted Harris in front of other employees with such remarks as, "You're a woman, what do you know," and by referring to her as "a dumb ass woman."[9] Moreover, Hardy directed a

---

[5]42 U.S.C. 200⁰e-2 (a) (1).
[6]*Spenser v. General Electric Co.*, 894 F.2d 651, 658 (4th Cir. 1990).
[7]29 CFR 1604.11(a) (3) (1992).
[8]114 S.Ct. 367 (1993).
[9]114 S.Ct. at 369.

number of sexual innuendoes at Harris and other female employees, commenting on their clothing and asking them to get coins from his pants pocket. Hardy also suggested that he and Harris go to a motel to discuss her request for a raise.

The trial court found that the comments were offensive to a "reasonable woman," but were not serious enough to affect Harris' psychological well-being or interfere with her job performance. As a result, Harris could not establish a viable claim for sexual harassment. The U. S. Court of Appeals for the Sixth Circuit agreed.

The U.S. Supreme Court rejected the psychological harm standard, holding instead that "so long as the environment would reasonably be perceived, and is perceived, as hostile or abusive ... there is no need for it also to be psychologically injurious."[10] The Court emphasized that federal sexual harassment law "comes into play before the harassing conduct leads to a nervous breakdown."[11] The Court declined to set forth a precise test for when conduct creates a hostile environment. Rather, the Court wrote that the determination could only be made by considering all the circumstances of a given case, including the frequency of the offensive conduct, its severity, and the extent to which it interfered with the plaintiff's job performance. The Supreme Court remanded the *Forklift* case for further proceedings in accordance with the Court's opinion.

Although the *Forklift* case does not set forth a clear and unequivocal rule as to when a workplace becomes hostile, it does suggest that the conduct necessary to create a hostile environment need not be as severe as some courts and lawyers had thought. By emphasizing that no nervous breakdown was necessary for a hostile environment to exist, the Court opened the door for plaintiffs to get their cases before a jury if a factual dispute exists as to the severity of the harassment. As one plaintiff's lawyer said of the *Forklift* decision: "This decision will certainly increase the number of cases that can get to a jury, and where a judge will say, 'I can't decide whether these facts are oppressive enough.' "[12]

VICARIOUS LIABILITY

The common-law doctrine of vicarious liability is very old.[13] The doctrine, also called *respondeat superior* ("let the master answer"), holds that wrongs committed by a servant are imputed to the master. In the modern corporate

---

[10]114 S.Ct. at 371.

[11]114 S.Ct. at 370.

[12]Jan Hoffman, Plaintiffs' Lawyers Applaud Decision, *New York Times*, 10 November 1993, A14, col. 1.

[13]"The idea of vicarious liability was common enough in primitive law. Not only the torts of servants and slaves, or even wives, but those of inanimate objects, were charged against their owner." William L. Prosser, Law of Torts 458 (4th ed. 1971).

context, vicarious liability means that, under certain circumstances, torts—civil wrongs—committed by employees are chargeable to the organization. A variety of justifications for the doctrine have been advanced, but the principal reason seems to relate to who should bear the risk of wrongs committed by (often judgment-proof) employees. As noted expert Professor William Prosser explained the doctrine:

> What has emerged as a modern justification for vicarious liability is a rule of policy, a deliberate allocation of a risk. The losses caused by the torts of employees, which as a practical matter are sure to occur in the conduct of the employer's enterprise, are placed upon that enterprise itself, as a required cost of doing business.[14]

Although vicarious liability originated in the common law, it has been extended to various areas of statutory law, including Title VII sexual harassment suits. The general rule that has emerged from federal appellate courts is that companies are strictly liable for quid pro quo harassment by supervisory employees. Under strict liability, there is no need for a plaintiff to show that the company had notice of the harassment or did not try to prevent it. The mere fact that it took place is enough to assign liability to the company for the acts of its supervisory employees. For example, the U.S. Court of Appeals for the Sixth Circuit found strict liability applicable in a 1992 case involving harassment by a supervisor. In *Kauffman v. Allied Signal*,[15] the plaintiff's male supervisor assigned her onerous tasks when she rebuffed his suggestions that she show him the results of her breast enhancement surgery. The Sixth Circuit stated that "under a 'quid pro quo' theory of sexual harassment, an employer is held strictly liable for the conduct of its supervisory employees having authority over hiring, advancement, dismissal, and discipline, under a theory of [vicarious liability]."[16] Other federal courts of appeal have followed similar reasoning.[17] One treatise on the subject explained that strict liability applies in quid pro quo cases because

> the supervisor acts for the company by definition, and the employer's knowledge of harassment is imputed to it through its agent, the supervisor. The employer is also strictly liable for supervisory job benefit harassment that partially takes place after hours or off company property, if the employer had relinquished broad personnel authority over the victim to the supervisor.[18]

---

[14]Prosser, Law of Torts at 459.

[15]970 F.2d 178 (6th Cir. 1992).

[16]970 F.2d at 185–186.

[17]E.g., *Chamberlin v. 101 Realty, Inc.*, 915 F.2d 178 (1st Cir. 1990); *Carrero v. New York City Housing Authority*, 890 F.2d 569 (2d Cir. 1989).

[18]Employment Coordinator at 82,218 (1993).

Strict liability only applies in quid pro quo cases, however. In 1986, the U.S. Supreme Court decided that employers would not be strictly liable for hostile environment harassment by their employees in *Meritor Savings Bank v. Vinson*.[19] In the *Meritor* case, Vinson, a female bank employee, alleged that the bank's male vice president had harassed her constantly throughout her 4-year employment at the bank. The case was based solely on a hostile environment because both parties admitted that Vinson's advancement from teller-trainee to assistant branch manager was based on merit alone. Vinson claimed that the vice president had initiated a sexual relationship, in which she had agreed to participate for fear of losing her job. The vice president "thereafter made repeated demands upon her for sexual favors, usually at the branch, both during and after business hours; she estimated that over the next several years she had intercourse with him some 40 or 50 times."[20] Moreover, Vinson alleged that the vice president "fondled her in front of other employees, followed her into the women's restroom when she went there alone, exposed himself to her, and even forcibly raped her on several occasions."[21]

The Supreme Court recognized the legal validity of claims of hostile environment harassment, and proceeded to discuss the issue of when an employer could be held liable for the acts of its employees. The Court declined to issue a definitive rule on employer liability, but did state that a lower court had erred in concluding that employers were strictly liable for harassment by their employees—in this case, the vice president. The Court also rejected an argument by the bank that, because it had a grievance procedure that Vinson did not utilize, it should be shielded from liability because it could not have known about the harassment and taken corrective action. Instead, the Court reasoned that "Congress wanted courts to look to agency principles for guidance in this area."[22] This finding suggests that, rather than creating a special rule for hostile environment harassment, courts should look to general common-law principles for determining when vicarious liability applies. The particulars of how common-law doctrine should be applied in Title VII litigation are still being worked out in lower courts.

The *Meritor* majority also pointed out two flaws in the bank's grievance procedure and nondiscrimination policy. First, the bank's nondiscrimination policy did not specifically address sexual harassment. Second, the grievance procedure required an employee to complain first to his or her supervisor. In this case, the supervisor was also the harasser. The Court suggested that the policy should have provided some alternative means of reporting the harassment.

---

[19] 477 U.S. 57 (1986).
[20] 477 U.S. at 60.
[21] 477 U.S. at 60.
[22] 477 U.S. at 72.

Concurring in the judgment, Justice Marshall, joined by Justices Brennan, Blackmun, and Stevens, called for something closer to strict liability for an employer when a supervisor created a hostile environment. Justice Marshall's opinion recognized that some limitations on strict liability might be appropriate, but stated he would "hold that sexual harassment by a supervisor of an employee under his supervision, leading to a discriminatory work environment, should be imputed to the employer for Title VII purposes regardless of whether the employee gave 'notice' of the offense."[23]

Since *Meritor*, lower federal courts have applied a variety of standards for determining when a company should be vicariously liable for the creation of a hostile environment by one of its supervisors. It appears that most courts have adopted a standard holding a company liable when it knew of the harassment or should have known of it and did not take some immediate action to remedy the situation. For example, the Eleventh Circuit endorsed such a standard in 1989 in *Steele v. Offshore Shipbuilding*, when it found that "liability exists where the corporate defendant knew or should have known of the harassment and failed to take prompt remedial action against the supervisor."[24] In *Steele*, the plaintiff was a secretary at a shipbuilding firm who claimed that the vice president, Anthony Bucknole, frequently engaged in off-color and suggestive joking with female employees. "For example, Bucknole requested sexual favors from [female employees]. He commented on their attire in a suggestive manner and asked them to visit him on the couch in his office."[25] After the employees complained, the company reprimanded Bucknole and the harassment stopped.

The federal district court that initially heard the case found Bucknole had created a hostile environment and ordered him to pay nominal damages as well as attorneys' fees. However, the court found the company not liable for Bucknole's actions. The Eleventh Circuit agreed. The court of appeals stated that because the employer learned of the harassment and took prompt action (e.g., calling Bucknole back from Saudi Arabia to New York for a reprimand), it was not liable for his actions. "Of special importance," the Eleventh Circuit wrote, "Bucknole's harassment ended after the remedial action. The corporate employer, therefore, is not liable for Bucknole's actions under the doctrine of respondeat superior."[26]

Other federal courts of appeals have created similar standards.[27] Most do not require that the corporate employer have actual notice of the harass-

---

[23]477 U.S. at 78 (Marshall, J., concurring in the judgment).

[24]867 F.2d 1311, 1316 (11th Cir. 1989).

[25]867 F.2d at 1313.

[26]867 F.2d at 1316.

[27]For a thorough review of standards created by federal appellate courts after *Meritor*, see Hope A. Comisky, Prompt and Effective Remedial Action? What Must an Employer Do to Avoid Liability for Hostile Work Environment Sexual Harassment? 8 *The Labor Lawyer* 181, 182–84 (1992). See also, Justin S. Weddle, Note: Title VII Sexual Harassment: Recognizing an Employer's Non-Delegable Duty to Prevent a Hostile Workplace, 95 *Colum. L. Rev.* 724 (1995).

ment; it is enough that the employer *should* have known of the conduct by exercising reasonable care. The Tenth Circuit, for example, invoked section 219 of the Restatement (Second) of Agency for guidance on the question of corporate vicarious liability.[28] That section creates employer liability when "(1) the master was negligent or reckless, and (2) where the servant purported to act or to speak on behalf of the principal and there was reliance on apparent authority, or he was aided in accomplishing the tort by the existence of the agency relation."[29] This formulation would allow employer liability in cases in which the employer was negligent for not being aware of the hostile environment. A negligence standard introduces all the legal uncertainties associated with a jury determination of what a reasonable person or reasonable employer would have known or done in a similar situation.[30]

Regardless of the precise legal formulation, the general rule seems to be that companies should make every effort to monitor the workplace to ensure that a supervisor is not creating a hostile environment for employees. If such a situation develops, the company must quickly take action to remedy the harassment.

As the prior discussion demonstrates, companies can be held vicariously liable for hostile environment sexual harassment by a supervisor. Not so obviously, they also can be held vicariously liable for a hostile environment created by coworkers. Coworkers, of course, could not commit quid pro quo harassment because they lack the power of hiring, firing, and otherwise affecting job benefits. However, coworkers can create a hostile environment.

EEOC guidelines state that vicarious liability for coworker harassment depends, as in supervisory hostile environment harassment, on the knowledge of the employer:

> With respect to conduct between fellow employees, an employer is responsible for acts of sexual harassment in the workplace where the employer (or its agents or supervisory employees) knows or should have known of the conduct, unless it can show that it took immediate and appropriate corrective action.[31]

The few federal appellate courts that have considered the matter seem to have adopted this standard.

---

[28]*Hicks v. Gates Rubber Co.*, 833 F.2d 1406 (10th Cir. 1987).

[29]833 F.2d at 1418, quoting Restatement (Second) of Agency 219 (2) (1958).

[30]Negligence is "the omission to do something which a reasonable man, guided by those ordinary considerations which ordinarily regulate human affairs, would do, or the doing of something which a reasonable and prudent man would not do." *Black's Law Dictionary* 930 (West 5th ed. 1979).

[31]29 CFR 1604.11 (d) (1992).

For example, in *Hall v. Gus Construction Co.*,[32] the Eighth Circuit in 1988 held that either actual or imputed knowledge of harassment by coworkers was sufficient to create employer liability. In *Hall*, female employees hired to work as traffic controllers at construction sites were subjected to vicious harassment by male members of the construction crew. The harassment included the male crew members verbally abusing and physically touching the female employees, as well as exposing themselves to the women. The male crew members also "would refuse to give the women a truck to take to town for bathroom breaks. When the women would relieve themselves in the ditch, male crew members observed them through surveying equipment."[33]

The construction company argued that the male crew members were not its agents for purposes of vicarious liability, and that they acted outside the scope of their employment. The Eighth Circuit disagreed. The *Hall* court cited cases involving racial harassment by coworkers, in which employers were held liable if they had reason to know of a pattern of harassing conduct and did not prevent it. In *Hall*, a supervisor, Mundorf, was aware of some of the incidents, and should have been aware of the poisoned atmosphere of the workplace, the court reasoned. The court stated as follows: "[Mundorf] knew that the men bombarded the women with sexual insults and abusive treatment. Even if Mundorf did not know everything that went on, the incidents of harassment here ... were so numerous that Mundorf and Gus Construction Co. are liable for failing to discover what was going on and to take remedial steps to put an end to it."[34]

Conduct by nonemployees also may result in vicarious liability for an employer if the employer knows or should have known of the harassment and takes no action. For example, a restaurant was found liable in a case in which a waitress was harassed by regular customers and the employer did nothing to prevent the harassment.[35] In another nonemployee case, an employer was held liable for harassment of a female lobby attendant by the general public after it required her to wear a sexually revealing uniform.[36] The attendant was subjected to a variety of lewd comments and propositions. The employer had notice of the harassment, but nonetheless required the attendant to wear the outfit. In the media context, it is possible to envision harassment by such nonemployees as frequent journalistic sources (e.g., government officials[37]), or by advertisers buying space or time from

---

[32]842 F.2d 1010 (8th Cir. 1988). See also, *EEOC v. Hacienda Hotel*, 881 F.2d 1504 (9th Cir. 1989).

[33]842 F.2d at 1012.

[34]842 F.2d at 1016.

[35]EEOC Decision 84-3 (1984). See also, Robert J. Aalberts and Lorne H. Seidman, *Sexual Harassment by Clients, Customers, and Suppliers: How Employers Should Handle an Emerging Legal Problem*, 20 *Employee Relations L. J.* 85 (1994).

[36]*EEOC v. Sage Realty*, 507 F. Supp. 599 (S. D. N. Y. 1981).

[37]See also, e.g., Carol D. Rasnic, *Illegal Use of Hands in the Locker Room: Charges of Sexual Harassment and Inequality from Females in the Sports Media*, 8 *Ent. & Sports Law.* 3 (1991).

print or electronic media, or by clients of advertising or public relations firms.

Thus, supervisor, coworker, and nonemployee hostile environment cases can give rise to employer vicarious liability when the employer knew or should have known of the harassing conduct and refused to take action. These cases suggest that an employer may not simply look the other way and then claim that it was unaware of a hostile climate in the workplace.

SEXUAL HARASSMENT IN MEDIA ORGANIZATIONS

Although no reported trial or appellate cases have yet dealt squarely with the vicarious liability of a media organization, the problem of sexual harassment is no stranger to the media. A number of (unsuccessful) cases have been reported, whereas other media cases have resulted in settlements prior to trial and thus are not found in reported decisions.

One of the reported cases that found no harassment was the 1991 decision in *Schneider v. NBC New Bureaus*,[38] in which an NBC sound technician alleged that she resigned because of a hostile workplace environment. The plaintiff, Deborah J. Schneider, claimed that poor assignments and a generally hostile atmosphere based on her gender led to her resignation. The U.S. District Court for the Southern District of Florida found that Schneider's failure to receive some assignments was primarily due to her poor attitude and job skills. The district court also found that Schneider "failed to show the creation or maintenance of a sexually hostile working condition."[39] The plaintiff had complained of, among other things, sleeping arrangements on various assignments, suggestive posters and videotapes in the workplace, and at least one incident in which the plaintiff was propositioned by a fellow employee. The court placed considerable reliance on the plaintiff's failure to complain contemporaneously with these events. Because the court found the plaintiff had not made a sufficient showing of a hostile environment, the court did not consider the issue of vicarious liability.

Another media case in which a district court refused to find sexual harassment was the 1988 decision in *Silverstein v. Metroplex Communication*.[40] The court also expressly addressed the vicarious liability issue and found the corporation blameless. Linda Silverstein, a sales manager for a top-40 FM radio station, claimed that coworkers and supervisors created a hostile environment, from which she was eventually fired.

---

[38]801 F.Supp. 621 (S. D. Fla. 1991).
[39]801 F.Supp. at 633.
[40]678 F.Supp. 863 (S. D. Fla. 1988).

The U.S. District Court for the Southern District of Florida rejected the claim, as well as related claims of discrimination. The court noted that the plaintiff did not achieve the sales goals set forth by the station, whereas the plaintiff's predecessor in the position had always exceeded the sales goals. The court also noted that the plaintiff had trouble getting along with the station's national sales representative firm—an organization that sold advertising for the station to national advertisers. The court found that the plaintiff was inaccessible to the national sales firm, did not return telephone calls, and damaged the station's relationship with the firm.

Silverstein claimed that Matthew Mills, general manager of the station, joked about a vibrator in Silverstein's presence. The court expressed doubt about whether that event occurred. The court also regarded as insignificant claims that Mills asked about "the well-being of Plaintiff's boyfriend," or that "on one occasion, while on a business trip, he may have asked Plaintiff to hold for him his newspaper or wallet."[41] Silverstein also claimed that several salespeople made sexual remarks to her, including one salesperson who telephoned her and tried to persuade her to spend the night with him. The court regarded as significant Silverstein's failure to complain about the alleged harassment. The court also stated that it was not convinced that all the conversations Silverstein alleged took place.

On the issue of the vicarious liability of Metroplex, the corporate owner of the station, the court said Silverstein failed to complain to Metroplex representatives, who "were available to hear Plaintiff's grievances. Also, the harassment was not so pervasive as to put Metroplex on constructive notice of the conduct."[42] The court thus concluded that the corporation was not responsible for any harassing conduct that did take place.

Although information about unreported media harassment cases is difficult to come by, some reports of the problem have suggested that a significant number of media cases are settled prior to trial, often with agreements forbidding the parties to discuss the case publicly. For example, writer Carolyn Weaver reported that "interviews with nearly 100 reporters, editors, and producers at more than 30 newspapers, magazines and broadcast outlets reveal a largely untold story of sexual harassment within the media." In "A Secret No More," a study of sexual harassment that appeared in *Washington Journalism Review*, Weaver wrote that media harassment is "a story—oddly enough in an industry dedicated to uncovering the facts—of a lot of little coverups."[43]

Weaver's research found that, of eight harassment suits either filed or threatened against media organizations between 1985 and 1992, six were settled with a provision that the settlement remain confidential. For example, Weaver reported that a 1986 lawsuit by seven women at CBS working

[41]678 F.Supp. at 867.
[42]678 F.Supp. at 870.
[43]Carolyn Weaver, A Secret No More, *Washington Journalism Review*, September 1992, at 24.

on the overnight news program "Nightwatch" resulted in a confidential settlement. According to Weaver, the women "had been sexually harassed and sexually assaulted, despite repeated requests for help from top managers."[44] If this version is correct, there would seem to be little question that the case would have involved a strong likelihood of vicarious liability had it gone to trial.

Weaver also described a confidential settlement by a deputy national editor at the *Kansas City Star* in a case that reportedly involved sexually derogatory language and inappropriate touching by other employees. The *Star*, responding to Weaver's report, said that its own investigation revealed that no harassment occurred, and that the paper settled to resolve the matter. Numerous other allegations of sexual harassment in media organizations have been reported.[45]

Anne P. Pomerantz reported other media harassment cases that never reached trial in a 1989 article in the *Cardozo Arts & Entertainment Law Journal*.[46] For example, Pomerantz reported the case of Elissa Dorfsman, a sales manager for CBS, who sued CBS and a top sales executive after alleging harassing conduct at a company sales dinner. According to Pomerantz, CBS privately reprimanded the executive, but took no other action. Eventually, Dorfsman settled the case "for a purported $250,000."[47]

Another settlement came in a case involving an employee who worked for Playboy's cable channel.[48] Stephanie Wells, director of the channel's On Air Promotions department, brought suit after "paint[ing] a picture of a company that scorned repeated complaints over a four-year period by Wells and several other women who were often reduced to tears by harassment by a male executive."[49] Playboy had argued, among other things, that sexually suggestive comments and other conduct could not have offended Wells because she produced adult programming as part of her job. The amount of the settlement was not disclosed.

Clearly, the evidence of widespread harassment in media organizations is anecdotal at best. Nonetheless, it strains credulity to suggest that harassment is not a problem for the media, as it appears to be for nearly all businesses.

---

[44]Weaver, A Secret at 25. See also Anne P. Pomerantz, No Film at 11: The Inadequacy of Legal Protection and Relief for Sexually Harassed Broadcast Journalists, 8 *Cardozo Arts & Ent. L. J.* 137, 156 (1989).

[45]See, e.g., M. L. Stein, Sexual Harassment Flap in Denver, *Editor & Publisher*, 28 March 1992, at 12; Sexual Harassment Allegation at Student Newspaper, *Editor & Publisher*, 30 January 1993, at 20; Susan Fry Bovet, Sexual harassment; What's Happening and How to Deal With It, *Public Relations Journal*, November 1993, at 26; Katie Maddox, Sex Harassment in the Media, *Electronic Media*, 9 December 1991, at 1.

[46]Anne P. Pomerantz, No Film at 11: The Inadequacy of Legal Protection and Relief for Sexually Harassed Broadcast Journalists, 8 *Cardozo Arts & Ent. L. J.* 137, 153–156 (1989).

[47]Id. at 155.

[48]Susan Seager, Playboy Settles Suit by Former Producer, *Los Angeles Daily Journal*, 10 Nov. 1992 at 3.

[49]Id.

Media organizations must respond seriously and in a legally appropriate manner to the problem. The next section describes some appropriate legal responses, which also happen to be sound methods of making employees feel safer in the workplace and discouraging discrimination in general.

COMBATING VICARIOUS LIABILITY

Media organizations, like other employers, should rightfully be concerned about the possibility of vicarious liability for sexual harassment. The EEOC suggests that "prevention is the best tool for the elimination of sexual harassment."[50] The agency's guidelines state that employers

> should take all steps necessary to prevent sexual harassment from occurring, such as affirmatively raising the subject, expressing strong disapproval, developing appropriate sanctions, informing employees of their right to raise and how to raise the issue of harassment under Title VII, and developing methods to sensitize all concerned.[51]

Companies may take a number of steps to minimize the possibility of sexual harassment, and thus minimize the likelihood they will be held vicariously liable for hostile environment sexual harassment. As noted earlier, employers are strictly liable for quid pro quo harassment, so preventive measures cannot operate to limit vicarious liability after the fact, although they can serve as a deterrent to would-be harassers. Most commentators suggest detailed sexual harassment policies that outline forbidden conduct and warn of sanctions if harassment occurs. For example, one authority advocates the following steps: (a) issuing a policy statement that defines sexual harassment and makes it clear that harassment will not be tolerated and will result in appropriate sanctions, (b) defining sexual harassment to include both physical and verbal conduct that results either in quid pro quo or hostile environment harassment, (c) adopting a complaint procedure that assigns a specific employee to hear complaints, (d) educating supervisors as to the law and company policy, (e) investigating complaints, and (f) taking appropriate action after the investigation.[52]

The issues of the policy and the complaint procedure may be problematic, as demonstrated by the Supreme Court's decision in *Meritor*—the case involving the female bank employee and her supervisor. First, the Court rejected the bank's claim that "the mere existence of a grievance procedure and policy against discrimination, coupled with [the harassed employee's] failure to invoke that procedure, must insulate [the bank] from liability."[53]

---

[50]29 CFR 1604.11 (f) (1992).
[51]29 CFR 1604.11 (f) (1992).
[52]Employment Coordinator at 141, 101–141, 102 (1991).
[53]477 U. S. at 72.

A grievance procedure and policy could be relevant to the determination of vicarious liability, but their existence was not sufficient by itself to allow an employer to avoid liability, the Court reasoned. Second, the bank's policy in *Meritor* addressed discrimination in general, but not sexual discrimination in particular—an omission the Court pointedly noted. Third, and perhaps most important, the Court stated that the bank's grievance procedure required a harassed employee to complain first to his or her supervisor—in *Meritor*, the harasser. The Court noted that the bank's contention that the employee's failure to complain "should insulate it from liability might be substantially stronger if its procedures were better calculated to encourage victims of harassment to come forward."[54]

The exact nature of appropriate action after the complaint has been made and found legitimate is still being determined by the courts.[55] For example, in *Ellison v. Brady*,[56] a 1991 Ninth Circuit case, the court of appeals suggested that an employer's remedy could be inadequate if it allowed a harasser to return to the same workplace as the victim, even after a separation. In *Ellison*, an Internal Revenue Service (IRS) employee was harassed by notes and letters from a coworker who seemed obsessed with her. After a 6-month cooling-off period, the coworker was allowed to return to the office. "We believe that in some cases the mere presence of an employee who has engaged in particularly severe or pervasive harassment can create a hostile working environment,"[57] the Ninth Circuit court wrote. The court also questioned the IRS' action of allowing the harassed employee to transfer to a less desirable location to avoid the harasser. "We strongly believe that the victim of sexual harassment should not be punished for the conduct of the harasser," the court wrote.[58]

To avoid vicarious liability for hostile environment harassment, a company must do all it can to discourage harassment, to ensure rapid and effective procedures when it is alleged to have occurred, and to mete out appropriate sanctions when proven. As noted earlier, these policies not only make sense from a legal perspective, but also further socially responsible goals of eliminating all forms of discrimination from the workplace.

CONCLUSION

Although awareness of sexual harassment seems to be growing as a result of notorious cases, the problem appears to be a pervasive one. Despite the

[54]477 U.S. at 73.
[55]For a thorough examination of this issue, see Hope A. Comisky, Prompt and Effective Remedial Action? What Must an Employer do to Avoid Liability for Hostile Work Environment Sexual Harassment? 8 *The Labor Lawyer* 181 (1992).
[56]924 F.2d 872 (9th Cir. 1991).
[57]924 F.2d at 883.
[58]924 F.2d at 882.

lessons of Tailhook, Senator Packwood, and the Thomas nomination, sexual harassment is alive and well. The stubborn nature of the problem suggests that media organizations should be aware of and respond appropriately to harassment, both for selfish and more noble reasons.

Media organizations, like other employers, are subject to strict liability for quid pro quo harassment by supervisors. In cases of hostile environment harassment, whether the harassment originates from supervisors, coworkers, or nonemployees, media organizations can be held vicariously liable if they know or should have known of the harassment and do not take immediate and effective steps to remedy it. Clearly, media companies need strong policies and, perhaps more important, a genuine and clearly communicated unwillingness to tolerate any form of harassment in the workplace. Such a commitment not only helps to protect the company from legal liability, but it also should result in a workplace that is more humane and productive.

Chapter 6

A Proactive Model for Solving Ethical Dilemmas

Val E. Limburg
Washington State University

Even the best broadcast managers—those with congenial, efficient, profit-oriented, successful management styles—are often confronted with ethical dilemmas. Some have discovered that a proactive stance in solving those dilemmas has not only worked, but has enhanced a successful managerial style.

Within the last decade, the thinking of business scholars, marketers, philosophers, and media ethicists have merged to consider the field of applying ethics to business. In one anthology on the subject, Serafini (1989) observed:

> ... during the last decade the intensity of interest in the subject of business ethics has surprised even the most ardent defenders of the movement to study them. It is easy for a practitioner to become ecstatic over such developments. But the fact is that the movement stands at a crossroads. The key to success is dependent upon a multi disciplinary approach that relies on cooperation among faculty in the academy and in business. This will ensure a mix of theory and practice. (pp. 299–300)

Although he noted that "perhaps ... the field of ethics as defined by the philosophers of the past five centuries is too abstract to do justice to business" (p. 301), nevertheless, related literature has made concerted efforts to bridge this gap (e.g., Bartels, 1967; Ferrell and Fraedrich, 1981; Gibson, 1986; Hensel, 1986; Moser, 1986; Roberts, 1986; Schmidt, 1986).

In considering ethics, specifically in marketing management, "Value Marketing" (1991) described the concept of value marketing and related it to proactive marketing and management. The key components are thought to not only offer profits in the marketplace, but to also build relationships in organizations and increase quality of life of those involved.

The characteristics of this proactive marketing plan have been further elaborated by Samli (1992). These specific characteristics differ only slightly from the more general qualities of a proactive plan in media management described later, but the perspective or philosophy seems much the same.

The following is a case study that reflects effective proactive management. Although it is of most interest to the broadcasting and advertising industry, the principles gleaned from it are perfect illustrations of the characteristics of ethics in proactive management in many forums. This chapter looks at how one broadcast corporation worked with the threat of removal of beer and wine advertising from radio and television. There is then analysis in terms of the application of proactive elements. This, then, becomes a viable model for solving further ethical dilemmas in media management.

CASE STUDY: POTENTIAL BANNING OF ALCOHOL ADVERTISING IN THE BROADCAST MEDIA

Ever since the banning of tobacco products on radio and television in 1971, the broadcast media have faced the prospects of having other harmful products prohibited from being commercially promoted over the air. Some broadcasters have only thought of the potential economic loss, and have fought the proposed ban without regard to its reasons or the substance of the arguments. Other thoughtful business leaders have considered what they might do to address the concerns of those fighting alcohol advertising without actually advocating the ban.

Arguments to Curb Alcohol Advertising

Alcohol abuse kills over 300 people every day, 365 days of the year (Hacker, 1987). Problems of broken homes, child abuse, and crime often are linked to alcohol abuse, whereas conventional medical evidence linking alcohol with assorted health hazards is overwhelming and uncontrovertible.

Breweries and wineries spend billions of dollars each year, much of it in the broadcast media. Those channeling the advertising budgets apparently feel that these media are effective in reaching their target market. If these media sell beer and encourage beer drinking, especially among the youth, should it be held responsible for helping to promote a source of many social ills? Can broadcasters keep their lucrative income from beer and wine advertising and remain guiltless in promoting a social activity that is often destructive to both individuals and society?

Health organizations, including the American Medical Association (AMA; Todd, 1987), have called for an outright ban on beer and wine advertising on television, especially during the telecasting of sports events, which are seen by large numbers of teens. Groups that stop short of an outright ban insist that a health hazard warning label should be put on both labels and advertising. Such groups assume that beer advertising has a strong persuasive influence on young consumers. The models in TV commercials appear to be young, fun-loving, attractive, and engaged in activities desirable to many young people. Although it is illegal in most states for anyone under 21 years to purchase and consume alcohol, advertising often appears to be targeted to such youth. According to the National Clearinghouse of Alcohol and Drug Information, U.S. college students (the majority of which are under 21) spend some $4.2 billion a year on alcoholic beverages.

Moreover, critics point out, alcohol advertising contains mostly imagery associated with happy times and little valuable consumer information. The purchase of a six pack offers the hope of good times and social acceptance—an escapist promise that often leads to addiction and sometimes alcoholism.

Arguments to Keep Alcohol Advertising on the Air

There are several compelling arguments against interfering with the existing setup of alcohol advertising on radio and TV.

1. Fundamental to this whole problem is the First Amendment which prohibits any interference by the government with speech or press; advertising has been included in this protection. (*New York Times v. Sullivan* [1964]; *Bigelow v. Virginia* [1975]; *Virginia State Board of Pharmacy v. Virginia Citizens' Consumer Council, Inc.* [1976]; *Central Hudson v. Public Service Commission* [1980]). Even if one believes that there is a problem with alcohol advertising, the real issue is what to do about it. Many legal experts and case law determine that the government could not constitutionally impose such a ban, unless the courts find clear evidence that by doing so it is protecting the general welfare of the nation.

2. Our society depends on the judgment of an informed electorate or consumer. This is Milton's (1951) idea of self-righting process that truth will be found and prevail. This holds true economically as well as ideologically. If a product causes harm or is inherently evil, consumers will reason that out and shun the product. This perspective reasons that the decision to screen something out should be made on the consumer or citizens's end, not on that of government.

3. The slippery slope idea suggests that if beer and wine advertising is banned, what is to prevent the censor's ax from falling on other products at will—perhaps those whose consumption presents health risks of one kind or another (e.g., sugared cereal, meat or milk with fat content, or even automobiles in which tens of thousands of American die every year)?

4. Those arguing against alcohol advertising in broadcasting assume some kind of relationship between advertising and use of the product, particularly abuse. If advertising did not affect consumer purchasing behavior, those favoring a ban argue, breweries would not spend millions of dollars each year in such ventures. To this, advertisers and marketers will reply that such advertising does not necessarily induce consumption, but only encourages those already consuming beer to use the brand that is being advertised—market positioning.

5. Perhaps the most important consideration of all involves the enormous economic stake in the continuing of advertising—on the part of both manufacturers and the media. The profits trickle down to not only the associated industries of the breweries and wineries, but all the media services as well (e.g., advertising agencies, creative and production people, etc.). It is probably not an overstatement to say that the loss of alcohol advertising would be a devastating economic blow to the media.

The decisions concerning this large-scale problem may go back to anticipatory proactive action by media management. How fully and completely can a manager be an agent for social change—in this case, fight the problems of associated with the promotion of alcohol—without harming the profitable free enterprise involved in the advertising of beer and wine? One working model of proactive management of the dilemma started with a TV station general manager who knew of the issues of this particular problem. He had been personally troubled by some of the problems involved in alcohol abuse, and yet felt strongly about the need for freedom for the media to choose in dealing with the problem on their own. He was increasingly the target of consumer groups insisting on the removal of alcohol advertising from his station. He deliberated on the problem. Then it occurred to him to implement some of the characteristics of proactive handling of the problem.

First, he started with the idea of doing something about the problem before it came to be a law-making issue. Then, he formulated, democratically, a means to implement action to address the problem. He solicited the help of community and business leaders and formed a broadcasters' alcohol task force. The goals of the task force are identified in a Community Outreach Handbook of the Washington State Association of Broadcasters, "Tough Choices: Tackling the Teen Alcohol Problem" (1991), and include the following: (a) Provide accurate and current information about alcohol use and abuse, (b) identify approaches to abuse prevention and develop criteria for broadcast materials so that air time would be effectively used for consistent communication on the issue, (c) advise substance abuse experts about the most efficient uses of radio and television, (d) provide an advisory group to assist with research and development of useful materials, and (e) work with advertising agencies, breweries, and wineries to help them produce commercials that would discourage the appeal of alcohol consumption by young people ages 15–20.

The task force conducted extensive research, using focus groups of teens. Four focus groups uncovered teens' thinking about beer and beer advertising. Interestingly enough, one of the many findings was that teens like to hear about proactive solutions (like designating a nondrinking driver), rather than just messages of "don't drink." The teens suggested designs of the public service announcements to help educate viewers/listeners about alcohol and its abuse. It brought forth mottos and slogans, and even had local high schools participate in making the public service announcements. The teens, of all people, suggested that viewers not be told what to do or not do—Rather, give the audience options. Show reality, they said.

Using these ideas, the task force encouraged broadcasters to look at their programming and showed them ways to cover the issues, coordinate the sales department, and look at the various aspects of their public service. It also gave helpful suggestions on newsroom policies and strategies for covering the news on related issues. It furnished further national resources for the broadcasters, identified people in the various communities to contact, and suggested some station project ideas.

The project has received national recognition for its innovations in tackling a problem without partisan dogmatism. It has become a model for the National Association of Broadcasters (NAB) in developing strategy for addressing the problem. The work showed genuine concern and may have fended off legislative action moving toward the outright banning of beer and wine advertising from radio and TV.

What are the lessons from all this? Broadcasters, like the TV general manager in this case study, can practice ethics and strikingly demonstrate proactive business leadership. These characteristics parallel other dissimilar business settings, and appear to be universal. They may be partly intuitive. But intuitive or not, there are at least five general principles of proactive management that appear to be applied here in this potentially ethical dilemma. Each is formulated here with direct lessons drawn from this case study. Learning and applying these proactive principles and focusing on values of social concern (but not ignoring the economic factors) turned out to be a pragmatic and intelligent approach.

CHARACTERISTICS OF PROACTIVE MANAGEMENT POLICIES INCORPORATING ETHICS

Introspection of Personal Values

Development of proactive ethics policies begin with individual values. Ethics come from the heart, rather than a book. A manager seeking such an approach may begin with an examination of his or her own values. Plato noted that an unexamined life is not worth living. Policies that reflect ethics are often of an individual nature, as opposed to some kind of collective wisdom. Ethical perspectives rely on personal value judgments, and what constitutes desirable qualities may differ from situation to situation. The application of this in business has been considered by Ferrell and Fraedrich (1981) and Ferrell, Gresham, and Fraedrich (1989), among others. More recently, Goleman (1995) described how an individual's emotional intelligence (EQ) may be an unrecognized key to success and ascension in the corporate world. From the descriptions of this case study, there appears no evidence of thorough introspection on the part of the manager. However, this author's familiarity with the manager, the situation, and the process could lead us to imply such a first step.

Anticipating Ethical Problems

Like statutory laws, those policies that anticipate problems or ethical dilemmas before they arise is the critical first step in formulating proactive company policy (i.e., good proactive policies anticipate problems before they become problems). They glean from the experience of the past and determine what kinds of problems will arise, and formulate policies based on values that are embraced by the company. In business marketing, Samli (1992), in his work *Social Responsibility in Marketing*, pointed out that " ... those who are ahead of such developments or those who can cope with these developments are likely to develop substantial powers, whereas those who are not equally versatile are likely to get even further behind" (p. 54).

In this case, broadcasters have learned from experience that tobacco has been considered enough of a health menace that Congress banned it from radio and TV advertising, beginning in 1971. This scenario could well prompt some broadcasters to be wary of the same kind of process beginning to appear with the advertising of alcohol, specifically beer and wine advertising. Because such advertising comprises a large part of national spot and network advertising for radio and TV, broadcasters are learning to anticipate the threat of such prohibitions. Significantly, in this case, the broadcasters have taken to work on the problem before federal legislation became a real threat. It is this anticipation, with an eye to addressing options, that has won respect from both sides of the issue.

Ability to Activate Implementation

Even the best intentions with sophisticated anticipation will not work unless there is some means of actively putting forth ideas into action. A successful manager would be burned no more than once (if at all) from seeing the problem, but having no policy to help solve it. Being negligent in implementing such a policy is often regarded as a sign of poor management by boards, stockholders, or owners in determining retention. The power to execute policy is an expected duty of management. The manager should know of the issues and problems that he or she might face, and should consciously build station or company policy that can be implemented.

Even if not a formalized policy, there can be a guiding mission statement. Warner and Buchman (1991) noted: "A mission statement is a primary source of pride, self-esteem, and self-confidence for employees—they have confidence in knowing that their company knows where it's going and why it is going there. ... Once a meaningful mission statement is written, a code of ethics becomes easy to write and to follow.... Purpose gives meaning to work" (p. 347).

In this case study, the issue became one of overriding concern for a manager who initiated plans for a task force with its focus groups and its subsequent recommendations. The manager's power to seek out options and choose one that incorporated unique approaches gained respect and became part of the definition of leadership. Such initiative is especially important when no visible solutions or national professional codes exist. Earlier, a solution for this case study may have been found in the Code of Good Practice of the National Association of Broadcasters, with its formulated rules for what could and could not be properly advertised. But in 1982 courts ruled that parts of such policies violated antitrust laws. The code was dropped, leaving more responsibility and initiative in the hands of the individual managers and companies (Limburg, 1989).

Formulating by Democratic Participation

In many organizations, egalitarian qualities and willingness to allow employee input or participation create efficient management and a spirit of congeniality. In a democracy, those who are affected by the laws and policies participate in their formation. Likewise, in public relations, organizational communication, and business management, this applied theory advocates the use of ideas from the participants, or those who will be governed by the rules. In Adam Smith's (1779) ideal, performance of the market and decision making is a rational activity that revolves around individual utility and satisfaction. More than in just consumer markets, the Smith market ideal is applicable in management of both employees and the public. The economic growth and well-being, whether for a company or for the company's clients, stem from the people's efforts to satisfy their self-interests.

This case study offers the ideal of all parties to the issue—business leaders, media, pressure groups, and teens—who were all pulling together to create a synergetic policy, where the product is greater than the sum of its parts. Also included were the singular effort of a manager. If the manager were to have formulated a *unilateral* policy, no matter how friendly to the other parties' perspective, the efforts would have been suspect at best and likely dismissed, for they might then have been considered dictatorial and imposed, because they were not democratically formulated.

Under this element of proactive ethics policy, the manager also recognized individual employees who were concerned with doing the right thing—those who are honest and have integrity, even at the risk of being overly frank or outspoken. Managers attentive to ethics in their policies will respond to remedial voices and even encourage criticism in their organizations.

Clarifying Ambiguous Practices by Value Reference

Illegal practices would obviously not be tolerated in company policy. For example, Dow Jones and Company published a "Conflicts of Interest Policy" (1995), identifying some taboo illegal activities like "insider trading," even in this internal company policy. But most policies address something less ambiguous than illegal practices. Moreover, unproductive decision-making is not tolerated in most business settings. Such is the question that drives the title of a 1989 article in *Business and Society Review,*—"Do Good Ethics Ensure Good Profits?" In this case study, it can be noted that the manager was aiming to solve the problem for everyone, not just insisting on keeping the profitable advertising. (The results actually brought about the keeping of such profitability anyway.) The value of having sensitivity to others' perspectives is displayed here. Other values include a vision of the greater social good. A declaration of concern to solve the problem by taking into consideration others' feelings and values became part of the policy. There was value reference.

In ethical dilemmas, policies may be in the form of an attitude or philosophy, and refer to the dominance of a key principle or value. Such a perspective is often economic, and has been labeled *pocketbook ethics* (Samli, 1992). Such policy references tend to answer any ambiguity not specifically addressed in the wording of the written policy. Making ethical decisions involves not only applying values to professional conduct, but deciding which values have higher priority than others. Sometimes two values may have virtue, but behavior will dictate the necessity of choosing one over another. For example, if honesty dominates over profit, then that becomes the referent in ethical problem solving.

If the principles in ethics policy incorporate values—if they provide for the spirit of the law, not just exact rules—then they can set forth a tone, spirit, or atmosphere that can guide more specific conduct.

THE PROBLEM OF AUTHORITY IN ETHICS

Models have been derived for outlining accountability in business ethics (Goodpaster, 1989). As was illustrated in this case study, accountability may be defined not only in terms of individual moral accountability, but also in terms of the compounding efforts of management involved in moral decision making. In organizational ethics, the responsibility rests on the shoulders of the manager. It becomes his or her authority, and may be done without lessening the autonomy of the individual's value judgments.

In most commercial settings, it is understood who the boss is and where lines of authority are derived. The best ethical policies may carry the clout of what the boss says. Although they are created or endorsed by someone with high authority, the essential element is that everyone understands them and agrees to abide by them, or suffers the consequences, including, perhaps, job loss.

It is this element of enforcement that puts teeth into any ethics policy. The general problem with self-regulatory ethical codes or policies is that, because they are internal, there is no provision for outside monitoring, and thus there is difficulty in enforcement. Without some internal means of control—a penalty, consequence, or negative effect—it may be difficult to have authoritative clout in keeping the policies. Threat of job loss may be enough, as long as it is clearly laid out as a consequence in the policy. Otherwise, there may be threat of legal retaliation with an employee's dismissal.

From this case study, it should be apparent that a heavy-handed enforcement or an authoritarian overseeing would spoil the spirit of ethics, which is based on performance driven from within the individual, from his or her personal value system. Yet the professional, no matter what the status, is partly shaped by professional expectations. Just the thought of derision by respected peers may incur a wrath that can have as strong an effect as firing.

Some democratic managers formulate policies in a way that they do not appear to be imposed, but rather are something that trusted professionals are expected to practice. Leadership personality traits may determine where, along the scale of authoritarian and total autonomy, dichotomy is the best fit for policy formulation. If a policy is democratically formulated, it may be able to have demanding consequences without serious repercussions.

SUMMARY

Proactive approaches in broadcast management have been shown to be effective and productive. Moreover, they can address thorny ethical problems, sometimes even before they arise or become serious. Such approaches become recognized as a good will, positive effort by the audience the broadcaster serves, and can enhance a public relations image as much as a deliberate promotional strategy.

The characteristics of the proactive model are sometimes second nature to some managers: a positive, friendly, assertive style of leadership that has been intuitively used for decades, but only more recently identified in coming to grips with ethical problems that will often surface. Definitive characteristics identified here include a manager's ability to: (a) introspect personal values, (b) anticipate ethical problems, (c) activate means of implementation, (d) formulate democratic participation, and (e) clarify ambiguous practices by value reference.

Because the public is becoming more keenly aware of ethical activity, business must become increasingly sensitive in positively handling the problems, both individually and collectively as a business. Today, this is becoming the hallmark of reputable management and leadership.

ACKNOWLEDGMENTS

Parts of this chapter are from the author's recent work, *Electronic Media Ethics*, published by Focal Press, 1994. Acknowledgment is given to Focal Press for permission to include material from chapter 10, "Ethics and Proactive Management" (Limburg, 1994).

REFERENCES

Bartels, R. (1967). A model for ethics in marketing, *Journal of Marketing*, *31* 20–25.

Bigelow v. Virginia, 421 U.S. 809 (1975).

Central Hudson v. Public Service Commission, 447 U.S. 557 (1980).

Dow Jones & Company (1995). Conflicts of interest policy. In C. Fink (Ed.), *Media ethics* (pp. 319–322). Boston: Allyn & Bacon.

Do good ethics ensure good profits? (1989). *Business and Society Review* (Vol. 70, Summer), 4–10.

Ferrell, O. C., & Fraedrich, J. (1981). *Business ethics* (Vol. 19). Boston: Houghton Mifflin.

Ferrell, O. C., Gresham, L., & Fraedrich, J. (1989). A synthesis of ethical decision models for marketing. *Journal of Macromarketing*, 55–64.

Gibson, R. F. (1986). Corporations, persons and moral responsibility. *Thought*, *21*, 17–26.

Goleman, D. (1995). *Emotional intelligence*. New York: Bantam Books.

Goodpaster, K. E. (1989). Toward an integrated approach to business ethics. In A. Serafini (Ed.), *Ethics and social concerns* (pp. 321–346). New York: Paragon House.

Hacker, G. (1987). Statement in panel, "Free Speech and Advertising—Who Draws the Line?" Boston: Boston University Institute for Democratic Communication transcript.

Hensel, P. J. (1986). Ethical dilemmas in marketing: A rationale. *Journal of Business Ethics*, *5*, 63–67.

Limburg, V. E. (1989). The decline of broadcast ethics: U.S. v. NAB. *Journal of Mass Media Ethics*, *4*(2), 214–231.

Limburg, V. E. (1994). *Electronic media ethics*. Boston: Focal Press.

Milton, J. (1951). *Aeropagitica*. New York: Appleton-Century- Crofts. (Original work published 1644)

Moser, M. R. (1986). A framework for analyzing corporate social responsibility. *Journal of Business Ethics*, *5*, 69–72.

New York Times Co. v. Sullivan, 376 U.S. 254 (1964).

Roberts, D. (1986). Moral managers and business sanctuaries. *Journal of Business Ethics*, *5*, 203–208.

Samli, A. C. (1992). *Social responsibility in marketing*. Westport, CT: Quorum Books.

Schmidt, D. P. (1986). Patterns of argument in business ethics. *Journal of Business Ethics*, *5*, 501–509.

Serafini, A. (1989) *Ethics and social concern*. New York: Paragon House.

Smith, A. (1779). *Wealth of nations*. London: Routledge.

Todd, J. S., (1987). *Free speech and advertising—Who draws the line*? Boston: Boston University Institute for Democratic Communication.

Tough choices: Tackling the teen alcohol problem. A community outreach handbook. (1991). Seattle: Washington State Association of Broadcasters, Alcohol Task Force.

Value marketing. (1991, November 11). *Business Week*, pp. 132–140.

Virginia State Board of Pharmacy v. Virginia Citizens' Consumer Council, 425 U.S. 748 (1976).

Warner, C., & Buchman, J. (1991). *Broadcast and cable selling*. Belmont, CA: Wadsworth.

Chapter 7

Short-Circuited Mergers in the Mass Media: Credible and Incredible Evidence

Patricia T. Whalen
Barry R. Litman
Michigan State University

Numerous studies have evaluated the success of mergers based on the financial performance of the combined firm. This chapter examines collapsed mergers—those that have been publicly announced, but that do not come to fruition. The chapter specifically focuses on the mass media and some unique financial and technological issues that may explain the recent boom in media mergers and the potential for some of them to collapse before completion. The chapter examines five recent, highly publicized media megamergers that ultimately collapsed: Bell Atlantic/TCI, Southwestern Bell/Cox Enterprises, Contel/COMSAT, Turner Broadcasting/NBC, and QVC/CBS. It strives to determine what factors they shared, and if they could be linked to factors that have been shown in other merger studies to contribute to the failure of completed mergers. The chapter concludes that, although changes in the market price of the firms' stock, the presence of large individual shareholders, and firm size and relatedness may be important in the demise of the negotiations, conflicts in corporate culture and personality clashes play the largest role in short-circuiting a media merger.

Newspaper headline writers had a field day on August 1, 1995, when Walt Disney announced its intention to acquire Capital Cities/ABC. Even the stoic *Wall Street Journal* could not resist such lines as, "All Ears: Disney's Deal for ABC Makes Show Business a Whole New World" (Landro, Jensen, & King, 1995), when it wrote about the second largest merger in U.S. history, after the $25 billion R. J. Reynolds/Nabisco merger.

One day later, Westinghouse announced its long-awaited $5.4 billion acquisition of CBS, Inc. Immediately following these announcements, the business press began to publish articles that hailed a whole new strategic focus on mergers in the entertainment industry. It was reminiscent of the 1980s, when the term *merger mania* was used extensively in relation to the media industry.

MEDIA MERGER BOOM

The current media merger boom began in earnest in early 1993, and has continued unabated through 1995, after a previous 4-year slow down in merger activities. The *Wall Street Journal* reported that the number of mergers and acquisitions in the United States doubled between 1992 and 1993, and media mergers played an important role in the increase (Smith, 1993). One should recall that it was in 1993 that the American Telephone and Telegraph Co. (AT&T) announced its $12.6 billion acquisition of McCaw Cellular Communications Corp. (August 1993), and the $9.5 billion battle began between two cable network companies, QVC, Inc. and Viacom Inc., for the movie and publishing giant, Paramount Communications Inc. (September 1993). At the same time, Paramount, although the target of that acquisition battle, aggressively pursued and ultimately won its $552.8 million offer for book publisher Macmillan.

The following year, 1994, began with Viacom announcing its $8.4 billion acquisition of Blockbuster Video (January 1994). That year also saw the AT&T/McCaw Cellular and Viacom/Paramount deals completed. By October 1994, the National Cable Television Association reported that there were no fewer than 23 major media and telecommunications deals on the table that focused just on converging media industries such as cable, telephone, and cellular. By all indications, the United States was clearly in the midst of a full-fledged media merger wave.

FAILED MEDIA MERGERS

But not all the deals made it to completion. Two of the largest potential media mergers, initially announced in 1993, ultimately collapsed in 1994, within a few months of their announcement. The first was the highly touted $29.3 billion[1] Bell Atlantic/Tele-Communications Inc. (TCI) megamerger, which, had it been successful, would have been the largest in U.S. history. That announcement sparked widespread speculation about a number of similar merger hopefuls intent on joining the crest of the wave toward convergence of the cable-TV and telephone industries.

---

[1]The value of the Bell Atlantic/TCI deal has been estimated at various levels, depending on the stock value at the time of the article and whether the assets of Liberty Media were included, from a low of $19 billion (*The Wall Street Journal*, Oct. 14, 1993) to a high of $33 billion (*Mergers and Acquisitions*, May/June 1994).

One of these was the $4.9 billion Southwestern Bell/Cox Enterprises joint venture, which would have merged the firms' telephone and cable-TV expertise into a new business venture—Cox Cable. That venture also failed to materialize.

These failures are reminiscent of how fragile a merger can be, and that an announcement of a pending merger or acquisition does not ensure a completed deal, no matter how much publicity it receives or how advantageous the synergies of the merged firm seem to be. In fact, *Mergers and Acquisitions* reported that, "on a market-wide basis, the number of short-circuited deals was up substantially in 1993, to 252 from 204 in 1992" ("Crash on the Highway," 1994, p. 29). The publication also speculated that the actual number of failed deals was much higher than reported, because a large number of proposed transactions are negotiated in secret and are never announced if an agreement is not reached.

This chapter addresses the phenomenon of the failed merger—those that collapse after the firms have publicly announced their intent to join forces, but before coming to fruition.

RESEARCH SCOPE

The study examined five recently failed megamergers within the mass media industry to identify common elements that may have caused the merger negotiations to collapse. The five failed mergers include two telephone company/cable deals—Bell Atlantic/TCI and Southwestern Bell/Cox Enterprises; a potential merger between a domestic telephone company and an international satellite carrier—Contel/COMSAT; and two programming supplier/broadcaster agreements—Turner Broadcasting/NBC and QVC/CBS. These merger collapses were selected because they were all relatively recent, the values of the proposed merged firms all well exceeded the $1 billion mark that popularly classifies them as "megamergers," all 10 of the firms involved operated within the mass media or telecommunications arena, and they all were highly publicized with little speculation that they might not succeed.

Although the sample of firms is not large enough to generalize the results or conduct sophisticated statistical analysis, the study does raise some interesting questions about what the key factors are in completing merger negotiations. Identifying these factors may be useful in assessing the likelihood of future mergers encountering pitfalls that could derail the future negotiations.

Research Questions

Each proposed merger was explored for such specific factors as: (a) type of merger and the cultural fit, (b) whether the two negotiating firms were related or unrelated, (c) the size of the firms, and (d) the market changes in their individual stock prices. The study also examined the specific explanations publicly given by the firms for the collapse of the deals, and summarized what others have speculated may be the "real" reason for the collapse. Finally, it looked for patterns to suggest the possibility of predicting future negotiation failures.

Two key questions guide this study:

1. Can the observations from the literature on the success or failure of completed mergers be generalized to the premerger negotiation stage?
2. Is there a relationship between how the market reacts to the two firms' stock after a merger is announced and the ultimate collapse of the merger negotiations?

Definitions

The following definitions and assumptions are used throughout this chapter. *Mass media companies* are those operating in television or radio broadcasting, cable television, newspaper, magazine or book publishing, or the production and distribution of films and television programming. Because of recent technological changes in how programming may be delivered to the home (i.e., across fiber-optic cable and via small satellite dishes) and the interest in convergence of some mass media companies with telephone companies, telecommunications firms have also been included in this category for this article.

The terms *merger* and *acquisition* are used interchangeably in a broad sense to refer to any transaction where a company goes outside its own organization for investment purposes and acquires or combines with a second company. For this chapter, the terms encompass the more specific terms of *integration, joint venture,* and *consolidation.*

Leverage means the use of debt to finance an acquisition, and pledging the acquired company's assets as collateral for the loans. *Equity financing* means using company stock—either existing or newly issued—to pay for an acquisition. The market value of the stock is usually determined and a stock-for-stock trade takes place, sometimes with an additional amount of cash attached to each share.

The following system is used to classify the type of merger: *Horizontal* means that both companies are in the same industry, with approximately the same customers and suppliers. *Vertical integration* means that the firm being acquired is a major supplier or customer of the buying company and in the same industry. *Concentric marketing* means that both firms have the same customer types, but the firms use a different technology. *Concentric technology* means that both firms use the same technology, but have different customer types. A *conglomerate* merger is one where a firm acquires another that has different customers and technology than its own, usually indicating that the firms operate in different industries (Kitching, 1967). It is interesting to note that the Federal Trade Commission (FTC) classifies mergers into just four types, collapsing the horizontal and market concentric mergers into one category.

PAST RESEARCH AND A NEW ENVIRONMENT

A review of the literature on merger successes and failures suggests that most of the analysis on mergers to date has been focused on applying specific financial goals to an already merged organization—either in terms of an increase in stockholder value (Lubatkin, 1987; Shelton, 1988) or by using financial ratios and other criteria for determining financial success (Bielinski, 1992; Hogarty, 1978; Lee & Cooperman, 1989; McGann & Russel, 1988; Mueller, 1977; Stevens, 1972). The performance of the pre- and post-merger firms are then compared to determine if the merger should be deemed a success or a failure.

Some studies have used surveys, observations, and interviews with corporate executives to obtain subjective opinions about how successful a merger is perceived to be from within the organization (Chatterjee, Lubatkin, Schweiger, & Weber, 1992; Kitching, 1967; Levinson, 1973). Those studies focused on issues of cultural fit and how mismatched corporate cultures and personality factors can affect a merger's success. Although the popular business press has occasionally addressed why some proposed mergers fail to materialize (Callahan, 1986), the academic literature has virtually ignored the causes or characteristics of collapsed mergers.

Why Do Media Firms Want To Merge?

Litman and Sochay (1994) noted that "there is a growing perception in the communications industry that to survive in the marketplace, it is essential to become a global media colossus" (p. 234). As evidence of this trend, they cited the merging of four of the top seven Hollywood movie studios into other corporate conglomerates in the late 1980s. "By merging or consolidating, an entertainment company can not only spread its risk, but through vertical integration can back up its product with distribution and sales outlets as well" (p. 234).

In addition, there have been a number of recent changes in 20-year-old federal regulations that, in the past, limited the number and type of mergers that could take place within the various media industries. For example, established regulations barring movie studios from owning television networks recently changed, thereby facilitating the recent Disney/ABC announcement. Similarly, the networks are now allowed to own more of their programming sources, and will soon be able to syndicate shows directly to local stations, as well as their own studios. This opened the door for such recent ventures as Capital Cities/ABC forming a production studio with DreamWorks, the new venture formed by Jeffrey Katzenberg, Steven Spielberg, and David Geffen. It also led to News Corporation's, Fox division owning a network, local television stations, and a movie studio, while Time Warner and Viacom Inc., which both own movie studios, were able to start new broadcast networks (Jensen & Landro, 1995). This new level of competition, stimulated by the relaxation of the regulations, most certainly was the impetus for early TBS/NBC discussions and the 1996 acquisition of Turner Broadcasting Systems (TBS) by Time Warner. Other regulatory changes, which allowed the regional Bell Operating Companies to provide services with cable-TV companies (at least outside their own service areas), may have precipitated the Bell Atlantic/TCI and Southwestern Bell/Cox Cable merger negotiations, as well as a host of others in various stages of negotiation.

Behind this strategy is the concept of synergy, or the notion that the sum is greater than the parts and that the combination of two firms will produce greater efficiencies than either of the two firms can achieve alone. Literally hundreds of articles have been published in the popular business press and in academic journals on the concept of merger synergies. Bielinski (1992) provided a summary table that highlights most of the potential synergistic effects from mergers (see Table 7.1), but he warned that many firms overestimate the actual synergies that will be achieved, and, consequently, they pay too much for their acquisitions.

Current Mergers Versus Past Mergers

To explore the phenomenon of current media mergers and their successful or unsuccessful completion, it is important to compare the way they are

TABLE 7.1
Some Synergistic Sources Within Mergers

New markets for acquirer's products
New markets for target's products
Stronger combined product line
Manufacturing efficiencies (higher volume, focused factories)
Buy raw materials in larger volume—better prices
Eliminate duplicate general and administrative functions and departments
Eliminate duplication where suppliers are few and common to acquier and target
Eliminate duplication where customers are relatively few and in similar geographic territories
Tax benefits
Avoid additional capital expenditures through use of acquired warehouse or manufacturing capacity
Lower cost of money
Sale of unneeded assets (e.g., office space)
Risk and cost reduction through vertical or horizontal integration

From D. Bielinski, "Putting a realistic dollar value on acquisition synergies." *Mergers and Acquisitions,* November/December 1992, pp. 9–12. Reprinted with permission.

being conducted today with the recent past. Mergers of the 1970s and early 1980s tended to focus on spreading risk through diversification in nonrelated businesses, whereas those proposed today focus more on synergies and staying in related industries (Smith, 1993).

In addition, the 1970s and 1980s witnessed extensive use of antitakeover provisions because many of the mergers were the result of unfriendly raids. Today, corporate boards are more cognizant of maximizing shareholder value even if it means merging (Vogel, 1995). The past focus on diversification has given way to greater concentration on core businesses and on growing large enough to dominate a market.

But even when interested in expanding a core business, depressed stock prices in the 1970s and 1980s often made it "cheaper to purchase a company than to grow through internal investment ... and firms found new sources of capital for highly leveraged transactions—most notably high-yield 'junk bonds'" (Ozanich & Wirth, 1993, p. 119). The use of junk bonds rose to nearly $30 billion by 1987 and fueled a great many of the mergers and acquisitions of the 1980s, causing significant problems with making debt payments when expected revenues failed to materialize.

Today's mergers are being funded primarily by equity financing, which, although potentially risky if stock prices suddenly plunge, is currently being aided by a strong bull market. Another important trend today is the bypassing of investment bankers to complete the deals. The merger wave is now motivated by the companies, not financial entrepreneurs merely seeking to profit from the transaction, regardless of how much sense it makes.

There are some risks, however, from the new financing methods. The emphasis on stock makes the fluctuations in the acquirer's stock price a critical issue in completing the deal, as does the importance of large shareholders who need to be convinced of the value of the merger at the outset and placated throughout the merger negotiations. The lives of the executives of the merging firms become much more complicated when they have to deal with dozens of large shareholders, instead of a handful of investment bankers.

FIVE MEDIA MERGERS THAT NEVER WERE

The following summarizes the five failed mergers examined in this chapter.

Bell Atlantic/TCI

This $29.3 billion deal, which was announced in October 1993 and formally discontinued in February 1994, would have had Bell Atlantic acquire the assets of TCI Cable Systems and its Liberty Media subsidiary. The acquisition was to launch Bell Atlantic into the forefront of the interactive video world for the 21st century and diversify its business operations outside its traditional Bell operating region by providing a broad range of information and shopping services. The advantage to TCI was the infusion of cash that it needed to continue expanding its cable operations. The deal would have made TCI CEO John Malone a billionaire stockholder in Bell Atlantic and vice chairman of the merged firm.

The formal reason given for the collapse of the merger was that Raymond Smith, chairman of Bell Atlantic, concerned about new cable regulations that would require an additional 7% reduction in TCI's rates, wanted to renegotiate a lower price, and John Malone rejected it. However, the *Wall Street Journal* reported that the collapse was as much due to "the sharply divergent cultures of [the two firms] and the stubborn convictions of their respective chief executives" (Kneale, Roberts, & Cauley, 1994, p.A1). Malone had publicly stated that he felt the Bell Atlantic culture was "stuck in the mud" conservative, and that one of the first things he would do when they merged was to reinvest profits and discontinue paying dividends, which Bell Atlantic had traditionally paid (Kneale et al., 1994). When the negotiations collapsed, both CEOs downplayed the cultural issues, and publicly blamed the Federal Communications Commission (FCC) and Washington, saying they would continue to look for ways to work together in the future.

Southwestern Bell/Cox Enterprises

The announcement of this joint venture came in December 1993 on the heels of the Bell Atlantic/TCI announcement, when the business media were giving a great deal of credence to the value of converging the telecommunications and cable industries. The plan was for Southwestern Bell, a division of parent SBC Communication, Inc., to infuse $1.6 billion in cash over 4 years into a new cable venture created by the privately owned Cox Enterprises, Inc. The new venture, which would have been publicly traded and called "Cox Cable, Inc.," would have used SBC's cash and the venture's debt capacity to acquire new cable and programming assets, and to offer future entertainment and multimedia services through existing cable systems.[2] In return, Southwestern Bell would have received a 40% stake in the joint venture (with an option to increase it to 50%), but no ownership in the Cox parent, Cox Enterprises (Brown, 1993). This true joint venture would have given Southwestern Bell an opportunity for national expansion and access to an interactive network capable of carrying movies, shopping, and games, as well as its traditional telephone service.

Cox would have contributed its $3.3 billion in cable assets to retain a 60% ownership in the joint venture and, after executing its further expansion plans, jump from being the sixth largest to the third largest Multiple System

---

[2]The information for the strategic direction of the Southwestern Bell/Cox joint venture came from the discussion section of the 1993 Annual Report of Southwestern Bell Corporation.

Operator (MSO) in the United States. In contrast to the Bell Atlantic/TCI management structure, where Bell Atlantic's Ray Smith would have been the top executive, Jim Robbins, Cox Cable President, would have been CEO of the joint venture (Brown, 1993).

The new venture was called off by Southwestern Bell's CEO, Ed Whitacre, in April 1994 (a little over a month after the Bell Atlantic/TCI deal was canceled), citing the same regulatory and rate concerns that Bell Atlantic expressed. The popular business press, however, widely reported, that once the Bell Atlantic/TCI deal fell through, there was no longer any pressure on the other regional Bell companies to push so quickly for national expansion (Bernier, 1994; "Crash on the Highway," 1994).

Contel/COMSAT

The merger between Contel Corporation, the third largest independent telephone company in the United States, and the Communications Satellite Corporation (COMSAT), the world's leader in international satellite communications, was announced in September 1986. The merged firm would have had combined assets of over $6 billion and $3.5 billion in annual revenues ("COMSAT & Contel Boards Approve Merger," 1986).

COMSAT was the smaller of the two firms, with revenues in 1986 of approximately $466 million. Its unique congressionally mandated monopoly in international satellite communications,[3] however, allowed it to carry over one third of the world's international telephone calls and virtually all of the U.S. broadcasters' international television signals. But by the mid-1980s, the U.S. government had made it clear that it would soon open the door to competition in the international satellite arena, so the company sought out a merger partner with marketing expertise in the telecommunications arena.

Contel was founded in 1961, when Charles Wohlstetter invested $1.1 million in a rural Alaskan phone company. Over the next 25 years, he bought more than 700 phone companies, making the firm a major competitor with the huge Bell system, and bringing its revenue to nearly $3 billion by 1986 (Cannon, 1987). The merger with COMSAT would have given the firm access to the international arena, plus all of the technology of the COMSAT laboratories. In addition, it would have been protected from any hostile takeover attempts in the future by retaining the protective umbrella of the congressionally mandated COMSAT.

---

[3]See the Communications Satellite Action of 1963 for an explanation of COMSAT's charter and its U. S. signatory role in the International Telecommunications Satellite Organizations (INTELSAT).

Despite approval of the deal by the FCC, FTC, and both companies' shareholders and boards of directors, Contel announced on April 14, 1987, that it was ending the agreement due to a $62 million FCC order for COMSAT to refund overcharges for past international communications services ("Contel Says FCC Actions Pose Problems for Merger," 1987). *Business Week* reported, however, that "to industry observers, the government actions looked more like an excuse for Contel management than a reason for calling off the linkup" (Payne & Keller, 1987, p. 39). The magazine said that Contel had been well aware of the potential FCC actions for months, and that COMSAT had reported them in public filings that predated the merger agreement. The publication suggested that the real reason behind the merger's collapse was partly an ego issue for Wohlstetter. Paradoxically, although his company would play the larger role in managing the merged firm, it would lose its identity and assume the smaller company's name. Perhaps more important, there was a rift between Wohlstetter and Contel President John N. LeMasters. LeMasters had "pushed the deal through in the first place and ... Wohlstetter wouldn't let him participate in the decision to drop the merger" (Payne & Keller, 1987, p. 39).

Interestingly, COMSAT tried to force Contel to go through with the merger, but, finally, in August 1987, the dispute was resolved when Contel agreed to buy two of COMSAT's money-losing businesses—a data network service, and its satellite antenna manufacturing business—for $38 million. This was surely a strange marriage of convenience.

QVC/CBS

The friendly $7.2 billion merger agreement between QVC Network, Inc.[4] and CBS, Inc. involved another unlikely pairing—namely, 52-year-old QVC CEO Barry Diller and 71-year-old CBS Chairman Laurence Tisch. It would be one of the shortest combinations on record. The announcement was made public on June 29, 1994, and ended on July 13, 1994, the day before the CBS board was set to approve it.

The original announcement said that the two firms would merge, and, although on paper CBS would be dominant over QVC, Tisch promised: "Barry will be the boss" (Reibstein & Hass, 1994, p. 46). Tisch would have remained the CBS chairman for 2 years and then stepped down, but his family's Loews Corporation would have retained a 9.4% stake in the company. Diller would have been the CBS CEO. Existing CBS stockholders would have gotten 54% of the merged company plus a cash dividend of $175 per share, whereas QVC holders would have gotten a 46% share in the new firm (Schmuckler, 1994).

---

[4]QVC Network, Inc. has subsequently changed its name to QVC, Inc.

Although the initial media reports of the merger questioned any real synergies between the two companies and jokingly referred to the merger in such terms as "the Tiffany network meets cubic Zirconium" (Reibstein & Hass, 1994, p. 46), the stock market and business press generally hailed it as a good match. The advantage to CBS would primarily have been the experienced leadership of Barry Diller, who had a strong broadcasting and movie studio background and was considered an expert in programming. Many analysts felt that CBS, under Tisch's leadership, lacked strategic direction, and the QVC deal would enable it to move into cable and vertically integrate to obtain better access to programming.

The merger was killed after less than 2 weeks, when QVC's largest shareholder, COMCAST Corporation (which co-owned with Barry Diller 28% of QVC), felt left out of the deal and joined forces with TCI, QVC's second largest shareholder, to launch a $2.2 billion takeover bid for QVC.

COMCAST's Brian L. Roberts, in explaining why he played the spoiler in the QVC/CBS deal, publicly stated that he viewed the merger as a "sale of QVC to CBS," which "would have made us a disenfranchised minority investor" (Landler & Grover, 1994, p. 29). He was most concerned about his company's significant investment in QVC dropping to a 4.9% stake in the combined CBS/QVC entity and losing a seat on the company's board.

Turner Broadcasting/NBC

A formal agreement for the proposed merger between Turner Broadcasting System (TBS) and the National Broadcasting Company (NBC), owned by General Electric (GE) Company, was never reached in the same manner as they were for the previous four mergers discussed previously.

Although Ted Turner was quoted in *Electronic Media* as saying he had "struck a $5 billion 'basic deal' with GE for NBC a year ago" (Mermigas, 1994a, p. 47), GE denied that any agreement had been reached with TBS then or a year earlier. NBC President and CEO, Robert Wright, did, however, confirm that negotiations were underway with TBS. However, GE no longer wanted to sell NBC outright, but rather wanted to find a minority partner "whose operations and cash investment will enhance the network, its TV stations and cable services" (Mermigas, 1994a, p. 47).

The general agreement under consideration was that TBS would put up some cash, but primarily finance its purchase by giving GE a note for a 49% ownership interest in the $6 billion NBC. GE would retain a 51% ownership. The biggest complicating factor was that, although Ted Turner owned 26% of the TBS stock and controlled 63% of the votes, TBS had two large shareholders—Time Warner and TCI—who were often at odds with Turner and who had veto power on the TBS board.

Time Warner was also a potential merger partner with NBC, and Turner accused its management of a conflict of interest by purposely trying to kill the TBS/NBC deal (Mermigas, 1994b). By December 1994, both Time Warner and TCI agreed to support a merger between TBS and NBC, but only if a complex agreement could be worked out that would allow them to have some ownership in the newly merged firm's assets.

The publicly stated reason for ending the negotiations was an issue of control. Turner continued to negotiate with GE for TBS to acquire NBC outright, but with GE retaining a minority ownership of 35%. The deal was officially called off by Turner on January 13, 1995, when GE, still inflexible on its need to own at least 51%, made Turner an offer to merge his entire operation into a new NBC/TBS combined venture valued at approximately $11 billion (Mermigas, 1995).

By February 1995, another opportunity to merge arose when TCI announced that it might buy out Time Warner's share in TBS, and thereby take control of TBS. It was then speculated that a new threeway merger could arise among TCI, TBS, and NBC. In March 1995, however, TCI turned its attention to a new $4 billion joint venture with Sprint Corp., Cox Enterprises, and COMCAST, and announced that it would not be pursuing Time Warner's TBS stock ("Time Warner's Effort to Sell," 1995).

Turner said publicly that the negotiations were over with GE, but he left the door open for future discussions. In early August 1995, on the heels of the Disney/Capital Cities–ABC and Westinghouse/CBS announcements, the *Wall Street Journal* speculated that TBS might make a counteroffer for CBS (Narisetti, Robinchaux, & Trachtenberg, 1995). But by late August, the tables had once again turned with a reported buyout of TBS by Time Warner. That deal was ultimately completed in 1996.

LITERATURE REVIEW: FACTORS THAT MAY AFFECT A MERGER'S SUCCESS

Type of Merger

Past studies on mergers have suggested that the type of merger—vertical, horizontal, concentric, or conglomerate—might play a role in the likelihood of the merger collapse. Vertical mergers provide certain access to materials and markets that puts pressure on nonintegrated competitors to integrate as well. Litman (1979) prophesied about "contagious merger races where vertical integration may breed vertical integration apart from any gains in efficiency" (p. 228). That may explain why there was such a high level of merger activity within the telecommunications and cable industries immediately following the Bell Atlantic/TCI announcement, and the subsequent collapse of many of the discussions once the negotiations ended unsuccessfully.

The proposed Bell Atlantic acquisition of TCI and the proposed joint venture between Southwestern Bell/Cox Enterprise might, on the surface, be considered concentric marketing mergers, because each dealt with serving essentially the same customers—the U.S. consumer's home information/entertainment market—but with different technologies. Taking a long-term perspective on the industry, one might classify them more properly as vertical integrations, which would better explain the industry activities surrounding these merger announcements and collapses. This assumes that telecos wishing to provide a full range of communications and information services to the home will require the wiring of either fiber-optic or coaxial cable, which is an upstream step in the distribution process—hence, vertical integration.

In addition to contagious vertical mergers, the literature suggests that conglomerate and concentric mergers, when the acquiring firm has no experience in the industry of the acquired firm, may be more susceptible to regulatory and market events due to confusion about their impact on the business. This issue is closely tied to the concept of relatedness.

Relatedness

Shelton (1988) provided a fairly complicated method of determining whether target and bidder businesses are related. Relying on Rumelt (1974, 1982), Shelton suggested that researchers should examine technology, production, and distribution channels of both firms to determine whether and how the businesses are related to one another. Naturally, horizontal mergers are the most closely related of all the types because the firm already has experience in this industry segment.

Chatterjee, et al. (1992) used a simpler criterion, categorizing firms as related if they were in the same two-digit Standard Industrial Classification (SIC). Montgomery (1982) found a high degree of correspondence between the SIC method and the categorical classification system. Because of its small sample size, this study looked at both measures to determine relatedness.

Although the popular press has hailed the concept of greater synergies coming from mergers between firms that have similar markets and technologies, the academic literature review offered inconclusive evidence that the merging of related firms has a higher rate of success (Lubatkin, 1987). Confirming the relatedness hypothesis were studies by Rumelt (1974) and Singh and Montgomery (1988), which showed that related diversification strategies outperformed unrelated diversification strategies. However,

Lubatkin's 1987 study failed to uncover a positive relationship between product and market relatedness and the future value of the merged firms. Lubatkin cited Bettis and Hall's (1982) study, which refuted Rumelt's (1974) results, indicating that a merged firm's performance is less a function of relatedness than the industry in which it participates. He also cited Elgers and Clark's (1980) study, which also challenged the relatedness hypothesis, finding that both buyer and seller stockholders benefit more from conglomerate than from nonconglomerate mergers.

To determine how or if this factor played a role in the subject merger collapses, the five proposed mergers were classified as either related or unrelated. Four of the five mergers studied would be considered related if just the two-digit SIC codes for the largest line of business is considered for each of the 10 firms involved. Nine of the 10 fall under SIC 48, which is classified as "communications." Only QVC fell into a different SIC code, 59, which is classified as "miscellaneous retail." Therefore, the QVC/CBS merger would be the only one not considered related, using common SICs as the measurement criterion. Using the Shelton/Rumelt classification system, all five of the mergers would be considered related. Yet, despite this high level of relatedness, all five of the mergers failed to be completed.

Size of the Firms

Kitching's (1967) study, testing the critical mass theory first advanced by H. Igor Ansoff, showed that, in 84% of the acquisitions considered failures, the sales of the acquired company were less than 2% of the parent company's sales. This created what he called a "size mismatch," leaving many executives with one of two feelings: that "the acquired company was so small no one in corporate headquarters could get interested in it," or "we couldn't get these little entrepreneurs to think like big businessmen" (p. 92). In the five mergers explored in this chapter, size did not appear to have an effect on their ultimate collapse. For three of the five mergers, the sales of the firm being acquired or merged represented nearly one third of the acquirers' sales: 32% for Bell Atlantic, 26% for Southwestern Bell, and 38% for CBS (although CBS was 2.5 times larger than QVC, QVC was trying to position itself as the acquiring firm). There were two mergers where the percentage of sales was relatively small, but still not as low as Kitching's 2% figure. In the Contel/COMSAT merger, COMSAT's revenues represented only 15% of Contel's. In the TBS/NBC discussions, Turner Broadcasting, the smaller of the two, like QVC, was positioning itself as the acquirer. With NBC revenues at $3.3 billion and its parent, General Electric Company, at $39.6 billion, TBS's $2.8 billion in revenues represented 85% of NBC's revenues, but only 7% of the parent company's.

Although there does not appear to be a discernable pattern reflecting size and the collapse of negotiations, it is interesting that the two media merger negotiations that collapsed the quickest—QVC/CBS in 2 weeks and TBS/NBC in 3 months—were where the smaller organization was trying to act as the acquirer, dealing with a larger, more powerful organization. This was also the case in the Contel/COMSAT merger, at least in terms of the identity of the merged firm.

Capital Market's Reaction to the Merger

Traditional microeconomic theory suggests that, because the acquisition's market is perfectly competitive, the acquirer's stockholders will not have a permanent increase in their wealth position after an acquisition (Mandelker, 1974; cited by Lubatkin, 1987). At the time of the merger, competitors will see the value in the acquired firm, and thus will bid up its price until all of the incremental value of the merger goes to the stockholders of the acquired firm. If this happens, and it is widely reported in the popular press that it does, the acquiring firm's stock price will drop after a merger announcement, and the merging firm's stock price will rise. When the entire financing of the merger is based on stock price, the executives of the merging company may begin to feel that the deal is no longer as valuable as it once was. Hence, this market reaction can have a disastrous effect on completing the merger, unless price protections were built into the deal at the outset.

But this does not happen in all merger situations, as the recent Disney/Capital Cities–ABC deal demonstrates. The day after that announcement, Disney's shares climbed $1.25 to $58.625, despite its taking on over $10 billion in new debt, and Capital Cities' shares soared $20.125 to $116.25. Similarly, in a number of recent acquisitions, acquiring companies such as IBM, American Home Products Corp., and Burlington Northern Inc. saw their stock increase after multimillion dollar announcements ("Let's Get Together," 1995).

Lubatkin (1987) explained this in a merger contingency framework adapted from earlier diversification contingency frameworks (e.g. Rumelt, 1974; and Christensen, Berg and Salter, 1976): "Whether a buyer firm gains or loses from a merger is contingent upon the firm's competitive strengths, the growth rate of its markets and the degree to which these two factors achieve a logical or strategic fit with the competitive strengths and market growth rates of its targeted firm." (p. 40). This theory suggests that the higher the stock price increase for the acquiring firm, the better the fit between the acquiring and acquired firm's.

In the case of the five failed mergers, the market reaction over time was mixed. Table 7.2 summarizes the changes in stock prices for the nine firms (Cox, being a private company, did not have publicly traded stock). Immediately following the public announcement, the stock price of the acquiring firm went up in four of the five mergers. However, by the 10 days before the negotiations ended, four of the five acquirers' stock prices were lower than the premerger price.

TABLE 7.2

Stock Price Changes: Before and Immediately after Merger Announcement and Prior to Collapse

	*QVC/CBS announcement: 6/29/94 collapse: 7/12/94			*TBS/GE (NBC announcement: 10/3/94 collapse: 1/13/95			*Bell Atlantic/TCI announcement: 10/13/93 collapse: 2/23/94			*SW Bell/Cox announcement:12/8/93 collapse: 4/6/94		*Contel/Comsat announcement: 9/29/86 collapse: 4/14/87		
	QVC	CBS	S&P 500	TBS	GE	S&P 500	BA	TCI	S&P 500	SW Bell	S&P 500	Contel	COMSAT	S&P 500
MARKET'S IMMEDIATE REACTION TO ANNOUNCEMENT														
Average Stock Price 10 Days Before Vs. 10 Days After Announcement														
Before	$33.48	$262.61	$452.60	$19.01	$49.10	$462.93	$61.66	$26.53	$460.51	$42.10	$463.32	$32.08	$35.24	$232.83
After	$36.60	306.89	$447.10	$19.74	$48.43	$461.17	$64.16	$30.55	$465.88	$42.88	$464.69	$29.85	$31.00	$234.57
Gain/loss on share price	$3.12	$44.28	($5.50)	$0.73	($0.68)	($1.76)	$2.49	$4.03	$5.37	$0.78	$1.37	($2.23)	($4.24)	$1.74
% gain/loss	9.32%	16.86%	-1.21%	3.81%	-1.37%	-0.38%	4.04%	15.17%	1.17%	1.84%	0.30%	-6.94%	-12.03%	0.75%
Co. Stock Perf. vs. S&P	10.54%	18.08%		4.19%	-1.00%		2.88%	14.01%		1.55%		-7.68%**	-12.77%***	
MARKET'S LONGER TERM REACTION TO ANNOUNCEMENT														
Average Stock Price 10 Days Before Announcement Vs. 10 Days Prior to Collapse														
Before Announcement	$33.48	$262.61	$452.60	$19.01	$49.10	$462.93	$61.66	$26.53	$460.51	$42.10	$463.32	$32.08	$35.24	$232.83
Before collapse	$36.70	$307.88	$446.98	$16.73	$50.49	$460.51	$54.14	$25.84	$470.80	$40.04	$455.33	$31.72	$31.94	$292.50
gain/loss on share price	$3.22	$45.27	($5.62)	($2.28)	$1.39	($2.42)	($7.52)	($0.69)	$10.29	($2.06)	($7.99)	($0.36)	($3.30)	$59.67
% gain/loss	9.62%	17.24%	-1.24%	-12.01%	2.83%	-0.52%	-12.20%	-2.58%	2.23%	-4.89%	-1.72%	-1.11%	-9.36%	25.63%
Co. stock perf. vs. S&P	10.86%	18.48%		-11.48%	3.35%		-14.43%**	-4.82%**		-3.17%		-26.73%**	34.99%***	

Note. Based on average 10-day stock prices.

*Acquiring firm listed first; merging firm listed second.

**Negative market reaction to both acquiring and merging firms' stocks.

There are at least three possible explanations for this to occur: (a) One might speculate that the market caught wind of the impending collapse of the negotiations and reacted unfavorably toward the stock; (b) the economic theory stated earlier would suggest that the market did not believe that there was a strong strategic fit and, therefore, rejected the merger by lowering its valuation of the firms' stock; or (c) from an equity financing perspective, one could claim that the stock price changed for unrelated reasons, but its decline was the reason for the collapse of the merger due to a lowering of the value of the deal to the seller firm.

This chapter does not attempt to decide if any one of these explanations is the most accurate. It simply suggests that the negative market reaction may possibly effect the success of the negotiations and should be closely monitored by the merging firms.

Cultural Fit

There are only a limited number of academic studies that tie the concept of cultural fit to merger success or failure, and many of these rely on opinion surveys and interviews (Chatterjee, et al., 1992; Kitching, 1967). However, the popular business press suggests that cultural and personality issues may have more to do with the success of a merger than synergies or the financial well-being of either of the merging firms. The five failed mergers were examined to see if there were similar cultural and personality issues among them that might help explain why their negotiations collapsed.

The key factors highlighted in the literature were: (a) conflicts in management styles, especially merging conservative firms with entrepreneurial firms; (b) a lack of personal chemistry between the managements of the merging firms; and (c) a lack of understanding of the other firm's markets, technology, or regulatory environments.

Harry Levinson, in his book *The Great Jackass Fallacy* (1973), which among other things explored the psychological roots of merger failures, warned that the pivotal issue can become one of control. He suggested that in organizations that have become rigidly systematic in defining jobs, and in measuring, counting, and controlling matters, there is less room for individual initiative and spontaneity. The existing management becomes resistant to change and obsolescent. Therefore, to obtain new blood, the company buys an enterprising organization, but maintains a superior attitude toward the acquired firm. This can be destructive to the merged entity, driving out of the organization the very people the parent was trying to gain and, hence, stifling the initiative of the remaining people, ultimately causing the merger to fail.

This concept was applied to the failed merger negotiations to see if similar issues might be at play. In all five of the failed mergers studied, one of the pairs of the negotiating firms was an older, more dominant, and more conservative company looking to merge with or acquire a smaller, less structured, more entrepreneurial company. Bell Atlantic came out of the old and fairly rigid AT&T system, whereas TCI was run as a fast-paced, entrepreneurial organization through the vision of one man, John Malone. Southwestern Bell came out of the same type of background as Bell Atlantic, whereas Cox Enterprises was a private, family-run organization that had undergone dramatic growth in a rapid period of time. CBS was the granddaddy of all television networks, and was still referred to as the "Tiffany Network," whereas QVC was an upstart company that was an overnight sensation, run by the high-profile Barry Diller. In the Contel/COMSAT negotiations, Contel was the dominant, older, and more conservative organization, run by its original founder, 74-year-old Charles Wohlstetter. COMSAT's Chairman, Irv Goldstein, was a former Washington attorney, still in his 40s, as were most of his executive staff.

In the TBS/NBC negotiations, not only was NBC larger, older, and more conservative than TBS, but Ted Turner's brash, often controversial management decisions must have been an interesting counterpoint to the stoic management of General Electric, the parent of NBC and the real organization with which Turner had to negotiate.

Recalling this chapter's premise that premerger failures can be attributed to the same types of cultural and personality problems that have been attributed to completed mergers, clearly mismatched management styles and the absence of personal chemistry between the negotiators can be the basis for discontinuing negotiations, even if all other criteria look promising. Although it is difficult to find anything more concrete than anecdotal information from press reports, there does appear to be a relationship between corporate cultures/personal styles and the collapse of the media merger negotiations.

In addition, there was a common thread among at least three of the failed mergers: a lack of familiarity with the industry and regulatory environment of the firms they were acquiring. The failures of both the Bell Atlantic/TCI and the Southwestern Bell/Cox mergers were ostensibly blamed on the new 700 pages of FCC cable regulations and a forced 7% additional rate reduction, whereas the failure of the Contel/COMSAT merger was blamed on the FCC-imposed $62 million refund order for COMSAT. Although it would be premature to conclude that the merger failures were due to a lack of understanding of the regulatory environment, the study findings suggest that, had there been better understanding of the financial consequences of the regulations, the mergers might have succeeded.

Methods

A broad range of financial and organizational data were gathered on the 10 companies cited earlier. Although the number of mergers is too small for statistical analysis, patterns were explored to determine commonalities among these failed mergers in several key dimensions suggested by the literature review. Table 7.3 provides a summary comparison for each of the mergers. The data were grouped into three key classifications:

1. Merger Characteristics: This included factors that characterize the nature of the merger—what type and size it was; whether it was friendly or unfriendly; and whether the firms were in related industries and familiar with each other's markets, technology, and regulatory environment.

2. Cultural and Personality Issues: To determine those factors most closely related to corporate culture, personality, and ego issues, this study relied on both past research and anecdotal information in the popular press. The factors chosen were: relative size of the firms to each other; whether one or both of the firms' CEOs were highly visible, public figures; and how conservative or entrepreneurial they were. To measure this factor, this study assumed that conservative firms pay an ongoing dividend and would have an above-average Value Line safety rating, which is used to measure "the total risk of a stock" (i.e., its price stability and the company's financial strength; Value Line Industry Reports, 1982–1995). Entrepreneurial firms were assumed to be riskier due to their need to reinvest in themselves for growth, paying out few or only token dividends and having an average to below-average Value Line safety ranking.

3. Capital Market Issues: The last set of characteristics dealt with whether equity financing was planned to complete the merger, and, if so, what the market reaction was to the merger announcement, as represented by changes in the market value of the two firms' stock prices. Also explored was the presence of large individual shareholders that could potentially veto the agreement.

Measuring Stock Price Changes

Because only a rough measure of stock prices was examined for this convenience sample, a simple premerger average stock price was computed for each of the firms by obtaining the closing price of the stock for the 10 days immediately preceding the public announcement of the merger and dividing by 10. Two measures of the change in stock prices were then taken—one against an average for the 10 days immediately following the announcement, and one 10 days preceding the collapse of the merger to get a longer term idea of the market's reaction to the merger. A percentage increase or decrease from the premerger price was computed and compared against the average percentage increase or decrease of the Standard & Poors 500 price index for the same period (see Table 7.2).

DISCUSSION OF RESULTS

Because this study did not directly compare short-circuited mergers with mergers that were successfully negotiated (a control group), the conclusions

TABLE 7.3

STATISTICS ON COLLAPSED MERGER AGREEMENTS

Acquiring/Merging Firms	BA/TCI	SW Bell/Cox	QVC/CBS	TBS/NBC	Contel/COMSAT
Merger Characteristics					
Year merger initiated (publicly)	1993	1993	1994	1994	1986
Friendly/unfriendly	friendly	friendly	friendly	friendly	friendly
Type of Merger	concentric marketing/vertical	concentric marketing/vertical	conglomerate/vertical	vertical	concentric marketing/horizontal
Length of negotiation before collapse	4 months	4 months	2 weeks	3 months	9 months
Public reason for collapse	FCC/cable regulations	FCC/cable regulations	Unfriendly bid for acquirer	ownership control	FCC—refund order
Related/unrelated	related	related	related	related	related
Same primary two-digit SIC?	Yes—48	yes—48	no—59	yes—48	yes—48
Operate in same regulated environment	no	no	yes	yes	no
Capital Market Issues					
Stock price acquiring Firm: Percent +/- S&P 500	-14.4%	-3.2%	+10.9%	-11.5%	-35%
Stock price merging Firm: Percent +/- S&P 500	-4.8%	n/a	+18.5%	+3.35%	-35%
Valuation and Synergy Value					
Value of deal	$29.3 billion	$1.6 billion	$2.9 billion	$5 billion	$6 billion
Price equation: operating income x 10	$18.27	Unknown	$4.9 billion	$45 billion	$1.03 billion
Cultural Issues: Size, Ego, Management Style					
Revenue of acquiring firm	$12.99 billion	$11.62 billion	$1.4 billion	$2.8 billion	$3.07 billion
Revenue of merging firm	$4.15 billion (TCI)	$3.0 billion (Cox)	$3.7 billion (CBS)	$3.3 billion (NBC)	$39.6 billion (GE)
Size difference: rev. smaller firm/rev. larger firm	32%	26%	38% of CBS	7% of GE 85% of NBC	15%
High-profile leader: acquiring/merging firm	No/ Yes—Malone	No/ Yes—Cox Kennedy	Yes—Diller/ Yes—Tisch	Yes—Turner/ No	Yes—Wohlstetter/ No
Insider ownership: acquiring firm	nmf*	nmf*	28%	82%	.4%
Insider ownership: manufacturing firm	7.8% cl.A 61.2% Cl. B	100%	17.9%	1%	nmf
Dividends declared: acquiring firm/merging firm	$2.68/0	$.84/private	0/$.40	$.07/$1.49	$1.86/$1.20

nmf stands for no meaningful figure

drawn here must be taken with a certain grain of salt. Nevertheless, certain interesting relationships did emerge. To assess the relationship between the factors found in the existing literature about mergers that failed to live up to their expectations and the five short-circuited mergers, Table 7.4 was created to compare the two profiles. As one might expect, some factors fit the bill while others do not.

The first column of Table 7.4 identifies the major factors cited in either the popular business press or previous academic studies as playing some role in merger successes and failures. The second column then summarizes a predicted profile of a merger that would not be likely to succeed if the merger agreement was completed. Although there was not total agreement among the previous merger studies and the popular business press on which factors would be the least desirable in a merger, in general, the literature suggests that the most likely mergers to fall short of their expectations would be as follows: those that are conglomerate types, with both firms operating in unrelated industries and the acquiring firm being unfamiliar with the regulatory environment of the acquired firm. One of the firms would be very conservative with a high degree of price and earnings stability and a tradition of paying dividends. The other firm would be considered entrepreneurial, with less stable stock price and earnings and paying little or no dividends. One of the firm's top executives would be a very high–profile individual featured regularly in the national media, whereas the other would be unknown to most people outside the executive's industry. The acquired firm's revenues would be significantly smaller than the acquiring firm's revenues, representing less than 2%. The capital market's immediate and long-term reaction to the merger would be a downturn in the price of both the acquiring and acquired firms' stock prices.

The next column in Table 7.4 summarizes how each of the mergers was actually classified, and the last column shows if, based on these classifications, the factor appears to have any bearing on the merger negotiations collapsing. For example, the literature suggests that the most likely mergers to fail are those where the size of the acquired firm's revenues is less than 2% of the acquiring firm's. In this study, all five of the merging firms' revenues were greater than 2%, but the agreements collapsed nonetheless. Therefore, although this factor may be important once the merger is completed, the size of the merging firms does not play a role in the mergers collapsing during the negotiation stage.

Of the 12 factors analyzed, 5 appear to have played the most significant role in the collapse of the merger negotiations. Three of the five fall into the category of corporate culture and personality factors, one is associated with the relatedness issue and familiarity with the other's industry, and one is associated with shareholder and stock issues. These are summarized next in general terms, suggesting that they may be factors in any future media merger collapses.

TABLE 7.4

Summary Profiles of Failed Mergers

Variable	Predicted Profile of Failed Merger	Summary of Five Subject Mergers	Apparent Impact on Negotiations
Merger Characteristics			
Type	Conglomerate	4 Verticals/1 Horizontal	No
Friendly/unfriendly	Unfriendly	5 Friendly	No
Relatedness:			No
market/technology:	Unrelated	5 Related	No
two-digit SICs	Unrelated	4 Related/1 Unrelated	
Familiarity w/ regulatory environment	Unfamiliar	3 Unfamiliar 2 Somewhat familiar	Yes
Corporate Culture and Personality Factors			
Size: Revenues of smaller firm/larger firm	Less than 2%	5 Greater than 2% (3 Greater than 25%)	No
High-profile and Low-profile CEOs	High/low	4 High/low 1 High/high	Yes
Conservative/entrepreneurial	Conservative/entrepreneur	4 Conservative/entrepreneur 1 Conservative/conservative	Yes
Ego issues: smaller firm playing acquirer role	Yes	4 Yes (QVC, TBS, COMSAT, Cox)	Yes
Shareholder/Stock Issues			
Financing method	Leveraged w/heavy debt	2 Equity 2 Cash 1 Leveraged	No
Large shareholders	Yes	3 Yes (TCI, QVC, TBS)	Yes
Market reaction after announcement	Neg. for acquirer Neg. for merging	1 Neg. for both (Contel/COMSAT)	No
Longer term market reaction	Neg. for acquirer Neg. for merging	2 Neg. For Both (BA/TCI & Contel/COMSAT)	*Possibly

*No market reaction for Cox stock because it is a private company.

Factors In a Merger Collapse

1. When the acquiring firm's primary business operates in a different regulatory environment, and its management is therefore unfamiliar with the regulatory issues affecting the firm being acquired or merged. This would be particularly important when major regulatory changes occur, as in the cable rate decrease that affected Bell Atlantic and Cox, and the rate refund order imposed on COMSAT.

2. When one of the firms, especially the smaller firm, has a high-profile CEO regularly featured in the media, whereas the more dominant firm's CEO has a much less visible role. This was the case in four of the five collapsed mergers. Only in the case of the CBS/QVC merger, where both individuals had equally high profiles, did this not seem to play a role.

3. When one of the firms is classified as conservative and the other is entrepreneurial—again, true in four of the five mergers.

4. When the smaller firm is acting in the more dominant role or as the acquirer—as was the case in four of the five mergers: QVC, TBS, COMSAT, and Cox.

5. When either of the firms has a few large stockholders that need to be placated throughout the merger discussions. It was these stockholders who killed the deals for QVC and TBS. Little mention of stockholder issues came up during the Bell

Atlantic/TCI discussion; regardless, TCI does have some large individual stock-holders, and they may have played a role in the ultimate decision to not pursue the deal. Because Cox Enterprises is privately held, it obviously has one large share-holder, but this was not factored into the summary chart.

6. The last factor, the longer term market reaction to the stock, was listed only as "possibly" affecting the merger negotiations. This factor was cited often in the popular business press as a reason for the collapsed deals, but in only two cases, Bell Atlantic/TCI and Contel/COMSAT—did the stock price for both the acquirer and merging firm's go down in the long run. Of course, the Southwestern Bell/Cox Cable merger might have fallen into this category as well (Southwestern Bell's price did go down), but because Cox is private no comparison could be made.

Conclusion

This chapter, using a literature review of past research on completed merg-ers, has suggested that there is a direct relationship between certain factors that cause a merger to fail after its completion and those that cause merger negotiations to collapse prior to completion. It suggests a number of possi-ble factors that can affect the successful completion of merger negotiations. In addition to these factors, some other interesting conclusions may be drawn from the observations of the failed mergers:

1. Vertical mergers, like those announced by Southwestern Bell and Cox Enter-prises, which are hurried through as a competitive response to a highly publicized megamerger like the Bell Atlantic/TCI merger, are more likely to dissolve if the original megamerger dissolves.

2. Merging firms from different regulatory environments need to thoroughly explain the regulatory rules under which they operate to their future partners, and clearly explain the financial impact of any changes to the partner before negotiations get underway. Otherwise, if a significant negative regulatory event occurs during the negotiations, the talks may be short-circuited.

3. There is an ongoing need for publicity about the status of the merger in the marketplace, beyond the initial announcement. Firms cannot assume that, once it is announced and reported on the front page of the *Wall Street Journal*, the deal is done. If investors do not understand the value of the merger, they will reject it, and that will be reflected in a downturn in stock value, which could ultimately kill the deal.

Future Research

Although a number of these suggestions and hypotheses are open to debate, they would make an interesting starting point for the next step in researching failed merger negotiations. Other preliminary questions that can provide a foundation for further research are: (a) Has the rate of failed media mergers increased? (b) What happens in the industry after a major merger fails? Do all the me-tools drop out or continue with the strategy? (c)

What variables do failed merger negotiations have in common with successfully negotiated mergers? Where are there discrepancies?

Effects of Failed Mergers on the Industry:

Commenting on the sheer number of media mergers in recent years, an investment banker said, "Media companies these days have to be experts in mergers [because] the media business is all about mergers and acquisitions" (Lipin, 1995, p. A5). This chapter has attempted to show why that reliance on mergers exists, and to summarize the key aspects of today's media mergers—both successful and unsuccessful—to suggest how these activities may be conducted as efficiently and effectively as possible. This is important for the well-being of the specific companies involved in the negotiations, as well as entire industry.

Highly publicized merger agreements that ultimately collapse can profoundly change an industry. The announcement of a multibillion-dollar megamerger can send the stock prices of individual companies in an industry soaring, and thus put pressure on competing firms to form new alliances. This certainly was the case following the Bell Atlantic/TCI merger announcement. It was interesting to watch the Disney/ABC and Westinghouse/CBS negotiation announcements. The failure of either of those mergers could have had a serious impact on the media industry as a whole. It would be especially interesting to explore what impact the completion of these two mergers had on the completion of the Time Warner/Turner deal in 1996, despite the diverse cultures and personalities of those two firms.

Regardless of the completion of these recent megamergers, the overall lesson of this chapter is that media firms must recognize that there is an opportunity cost associated with each merger attempt that fails—in terms of lost time and management attention to ongoing business, as well as actual financial outlays and stock dilution that can weaken the value of the acquiring company for its individual investors. Firms might be able to avoid these costs if they are able to judge, in advance, the likelihood of the proposed merger being completed. If the characteristics of the venture are weak, firms may then either forego the deal altogether, or put plans in place early in the negotiation process to avoid the potential pitfalls.

REFERENCES

Adams, W., & Brock, J. (1989). *Dangerous pursuits—Mergers & acquisitions in the age of Wall Street*. New York: Pantheon.

Bernier, P. (1994, April 11). Are failed deals and new rules bringing convergence to a halt? *Telephony*, p. 10.

Bettis, R., & Hall, W. (1982).Diversification strategy, accounting determined risk, and accounting determined return. *Academy of Management Journal*, 45(2), 254–264.

Bielinski, D. (1992, November/December). Putting a realistic dollar value on acquisition synergies. *Mergers and Acquisitions*, pp. 9–12.

Brown, R. (1993, December 13). Southwestern Bell, Cox go shopping. *Broadcasting & Cable, 6*, 11.

Callahan, J. (1986, March/April). Chemistry: How mismatched managements can kill a deal. *Mergers & Acquisitions*, pp. 47–53.

Cannon, K. (1987, August 24). Cold feet. *Forbes*, pp. 110–111.

Carveth, R., Owers, J., & Alexander, A. (1993). The global integration of the media industries. In A. Alexander, J. Owers, & R. Carveth (Eds.), *Media economics: Theory and practice* (pp. 331–353). Hillsdale, NJ: Lawrence Erlbaum Associates.

Chatterjee, S., Lubatkin, M., Schweiger, D., & Weber, Y. (1992, January 17). Cultural differences and shareholder value in related mergers: Linking equity and human capital. *Strategic Management Journal, 13*, 319–334.

COMSAT & Contel boards approve merger. (1986, September 29). COMSAT press release, Washington, DC.

Contel says FCC action pose problems for merger. (1987, April 14). COMSAT press release, Washington, DC.

Crash on the highway—and other mishaps. (1994, May/June). *Mergers & Acquisitions*, pp. 29–30.

Elgers, P., & Clark, J. (1980). Merger types and stockholder returns: Additional evidence. *Financial Management, 9*, 66–72.

Gomery, D. (1993a). The contemporary American movie business. In A. Alexander, J. Owers, & R. Carveth (Eds.), *Media economics: Theory and practice* (pp. 267–281). Hillsdale, NJ: Lawrence Erlbaum Associates.

Gomery, D. (1993b). Who owns the media? In A. Alexander, J. Owers, & R. Carveth (Eds.), *Media economics: Theory and practice* (pp. 47–70). Hillsdale, NJ: Lawrence Erlbaum Associates.

Hogarty, T. (1978, Spring). Profits from mergers: The evidence of 50 years. *St. Johns Law Review, 44*.

Jensen, E., & Landro, L. (1995, January 19). To merger or not to merge, that is NBC's issue. *Wall Street Journal*, pp. B1, B4.

Kitching, J. (1967). Why do mergers miscarry? *Harvard Business Review, 45*, 84–101.

Kneale, D., Roberts, J., & Cauley, L. (1994, February 25). The undeal—why the megamerger collapsed: Strong wills and a big culture gag. *Wall Street Journal*, pp. A1, A16.

Landler, M., & Grover, R. (1994, July 25). COMCAST plays spoiler. *Business Week*, pp. 28–30.

Landro, L., Jensen, E., & King, T. (1995, August 1). All ears: Disney's deal for ABC makes show business a whole new world. *Wall Street Journal*, pp. A1, A12.

Lee, W., & Cooperman, E. (1989, Spring). Conglomerates in the 1980's: A performance appraisal *Financial Management*, pp. 45–54.

Lets get together: In today's explosion of mergers, one plus one must equal much more than two. (1995, August 1). *Wall Street Journal*, p. B1.

Levinson, H. (1973). The psychological roots of merger failure. In H. Levinson (Ed.), *The great jackass fallacy* (pp. 108–125). Boston, MA: Harvard Graduate School, Division of Research.

Lipin, S. (1995, August 2). Weeks's media megadeals put bankers in uncustomary spot: The back seat. *Wall Street Journal*, p. A5.

Litman, B. (1979, Fall). The television networks, competition and program diversity. *Journal of Broadcasting, 23*(4), 393–409.

Litman, B., & Sochay, S. (1994). The emerging mass media environment. In R. E. Babe (Ed.), *Information and communications in economics* (pp. 233–265). New York: Kluwer.

Lubatkin, M. (1987). Merger strategies and stockholder value. *Strategic Management Journal, 8*, 39–53.

McGann, A., & Russel, J. (1988, Fall). Hostile takeovers in broadcasting. *Journal of Media Economics*, 29–40.

Mermigas, D. (1994a, October, 3). NBC battle turns ugly, goes public. *Electronic Media*, pp. 1, 47.

Mermigas, D. (1994b, December 12). GE board to weigh NBC deal. *Electronic Media, 1*, 76.

Mermigas, D. (1995, January 23). TBS-NBC deal not dead yet. *Electronic Media, 1, 77.*

Montgomery, C. (1982). The measurement of firm diversification: Some new empirical evidence. *Academy of Management Journal, 25* (2), 299–307.

Mueller, D. (1977). The effects of conglomerate mergers: A survey of the empirical evidence. *Journal of Banking and Finance, 1,* 339.

Ozanich, G., & Wirth, M. (1993). Media mergers and acquisitions: An overview. In A. Alexander, J. Owers, & R. Carveth (Eds.), *Media economics: Theory and practice* (pp. 115–133). Hillsdale, NJ: Lawrence Erlbaum Associates.

Payne, S., & Keller, J. (1987, April 27). COMSAT is left in the lurch. *Business Week,* pp. 38–39.

Reibstein, L., & Hass, N., (1994, July 11). Barry Diller's greatest hit? *Newsweek, 124,* 46–47.

Rumelt, R. (1974). *Strategy, structure and economic performance.* Boston, MA: Graduate School of Business Administration, Harvard University.

Rumelt, R. (1982). Diversification strategy and profitability. *Strategic Management Journal, 3*(4), 359–369.

Schmuckler, E. (1994, July 4). CBS sets up shop with QVC. *Media Week,* p. 1.

Shelton, L. (1988). Strategic business fits and corporate acquisitions: Empirical evidence. *Strategic Management Journal, 9*(3), 279–288.

Smith, R. (1993, October 14). Rising tide: High stock prices are feeding a revival of merger activity. *The Wall Street Journal,* pp. A1, A14.

Stevens, D. (1972). *A multivariate analysis of financial characteristics of acquired firms in industrial mergers.* Unpublished doctoral dissertation, Michigan State University.

Time Warner's efforts to sell its stake in Turner Broadcasting is falling apart. (1995, March 28). *The Wall Street Journal,* p. 39.

Value Line Industry Reports, (1982–1995). New York: Value Line Publishing, Inc.

Vogel, T. (1995, August 2). Merger wave won't create debt swamp. *The Wall Street Journal,* pp. A2, A5.

Chapter 8

Should Rape Victims Be Identified in News Stories?

Virginia Whitehouse
Whitworth College
Caryl Cooper
University of Alabama–Tuscaloosa

News managers face numerous conflicts when considering when and whether to identify the victims of crime, particularly rape victims. The courts have clarified the media's freedom to name victims, and it is realistic to assume that some will use the privilege at least at times. Yet before that leap is taken, questions must be considered with each case: Is the victim in danger? What is the true motivation for identifying the victim if this is a sudden departure from policy? Is the victim being identified because of her social class or ethnicity? What are community expectations? Is the victim a public figure in her own right? News managers must base their decisions on options that do not burden their commitment to free speech or strip rape victims of their dignity and privacy.

In April 1989, a group of teenage boys attacked and raped a lone female jogger in New York City's Central Park. The jogger was described by *The New York Times* and *The New York Post* as a pretty blond investment banker with a future. Two African-American newspapers, *The New York City Sun* and *The Amsterdam News*, published the victim's name. The mainstream New York media choose not to follow suit (Benedict, 1992). *New York Post* Editor Jerry Nachman (1990) explained, "What we want to avoid is, a year from now, she buys a blouse from Bloomingdale's and hands her credit card to the clerk who says, 'Oh, yeah, you're the one who got gang-raped in Central Park'" (p. B3).

Two years later, another woman claimed she was raped on a beach in Florida. This time, the accused—William Kennedy Smith—was a medical student and the nephew of a former U.S. president. The alleged victim—Patricia Bowman—was described by *The New York Times* (1991) as an unwed mother, a partier, a social climber, and an unemployed woman "with a little wild streak" (p. A17).

After a series of London tabloids revealed Bowman's identity, a Florida tabloid did the same. NBC News and *The New York Times* followed. Michael Gartner (1991), then executive producer of NBC News, explained, "First, we are in the business of disseminating news, not suppressing it. Names and facts are news. They add credibility, they round out the story, they give the view or reader information he or she needs to understand the issues, to make up his or her mind about what's going on" (p. A6).

From the justifications given for naming or not naming the victim, one can logically ask: What factors contributed to the decision made in certain media organizations to break with tradition and name a rape victim? Is the word of an upwardly mobile executive so credible that her name and background need not be publicized? Is the word of an unwed mother automatically to be put up for public scrutiny? Attorney Susan Estrich (1991), herself a rape victim, noted that the mainstream media consistently avoided naming the Central Park jogger even up through the defendant's sentencing, which took place a month before the Kennedy compound incident. In a syndicated editorial, Estrich wrote:

> Has so much changed in the last month? Has the stigma magically lifted, as waves of rape victims begin marching to police stations? Or could it be that the difference is that the rape in Central Park was not a date rape by one man but a gang rape; not an acquaintance rape, but a rape by strangers; that an investment banker jogging alone in Central Park is a more deserving victim than a working-class girl who climbed up the social ladder and went for drinks at a man's home at 3:30 a.m. (p. A21)

Victims of crimes and natural disasters have long been newsworthy subjects (Gans, 1980), but the media tend to portray rape victims as either "virgins or vamps," said Helen Benedict (1992). Naming victims will not remove the stigma of rape, she maintained. "The only way to destigmatize rape is to change the way in which sex crimes are reported so that victims' reputations will not be automatically destroyed … " (p. 259).

However, the Bowman case had far-reaching effects. A 1911 Florida law barring dissemination of victims' identities was struck down after the *Boca Raton Globe* published her name. The U.S. Supreme Court indicated in an earlier decision that blanket legal restrictions could not be imposed. Florida editors were jubilant, *The St. Petersburg Times* reported in 1993. Most insisted that they would maintain existing nondisclosure policies, but were thankful for the freedom to alter that policy if a situation warranted it.

The Court has clarified and defined the media's legal right to publish and broadcast adult rape victims' names in most circumstances. Applying a Kantian approach and establishing an absolute rule to always publish is neither ethically nor legally viable. However, it is realistic to assume that more media organizations will reveal victims' identities in some circumstances. Although not wishing to encourage such action, the purpose of this chapter is to identify the standards and questions that should be considered before naming rape victims. The evolution of court decisions on this subject must be explored before the evolution of the ethics debate on this issue can be fully understood.

ALLOWING PUBLICATION

"Short of homicide, [rape] is the ultimate violation of self," U.S. Supreme Court Justice White wrote in a 1977 opinion (*Coker v. Georgia*, 1977). He quoted himself more than 10 years later in his dissent when the court overruled *Florida Star v. B.J.F.* (1989) and said the media prolonged the victim's horror by publicly identifying her. However, six other justices said First Amendment rights outweighed privacy rights, and made way for a Florida Appeals Court to strike down a state law barring publication.

The major cases that set the precedent for striking down the Florida law all involved information from police or court records. In *Cox Broadcasting v. Cohn* (1975), a Georgia television station broadcast the name of a rape victim who died during her attack. Her father sued, claiming his privacy had been invaded and the broadcast violated Georgia law. The U.S. Supreme Court held that the "interests of privacy fade when the information involved already appears on public record, especially when viewed in terms of the First and Fourteenth Amendments and in light of the public interests in a vigorous press" (420 U. S. 469, 1975).

In *Daily Mail Publishing v. Smith* (1989), journalists heard the name of a juvenile murder suspect broadcast over a police scanner and, with confirmation of witnesses, published the name without written approval of the juvenile court, as West Virginia law required. The U.S. Supreme Court ruled that, as in *Cox v. Cohn*, a newspaper could not be punished for publishing lawfully obtained information, and that publication of the names did not hold a high enough state interest to warrant prior restraint.

In *Florida Star v. B.J.F.* (1989), the victim's name was inadvertently included in open police files, although release of victims' identities was against department policy. Then the name was accidentally included in the newspaper's "Police Reports," although the publication of such names was also against *Florida Star* policy. B.J.F. won compensatory and punitive damages at the lower court level, but the verdict was overturned when the U.S. Supreme Court applied the *Daily Mail* principle, holding that less drastic means were available to safeguard police records than punishing a newspaper for truthful publication.

Notably, Kenneth Harrell, the *Boca Raton Globe* journalist, did not turn to government agencies for Patricia Bowman's name. Instead, Harrell employed "conventional investigation methods" (*Globe Communications v. Florida*, 1991). He interviewed those who had seen Bowman and the Kennedys the night of the alleged attack, and a woman who claimed William

Kennedy Smith had also raped her. Once discovering Bowman's address in Jupiter, Florida, he went to her home and found reporters from the *London Sunday Mirror*, a British tabloid, and the *Star*, an American tabloid, already camped outside. Within hours, they were joined by reporters from the *Boston Herald* and *The New York Post*. Eventually, the coordinator for the Palm Beach County Victim Services Section arrived and agreed to deliver a note from Harrell requesting an interview, thus confirming Bowman's address. Subsequent interviews with her former fiancé confirmed her identity.

More than a week before the *Globe* first hit the newsstands, four British newspapers published articles releasing Bowman's name, and one included her photograph. At least three of the four British publications were distributed in Florida at that time. The day after the *Globe* release, NBC announced Bowman's name on its evening news broadcast, and *The New York Times* followed the next day. Bowman's name officially did not enter public record until sexual battery charges were filed against Smith in Palm Beach County Circuit Court, more than 2 weeks after the *Globe*'s initial distribution.

In *Globe Communications v. Florida* (1991), the state argued that the Florida law protecting rape victims' identities encouraged victims to report sexual assaults to authorities by "shielding them from the full glare of media publicity." The Florida District Court of Appeals ruled that, although this result is desirable, enforcing such a law "collides with First Amendment claims of the press to comment freely on a matter of public interest … " (622 So. 2d, 1073). Bowman's safety was not threatened by the publication, nor was Smith's right to a fair trial hampered. Using the *Daily Mail* standard, the law was overturned as unconstitutionally overbroad. The law, not amended after *Florida Star v. B.J.F.*, also was not inclusive enough to penalize those outside the media who effectively can broadcast a victim's name, although the Florida Attorney General threatened in court hearings, "If Mrs. Jones gets a megaphone or copy machine, we'll prosecute her too!" Last, the court ruled that, regardless of whether the Florida law served as prior restraint or subsequent punishment, it concluded that absolute protection of rape victims' identities did not constitute a high form of state interest.

Therefore, this Court interpretation gives news organizations the freedom to choose whether to name sexual assault victims. The organizations must choose whether to take the privilege. To make a solid decision, news managers must know how they came to make those decisions and why. Without that grounding, they might appear ignorant of the influence their acts have on the communities they serve. Blindly leaping into decisions at deadline damages journalistic credibility for the individual organization and the profession as a whole. The decision to name a sexual assault victim further disrupts the privacy of an individual whose privacy has already been shattered. That decision cannot be made without considering the possible outcomes.

ETHICAL JUSTIFICATIONS

Although the concept may be an old one, Louis Brandeis and Samuel Warren (1890) are generally credited for synthesizing the concept of privacy from the First, Third, Fourth, Fifth, and Ninth Amendments in their 1890 *Harvard Law Review* article. *Privacy*, as it has come to be understood in contemporary times, can be defined as "the claim of individuals, groups or institutions to determine for themselves when, how, and to what extent information about them is communicated to others" (Westin, 1983). In his essay "The Journalist and Privacy," Hodges (1983) created a visual image for the concept of privacy consisting of three circles. The innermost circle includes the individual and those relationships based on strong trust. The middle circle contains those people the individual considers close, but not necessarily intimate. The outermost circle is the least private circle and encompasses all humanity. Rape is an act of humiliation in an individual's most intimate circle—an act of domination and violence. Making a rape victim available to public inspection exposes her "irrevocably to the stigma of intimate humiliation...without her consent [and] is nothing short of punitive" (Benedict, 1992, p. 254).

However, some feminists argue that the modern-day debate is paternal-istic—a dispute between some in male-dominated media management (Glaberson, 1991) who wish to scrutinize a victim's sexual history, as well as government and law enforcement officials who wish to play big Daddy (Appel, 1991; McKenna, 1991). The debate has become so complex and so heated that no news organization can make a decision in either direction without engendering heavy criticism. In 1990, *Des Moines Register* Editor Geneva Overholser asked sexual assault victims to come forward with their stories to help destigmatize rape. Nancy Ziegenmeyer, who was raped in her car by a stranger, answered the call and helped the *Register* win a Pulitzer Prize. Although she was grateful for the opportunity to reach out to other victims, Ziegenmeyer said she felt "dehumanized" when revealing her story. "To the prosecutors, she was a witness; to the newspaper, she was a source. To some in the small town of Grinnell, [Iowa], she became a sort of Hester Prynne, but the scarlet letter was an R, not an A" (Tackett, 1991, p. 19).

Although Overholser became a leading national advocate of disclosure, Ziegenmeyer lobbied for laws to bar media publication of victims' identi-ties. She said it took her 8 months to summon the courage to talk to the *Register*. She told the *Tribune* in 1991, "If I were raped now, without confi-dentiality laws, I wouldn't report the crime to the police" (Tackett, 1991, p. 19).

Meanwhile, Bowman told United Press International in 1991 that she felt "raped again" when her identity was publicized. Naming Bowman brought an avalanche of complaints as well as support from rape victims, rape advocacy groups, and feminists. In response, news managers have used four basic premises to defend naming sexual assault victims in general, and

Bowman in particular. First, as explained by NBC News, the news organizations can name sexual assault victims because they have the legal authority to do so. Followers of this argument equate ethics with the law. Second, naming victims levels the playing field of public opinion between the victim and the accused. "Many editors who do publish rape complainants' names say they are seeking to avoid giving complainants the power of anonymous accusers," and that to only publicize the accuser's name is tantamount to a "pretrial assumption of guilt" (Lake, 1991, p. 110).

Victims are also named on the justification that this helps remove the social stigma attached to rape and acts as a catharsis for the rape victim. By giving a name and a face to rape victims, the media lets other women know that they are not alone. This argument has some support from feminists. Karen DeCrow, former president of the National Organization for Women, wrote in 1990, "Now is the time for us to understand that keeping the hunted under wraps merely establishes her as an outcast and implies that her chances for normal social relations are doomed forever more. Pull off the veil of shame. Print the name" (p. A8). This argument assumes that rape eventually might become comparable to any other crime in society. However, Benedict (1992) said rape victims suffer a unique sexual humiliation:

> As long as people have any sense of privacy about sexual acts and the human body, rape will, therefore, carry a stigma—not necessarily a stigma that blames the victim for what happened to her, but a stigma that links her name irrevocably with an act of intimate humiliation. To name a rape victim is to guarantee that whenever somebody hears her name, that somebody will picture her in the act of being sexually tortured. To expose a rape victim to this without her consent is nothing short of punitive. (p. 254)

Nonetheless, the public needs to know any and all information available on crime. This argument puts the onus of ethical decision making on the public. In addition, satisfying the public's want for information may be an erroneous assumption made by the press. In a survey conducted by the Times Mirror Center for the People & the Press in 1991, 80% of those polled felt that the decision to release the name was commercially motivated, 70% disapproved publishing or airing an alleged rape victim's name, and only 9% felt that news organizations named the alleged rape victim to show that society does not attach shame to the victim. This poll indicates that the public strongly opposes naming rape victims.

A poll of 900 members of the American Society of Newspaper Editors showed that 54% believed a newspaper should not be legally protected when identifying rape victims. Thirty-six percent said the right should be protected sometimes, and 8% said it should always be protected (Case, 1991). This means that the vast majority of newspaper editors are at odds with the public at large.

Some news managers argue that omitting rape complainants' names leads to false reports of rape (Lake, 1991). However, rape statistics show that there are extremely few false rape reports. Only 2% of rape reports prove false. A larger percentage of rape victims never report the crime. Rape advocates believe that routinely naming victims will result in fewer rapes being reported. In a survey conducted by the National Victim Center, half of those who reported being raped said they would be more likely to report a rape if a law prohibited news media from releasing the names of sexual assault complainants. Clearly, the specter of public identification may reduce the number of reported rapes.

Yet the laws barring publication have been struck down. Renowned national commentator Carl Rowan supports general media policies to *not* reveal victims' identities, but does not want to be bound by "journalistic rules" or laws. Because of the extraordinary nature of the William Kennedy Smith trial, he strongly believes "this is a case where the media ought to put all the names, all the ascertainable facts, on the record" (Rowan, 1991, p. A13).

Regardless of whether the Bowman/Smith scenario constitutes an extraordinary case warranting a breach of journalistic tradition, it is reasonable to assume that other extraordinary cases will arise again. It is also reasonable to assume that more media outlets will consider using victims' names regularly. But most likely, some organizations will use victims' names only in some special circumstances. Lambeth (1992) called on news organizations to adopt a journalistic principle of humaneness when making ethical decisions. This principle maintains that journalists should consider the "humanness" of all people involved in any story and act humanely. To shut down the possibility of ever naming a victim robs the media of the freedom to determine what the humane act might be.

QUESTIONS BEFORE PUBLICATION

Although the ethical door for identifying sexual assault victims may only stand open a crack, the legal door opens wide. The National Victim Center's Media Code of Ethics asks that victims not be identified without their permission (Gersh, 1992). Because the courts have clarified the media's right to name victims, it is unrealistic to assume that journalists will not take the privilege in at least some circumstances. However, before taking that privilege, journalists must answer some questions.

Is the Victim in Danger?

For obvious ethical reasons, a victim should not be identified if the attacker has not been arrested. This does not mean an arrested suspect is assumed to be guilty. Rather, it means that the media recognize a certain moral obligation not to leave a victim open to further attack. Failing to recognize

that obligation means risking losing the opportunity to maintain professional ethical norms without court intervention.

For example, a Columbia, Missouri, bank teller was abducted off a
downtown street in 1980. She was not raped, and escaped without the
attacker learning her identity. The next day, both city newspapers published
the victim's name and address. Her assailant followed her to work and
harassed her at home. Although the victim was not attacked a second time,
she won a negligence suit for emotional distress against the first newspaper
that revealed her identity (*Hyde v. City of Columbia*, 1982). In this case, bad
news judgment and failure to consider the consequences of printing the
story led to a national legal standard, and left journalists stripped of the
opportunity for independent ethical decision making.

What Is the Social Value in Identifying Rape Victims?

Lake (1991) proposed using John Stuart Mill's "harm principle" as the basis
for any ethical decisions to be made by journalists: "Journalists must weigh
the harm publication will cause [the rape victim] against the benefit to be
gained [by the public]" (p. 114). News managers should ask themselves if
the good to be gained by naming the rape victim outweighs the harm
publication will cause. Lake contended that, in most cases, the answer is
"no." Lake said:

> The duty of the media is to inform, but that duty is only one part of the news
> media's broader responsibility to serve their public ... When considering the
> benefits and costs of publication, editors do not need rules. They need only
> to pause, reflect, and weigh their responsibility to society. In doing so, they
> ask the right questions and do what is right. (p. 115–116).

This argument, although extremely compelling, still offers no real guidelines for determining what actions are right, and to which segment of
society is media most responsible to at any given point in time. Yet to
narrowly define social value is to deny the individual news organization
the freedom to make independent judgments based on unique community
needs. Therefore, each journalist must determine the social value in each
case, however carefully.

What Are the Community Expectations?

Fishbein (1985) suggested that the courts consider newsworthiness as well
as social value to determine if a media outlet violated a rape victim's
privacy by publishing her name without her consent. Clearly, the media
industry should balk at the suggestion that the courts determine such news
values. The question of the newsworthiness of identifying rape victims
should be left in the place where all decisions about news are made—in the
newsroom.

Yet the sole reliance on newsworthiness in determining the publication of rape victims' names does not take into account the impact that publication will have on a victim or the community. Rawls (1971) explained that all human beings have the "natural duty" to help others and do no harm. Again, Lambeth (1992) related this duty to journalism, and called it "humaneness" and "stewardship." Therefore, a media organization, operating in a conservative community where rape victims are likely to be blamed for attacks, would be acting humanely by not identifying victims. This does not mean journalists in those communities should shy away from rape stories because they might be unpopular. Rather, Merrill (1977) insisted that independent journalists set their own standard, meaning that they "consider [the] consequences of journalistic action and take responsibility for it ... " (p. 54). But if the community is not prepared for such action, the results may be disastrous.

For example, the Marshall University school newspaper, *The Parthenon*, announced a rape victim disclosure policy in a frontpage editorial; and in the same edition, it published a story identifying a woman who told police a week earlier that she had been sexually assaulted. The community, which did not have the opportunity to react before the policy was implemented, responded in force following the publication. Student and faculty senates denounced the decision, and women's groups held candlelight vigils in protest. The student government president attempted to wrestle student fee monies away from the *Parthenon*. The university president took supervision of the newspaper out of the journalism department and appointed a student publications board (Anthony, 1992). As this case illustrates, the community as a whole may not accept or be willing to adapt to a journalist's decision on this issue, no matter how newsworthy the story is.

Is the Victim Particularly Vulnerable or Will the Victim Refuse to Prosecute?

Haughwout (1992), who served as attorney to the *Boca Raton Globe*, suggested that a nondisclosure law could still pass constitutional muster if the media only were barred from identifying victims in special circumstances (e.g., if the assailant were unknown and threatened retaliation; if the victim, because of age or a preexisting mental condition, would be especially traumatized by publication of her name; or if the victim refused to prosecute otherwise).

Even with these provisions, such a law would be difficult to enforce. Yet these suggestions offer solid ethical guidelines. Older and young sexual assault victims are more vulnerable, and the media should make some considerations. Aside from a legal responsibility not to hinder in the fair trial process, journalists serve their communities by creating an environment where justice can be carried out.

Is the Victim a Public Figure in Her Own Right?

Desiree Washington held a single interview after Mike Tyson was convicted of raping her. The beauty pageant contestant told Barbara Walters on "20/20" in 1992 that she wanted to clear up some misconceptions, then she slipped back into private life. NBC News was the only major media outlet to identify her before that interview (Johnson, 1992). Clearly, she was not the public figure in the case.

Public figures and elected officials have legal rights to keep some facts private, but sacrifice a certain amount of private life as a price of power (*Sidis v. F-R Publishing Corp.*, 1940). Similarly when considering ethical constraints, the zones of privacy (Hodges, 1983) around public figures are naturally smaller than those around a private individual. Therefore, if the victim happens to be a public figure, the public will know and remember her in contexts other than sexual torture. Thus, identifying a public figure as a victim does not place the same stigma as it would on a private individual. However, the notoriety of the victim or accused should not automatically force the victim into the spotlight.

If This Is a Sudden Departure From Policy, What Is the Real Motivation?

In other words, do not hide behind the "destigmatizing rape" argument when the real reason for publishing the victim's identity is that the story is too good to pass up. Brownmiller (1975) found that, even in the mid-1970s when most newspapers almost ignored sex crimes, tabloids published some selected accounts. That selection seemed to be based on the potential for luridness. Be wary of identifying a victim merely because the rape could be construed as a sexy story.

Has the Case Been Published Elsewhere? Is That Publication Credible Enough to Be Used as Reference in Other Types of Stories?

If a media organization will not quote a tabloid concerning alien space monkeys landing in Wyoming, then it should not use a tabloid's story to justify identifying rape victims.

If the Victim Grants Permission for Her Name to Be Published, Is She Aware of the Possible Consequences?

Boston Globe reporter Alison Bass interviewed seven rape survivors who went public with their stories in 1993. All but one said the decision brought great pain and an unexpected loss of privacy. Almost all received threatening letters and faced strong negative reaction from family and friends.

It is paternalistic to assume that all rape survivors are so traumatized by the event that, even years after the attack, they cannot make sound decisions on media publicity. Some news managers may follow Overholser and the *Des Moines Register*'s lead and ask victims to come forward by name. However, journalists, who should be aware of the trauma such media coverage may bring, should at least warn the victim of the possible consequences.

Is the News Story Written in a Way That Myths Concerning Rape Are Perpetuated?

Journalists struggle to give rape meaning because of the violent nature of the act and the privacy it invades. It is easy, even convenient, to rely on myths to explain the rape's occurrence. The media can play on the woman's attractiveness or age, implying that women somehow incite the assault through provocative clothing or behavior. The media can also contribute to the public expectation that women can avoid being raped by merely avoiding dark alleys and sleazy bars (Devitt, 1992). Journalists do not set out to discredit the victim, but the result is the same. The rape victim is turned into the villain, and the accused becomes the underdog whose name and actions deserve to be cleared.

These subjective elements need to be, and can be, eliminated from news stories. As educated persons, journalists generally are aware that rape is not just a crime of sex, but of violence. Nonetheless, the media is a part of the society that created these rape myths. If news managers are aware of these biases about rape, they can attempt to eliminate those biases from news stories. The cynicism that often pervades the profession must be replaced with empathy.

CONCLUSION

Media critics, including Benedict and Brownmiller, have contended that identifying rape victims has often been a social class dilemma: Wealthier women tend to be shielded, whereas women with more lurid backgrounds are exposed. This should not be. News managers must balance the right to identify victims of all crimes with the victims' safety and well-being.

They also must decide if naming rape victims constitutes a warranted invasion of privacy and, if so, under what conditions that decision is justified. To answer these questions, the media must take responsibility for its conduct toward rape victims. News managers must base their decisions on options that do not burden their commitment to free speech or strip rape victims of their dignity and privacy.

REFERENCES

Anthony, T. (1992, November). West Virginia campus explodes over naming of rape victims. *Los Angeles Times*, p. A1.

Appel, T. (1991, August 28). *Changes to proposed ban on publication of rape victims' names.* United Press International (Producer and Distributor).

Benedict, H. (1992). *Virgin or vamp: How the press covers sex crimes.* New York: University of Oxford Press.

Brandeis, L., & Warren, S. (September 1890). The right to privacy. *Harvard Law Review*, p. 196.

Brownmiller, S. (1975). *Against our will: Men, women and rape.* New York: Bantam Books.

Butterfield, F. (1991, August 16). Woman in Florida rape inquiry fought adversity and sought acceptance. *The New York Times*, p. A17.

Case, T. (1991, April 27). New York Times criticized for printing victims names. *Editor & Publisher*, p. 39.

Coker v. Georgia, 433 U.S. 584 (1977).

Cox Broadcasting v. Cohn, 420 U.S. 469 (1975).

Daily Mail Publishing v. Smith, 443 U.S. 97 (1989).

DeCrow, K. (1990, April 4). Stop treating rape victims as pariahs: Print names. *USA Today*, p. 8A.

Devitt, T. (March 1992) Media circus at Palm Beach rape trial. *Extra!*, pp. 8–10.

Estrich, S. (1991, April 18). A rape victim can suffer from treatment by the media. *St. Petersburg Times*, p. 21A.

Fishbein, E. B. (1985, Summer). Identifying the rape victim: A constitutional clash between the First Amendment and the right to privacy. *John Marshall Law Review*, p. 1012.

Florida Star v. B.J.F., 491 U.S. 524 (1989).

Gartner, M. (1991, April 22). Naming rape victims: Usually, there are good reasons to do it. *USA Today*, p. A6.

Gans, H. (1980). *Deciding what's news.* New York: Vintage Books.

Gersh, D. (1992, September 26). *National Victims Center media code of ethics.* New York: National Victims Center.

Glaberson, W. (1991, April 26). Times article naming rape accuser ignites debate on journalistic values. *New York Times*, p. A14.

Globe Communications v. Florida, 622 So. 2d 1066 (1991).

Haughwout, C. (1992, Summer). Prohibiting rape victim identification: Is it constitutional? *Toledo Law Review*, p. 750.

Hodges, L. (1983). The journalist and privacy. *Social Responsibility: Journalism, Law and Medicine*, 9, 5–19.

Hyde v. City of Columbia, 637 S.W. 2d 251 (Mo. App. 1982).

Johnson, P., Donlon B., & Graham, J. (1992, February 3). NBC News names Tyson's accuser. *USA Today*, p. D3.

Lake, J. B. (1991). Of crime and consequence: Should newspapers report rape complainants' names? *Journal of Mass Media Ethics*, 6, 106–118.

Lambeth, E. B. (1992) *Committed journalism: An ethic for the profession.* (2nd ed.). Bloomington, IN: Indiana University Press.

McKenna, W. P. (1991, May 9). Protect rape victims with the force of law. *USA Today*, p. 10A.

Merrill, J. (1977) *The existential journalist.* New York: Hastings House.

Nauchman, J. (1990, June 13). *The New York Times*, p. B3.

New York Daily News, Wolf pack's prey: Female jogger near death after savage attack by roving gang. (1989, April 21). p. 1.

New York Post, Nightmare in Central Park. (1989, April 21). p. 1.

Rawls, J. (1971). *A theory of justice.* Cambridge, MA: Harvard University Press.

Rowan, C. (1991, April 22). Media should name the Florida rape victim. *The Atlanta Journal and Constitution*, p. A13.

Sidis v. F-R Publishing Corp., 113 F.2D 806 (2d Cir. 1940).

St. Petersburg Times, Toward erasing a stigma. (1993, August 7). p. A22.

Swanson, J.A. (1992). *The public and the private in Aristotle's political philosophy.* New York: Cornell University Press.

Tackett, M. (1991, May 26). Iowa rape victim: Confidentiality vital. *The Chicago Tribune,* p. 19.

Washington, D. (1992, February 21). *Why she took on Tyson* ["20/20" interview with Barbara Walters].

Westin, A. (1983). The journalist and privacy. *Social Responsibility: Journalism, Law and Medicine,* 9, 5–19.

Chapter 9

How Much Is Ignorance of Libel Law Costing Your Organization?

Larry G. Burkum
University of Evansville, Indiana

Managers must protect their company against the risks of harm to its property or employees. Of special concern to news media managers are the risks associated with defamation by libel, including the costs of defending against potential lawsuits. Although the media often win on appeal, or win reductions in damages awarded by juries, such victories include the expense of large legal fees and loss of time better spent on news gathering (Gillmor, Barron, Simon, & Terry, 1990).

To protect their companies from costly lawsuits, news media managers must understand the basic principles of libel law while still reporting the news as completely as possible. It is this knowledge and understanding, not the law as it is interpreted by the courts, that govern how editorial decisions are made on potentially actionable material, and perhaps whether a libel suit will be brought against the company. But how much knowledge of libel law *do* media managers have? A recent survey of broadcast news managers, as well as several other studies, suggests it may not be enough.

LEGAL BACKGROUND

Libel may be generally defined as a publication or broadcast that is injurious to the reputation of another. Essentially, libel changes the way an individual is viewed by others (Gillmor, et al., 1990). Since the Supreme Court decision in *The New York Times Co. v. Sullivan* (1964), which brought libel law under the constitutional umbrella, the courts have viewed libel as a First Amendment issue that balances the right of free speech against the protection of an individual's or corporation's reputation.

Plaintiffs who successfully sue media organizations may recover three kinds of damages: compensatory, actual, and punitive. State laws and

Supreme Court decisions greatly affect the kinds of damages that may be awarded.[1] Compensatory damages are awarded for injury to reputation. A jury may set the amount of the award, which may be reviewed by a judge. Actual damages are meant to compensate for proven monetary loss suffered as a result of a defamatory statement. Punitive damages are meant to punish a media organization for communicating a defamatory statement. Punitive damages are high in order to serve as a deterrent to others who may consider publishing similar material, but they may also be a death sentence for small operations.

Hundreds of thousands of dollars, and a lot of precious time, can be lost just in the preliminary phases of libel cases. Pretrial issues of constitutional privilege and discovery, and the appeals that may accompany them, can take as long as 4 years. Those dollars are lost whether the news organization defendant eventually wins or loses the case, or, in some cases, settles out of court.

The Libel Defense Resource Center (LDRC) reported the average libel award rendered by a jury in 1990 and 1991 was $9 million ("Survey: Juries Hiking," 1992). Broadcasters won 41% of the libel suits tracked by the LDRC, compared with 33% for newspapers, magazines, books, and other print media. Radio companies won 36% and television companies won 43% of the libel suits brought against them (Sukow, 1992).

It is not just newscasts that can serve as a cause for action. Radio stations in Louisiana and Michigan have been sued for "pranks" played by announcers on unsuspecting listeners (Blodgett, 1988). The irreverent and sometimes abrasive behavior of shock jocks are the source of a large percentage of radio libel cases. Call-in shows are the next most common target (Sukow, 1992).

To reduce the risk of libel, news media managers could delegate editorial judgment to a libel lawyer, which would include the high cost of a retainer fee. An alternative is for the news media managers to be well versed in libel law principles.

THE SURVEY

Previous research relating to news managers' libel law knowledge focuses exclusively on print media. The present study measured the knowledge of broadcast news directors. Information was gathered through a questionnaire mailed to 189 radio and television stations listing a news director included in the 1994 Iowa Broadcast News Association Directory. This included stations located in states bordering Iowa whose signals can be

---

[1]For example, the Supreme Court ruling in *Gertz v. Robert Welch, Inc.* (418 U.S. 323, 1974) prohibits punitive damages if actual malice has not been demonstrated by the plaintiff.

received in Iowa. Because a plaintiff can bring suit in the state where the potentially libelous material was broadcast, and not just in the state where the station is located, these stations could face a libel suit in Iowa.

This population was selected because all prior similar research has used midwestern state-based populations, rather than random selections from a region or the nation. This allowed for some limited comparisons, especially to the Steffen (1988) study on Iowa newspaper editors.

The questionnaire contained a 20-item libel test, as well as demographic questions. The 20 statements in the libel test were all based on case law, and were evenly split among those that required respondents to have some knowledge of the legal aspects of libel law and those that dealt with practical libel situations news directors might reasonably confront in daily news gathering. News directors were asked if they agreed, disagreed, or were unsure with each statement. A copy of the libel test appears in the appendix.

A knowledge score—representing the percentage of correct answers—was created from each respondent's libel test answers. The higher the score, the more knowledge the respondent was defined as having. A response of *agree* for a true statement, or *disagree* for a false statement, was considered a correct answer. A not sure response was counted as incorrect, as was disagreeing with a true statement or agreeing with a false statement.

RESULTS

One hundred and eighteen news directors returned the questionnaire—a response rate of 62.4%. Responses were distributed among large and small radio and television stations in percentages similar to those that exist in the population of broadcast stations serving Iowa. Market size was determined using Nielson and Arbitron rankings as reported in the 1994 Broadcast and Cable Yearbook.

The mean libel law knowledge scores for all respondents were calculated and broken down by (a) market size, (b) gender, (c) education level, (d) whether respondents had taken a mass communication law course, and (e) years of journalism experience. On average, broadcast news directors answered about 60% of the libel test questions correctly. Splitting the responses among those dealing with legal concepts and those dealing with practical situations generated means of 50.9% and 69.1%, respectively. These percentages indicate that broadcast news directors have a greater knowledge of practical libel situations than legal concepts associated with libel.

News directors in large markets answered roughly the same number of questions correctly as did news directors in small markets (60.7% vs. 59.2%), although large-market news directors scored slightly better on legal concept questions (52.3%) than did their small-market counterparts (49.3%).

Male news directors, who made up nearly 80% of the respondents, had slightly higher mean scores on practical situation questions than their female counterparts (69.9% vs. 65.8%), whereas females had higher mean scores on legal concept questions (52.9% vs. 50.3%). Perhaps not coincidentally, females were more likely than males to have: (a) taken a mass communication law class, (b) a college education, and (c) fewer years of experience.

News directors who have taken a mass communication law class averaged more correct answers on legal concept questions (54.4%) than did those who have not taken such a course (47.5%). This is logical given that a news director would more reasonably be exposed to these concepts after taking a mass communication law course. This idea is further supported by the lack of difference between mean scores on questions regarding practical situations. A news director having taken a mass communication law course would not logically be any more likely to understand these practical situations than a respondent without such a class.

A college education may influence knowledge of libel law. News directors who are college graduates scored between two and three percentage points higher on the libel test and the legal concept and practical situation questions than did those who are not college graduates. Professional experience may also play a role in libel law knowledge. Respondents ranged from 1 to 51 years of broadcast news experience, with an average of just over 12 years. More experienced news directors consistently scored higher than less experienced news directors on the complete test, the legal concept questions, and the practical situation questions, although the differences were much less on the latter measure.

Gaps in Knowledge

The present study also sought to determine in what areas news directors lack libel law knowledge. This was accomplished by examining the distribution of scores for each question of the 20-item libel test. News directors clearly have difficulty with the legal concept questions, but do well on most practical situation questions. On 8 of the 20 questions, all but 1 a legal concept question, less than half of the news directors answered correctly. On half of the questions, seven of them legal concept questions, at least one fifth of the respondents answered incorrectly.

Two questions are worthy of special note. The first is a legal concept question where nearly two thirds of the respondents (61%) answered incorrectly that private figures need to establish actual malice to prove libel. Private figures must only show negligence. An additional 10% of the respondents were unsure of the answer. The second is a practical situation question, where nearly half (48.7%) of the respondents answered incorrectly that stations cannot be held liable for comments made by guests on talk shows. Another 8.5% of respondents were unsure of the answer.

The polled news directors seemed to have the most difficulty with questions associated with the level of fault necessary for a successful lawsuit, who defines this level, and what the station can be held liable for. Several of these principles are especially important to daily news gathering, yet more than 50% of the respondents either answered such questions incorrectly or were unsure of the correct answer.

Who Can Sue?

Understanding who can bring a libel suit and the level of fault such persons must show against the news operation are helpful in defending against libel suits for several reasons. The standard of fault (actual malice or negligence) is determined by whether the plaintiff is a public or private figure, and this in turn determines the types of damages that may be awarded. Plaintiffs must show actual malice on the part of the news organization to collect punitive damages. *Actual malice* is generally defined as knowingly publishing or broadcasting something that is false, or having reckless disregard as to the truth or falsity of the information. Thus, publishing or broadcasting a truthful statement cannot be considered actual malice, which mitigates the damages that might be awarded in a libel suit. Media defendants must only show that a statement charged as defamatory is substantially true, rather than proving every aspect of the statement to be true (Creech, 1993).

The Supreme Court has also ruled that only an extreme departure from standard journalist practices ordinarily adhered to by responsible publishers would constitute actual malice, although lesser errors might constitute negligence (*Curtis Publishing Co. v. Butts*, 1975). In addition, knowledge of such libel law principles may lead to a dismissal of a libel suit, or summary judgment for the defendant. If the defendant can show that one of the essential elements to libel is missing, the lawsuit can be dismissed without ever going to trial.

In some libel suits, after the plaintiff has presented his or her allegations before the court, the defendant may ask for summary judgment, which will be granted if the judge believes that a jury could not reasonably find in favor of the plaintiff. Often this is possible because the plaintiff cannot show actual malice (Creech, 1993).

What You Are Liable For

News media managers should also be aware of what they can be held liable for. For example, broadcast stations are responsible for everything they transmit, just as newspapers are responsible for everything they print. Thus, just as a newspaper can be liable for publishing a defamatory statement in a letter to the editor or in a direct quote, the broadcast station can

be held liable for defamatory statements made by talk show guests, participants in call-in programs, and in soundbites.

CONCLUSIONS

The results presented here are potentially foreboding for news directors at
radio and television stations serving Iowa, and worth noting by all news
media managers. Many are operating without an understanding of some
basic libel law concepts, such as that a station can be held liable for
comments made by guests on a talk show, or that private figure plaintiffs
do not need to show that misstatements of fact were made with actual
malice. The mean correct score for all respondents (60%) would barely rate
a D grade in any law course. The respondents would receive a failing grade
on questions dealing with legal concepts (with about 51% correct answers),
but about a C grade on questions dealing with practical situations (with
about 69% correct answers). Broadcast news directors also may not be very
confident in their understanding of libel law. At least one quarter of the
respondents answered *not sure* on 6 of the 20 questions, with 5 of the 6 legal
concept questions. It is extremely disturbing to discover that less than half
of the respondents understand that the degree of fault a plaintiff must prove
depends on whether the plaintiff is a public or private figure. This also
indicates a failure to understand the concepts of actual malice and negligence. Over half of the respondents also seemed unsure of who a public
figure is. These areas are especially important because so much of the
reported news involves governmental activities, and not all government
employees are considered public figures by the courts. There is great
potential for libel action resulting from assuming the degree of fault is the
same for public and private figures. Private figures must only show that the
news organization was negligent, or essentially made a mistake, whereas
public figures must show the mistake was made with actual malice (i.e., the
news organization knew the information was wrong, but reported it anyway). Actual malice is difficult to prove, and thus may protect the news
organization when covering public officials.

Additionally, half of the respondents did not know that information
contained in public records, such as official arrest reports and court documents, is protected under the defense of privilege. Again, news media
managers might save themselves a few headaches with this knowledge
because a large amount of news is gathered from such documents.

It was also disturbing that more than half of the broadcast news directors
did not know that their station could be held liable for comments made
during talk shows, and that more than one third did not know their station
could be held liable for defamation contained in a soundbite. More than
half also did not know that they could be sued for merely rebroadcasting

libelous statements, even if those statements were made by someone else. This is especially dangerous given the proliferation of talk radio programs and daytime talk television.

Over 55% of the respondents believe a person must be identified by name to successfully sue for libel. Working under this assumption, a reporter could easily believe that merely alluding to an individual without using his or her name, but who can easily be identified, will not result in a libel suit. It is indeed a very wrong, and potentially very costly, assumption.

Although respondents may be aware that truth is probably the best defense against libel, the majority did not know that they must only show that the defamatory statement in question is substantially true. The courts have held since *The New York Times Co. v. Sullivan* (1964) ruling that plaintiffs must prove that the offending statement is not true. Such knowledge offers perhaps the best preemptive protection for news media managers. However, professional experience appears to add to broadcast news directors' libel law knowledge. The mean knowledge level scores consistently increased across all measures with more years of professional experience.

It is also worth noting that the broadcast news directors averaged more total correct answers (60%) than the Iowa newspaper editors polled by Steffen in 1988 (46.7%). The broadcast news directors also averaged more correct answers to practical situation questions (69.1%) than the Iowa newspaper editors (37%). But the newspaper editors averaged more correct answers to legal concept questions (55%) than the broadcast news directors (50.9%).

However, these comparisons are only speculative. About 75% of the libel test questions were the same for both studies. The remaining questions applied specifically to either print or broadcast situations, or more truly measured a legal concept in the present study than did a similar question in the newspaper study. For example, newspaper editors were asked if the 1964 *The New York Times Co. v. Sullivan* decision was a setback for the press. Such a question would require knowledge of the actual court case, rather than the legal concepts that resulted from it. Instead, the present study contained questions on the burden of proving falsity and showing actual malice versus negligence without referring to specific court cases.

Unlike Steffen's (1988) finding that editors of daily newspapers had higher mean scores than weekly newspaper editors, large-market broadcast news directors did not have substantially higher mean scores than small-market news directors. Steffen also found that male editors outscored female editors—a finding not fully supported in the present study. However, both Steffen's study and the present study indicate that news media managers who have taken a mass communication law course have greater libel law knowledge than those without such training. And libel law knowledge generally increases with levels of education.

It is clear that broadcast news directors could use a refresher course in basic libel law concepts. Even some of the respondents recognize this, based on written comments that accompanied many of the questionnaires. But those comments also point out a disturbing belief held by a handful of respondents—that because they operate a small station in a small, rural community, they do not have to worry much about libel. Although the risk may be small, one lawsuit—even a frivolous one—could financially destroy a small, rural station.

It is impossible to know whether the news directors polled in the present study are representative of all broadcast news directors because only radio and television stations serving Iowa were included in the study, and a census was used, rather than a sample. The study did not include any major market stations, which may face the greatest threat of libel suits. But the findings presented here are fairly consistent with those from previous studies involving midwestern newspaper editors, all of which indicate a need for management-level news persons to either become more knowledgeable of libel law, frequently turn editorial judgment over to a libel lawyer, or risk losing hundreds of thousands of dollars or more in legal fees and/or damages resulting from a libel suit.

RECOMMENDATIONS

Managing a news department brings with it a number of legal pitfalls that involve possible financial sanctions against a media company. Among the more dangerous of these is the threat of libel action. But there are several things a media manager can do to help guard against this threat without turning editorial judgment over to a lawyer.

News media managers must have a good working knowledge of libel law for the everyday, routine newswork. Radio and television station managers and newspaper publishers can help ensure this in the following manner. After a news manager or reporter is hired, he or she should be given the libel test found in the appendix. He or she should then be given information about libel law (including this chapter) to read, and should then retake the test. All news personnel should be given the test on an annual basis to keep them fresh. Those scoring below 80% correct should take a refresher course in libel law.

The test should be updated periodically, and should use varied questions so that news personnel do not merely memorize the correct answers. This can easily be accomplished by scrambling the order of the questions and/or reversing the wording of some questions. For example, one time a test question would read "A plaintiff must be identified by name in order to sue for libel" and the next time the same question would read "A plaintiff need not be identified by name in order to sue for libel." Because the test is essentially in a true–false format, alternative wording is fairly simple.

Broadcast stations and newspapers might also offer a libel workshop on an annual or semiannual basis. An area university or community college may be willing to conduct such a workshop for a small fee. Perhaps one member of the news department could audit a media law course each year, and then conduct the workshop for other employees. This could be done on a rotating basis, and would help keep news personnel aware of changes in how the courts are interpreting libel law. Stations and newspapers might also wish to develop a "libel book" similar to a stylebook for their news personnel to consult. Again, an area university or community college might assist in producing such a manual.

This is not to say a lawyer should never be consulted, especially in borderline situations. But to seek approval on every story is overly cautious, and will greatly slow the news gathering process, which can be even more financially harmful in a competitive environment.

The past decade has seen a dramatic rise in the number of libel cases filed in civil courts across the United States, and some of the judgments sought are astronomical. Because of this rising interest in libel litigation by persons who feel they have been slandered, and because of the number of libel cases won by defendants, news media managers should be prepared for even the threat of libel action. The best preparation is a good understanding of libel law.

REFERENCES

Blodgett, N. (1988, February 1). Radio daze: Targets strike back; Stations sued for pranks that cause listeners distress. *ABA Journal*, p. 15.
Creech, K. C. (1993). *Electronic media law and regulation*. Boston: Focal Press.
Curtis Publishing Co. v. Butts, 388 U.S. 130 (1975).
Gertz v. Robert Welch, Inc., 418 U.S. 323 (1974).
Gillmor, D. M., Barron, J. A., Simon, T. F., & Terry, H. A. (1990). *Mass communication law: Cases and comment* (5th ed.). St. Paul, MN: West.
The New York Times Co. v. Sullivan, 376 U.S. 254 (1964).
Steffen, B. J. (1988). What Iowa editors know about libel law. *Journalism Quarterly, 65*, 998–1000.
Sukow, R. (1992, October 19). Libel plaintiffs find sympathetic jurors. *Broadcasting*, pp. 48, 51.
Survey: Juries hiking libel penalties. (1992, September 5). *Editor & Publisher*, p. 13.

APPENDIX: THE LIBEL TEST

The statements below are about aspects of libel law or about practical libel situations news directors confront from time to time. Please answer the questions in the context of your daily decision making regarding the news content of your station. Please answer true or false for each question. (Correct answers are indicated in parentheses.)

(T) 1. Libel suits must be filed within a set period of time after a statement has been broadcast.
(T) 2. Libel plaintiffs (those bringing the suit) must establish the falsity of a potentially libelous statement to win their lawsuit.

(F) 3. Private figure plaintiffs must also establish that misstatements of fact were made with actual malice.

(T) 4. A station can be held legally liable in a libel action for the comments a guest makes over the air during a talk show.

(F) 5. The good intentions of a reporter are a complete defense against libel.

(F) 6. Only individuals, not businesses, may sue for libel.

(F) 7. Video used in a television news story cannot be libelous.

(F) 8. Broadcast stations can only be sued in the state where their signal originates.

(F) 9. All employees of government agencies are considered public figures under libel law.

(F) 10. States are not allowed to independently define the standards of liability for libel law covering private individuals.

(F) 11. Stations cannot be held liable for libelous statements made by others in soundbites.

(F) 12. Plaintiffs who successfully sue broadcasters may only recover actual damages.

(T) 13. A plaintiff cannot win a libel suit when the libelous material consisted of accurately reported statements made by witnesses in a court case.

(T) 14. In order to use truth as a defense in a libel suit, the defendant must only show that the statement charged as libelous is substantially true.

(T) 15. Rebroadcasting libelous statements is grounds for an additional libel suit.

(F) 16. An individual reporter cannot be held liable in a libel suit.

(F) 17. A plaintiff must be identified by name in order to sue for libel.

(T) 18. Information found in public records, such as official arrest reports and court records, is protected under the defense of privilege.

(T) 19. The Supreme Court has said that failure to follow standard journalistic practices is not sufficient proof of actual malice.

(F) 20. It would be negligent for a news person to broadcast a story, without further checking, from the Associated Press.

Chapter 10

Delivery System Disaster: Circulation Problems of the *St. Louis Sun*

James E. Mueller
The University of Texas at Austin

Nothing, it seems, is simple about circulation except the basic adage: Circulation increases come one at a time, but circulation drops come in droves.—(*Thorn & Pfeil, 1987, p. xv*)

This chapter uses the case study method to examine the role that circulation delivery problems played in the death of the *St. Louis Sun*, an innovative metropolitan daily that lasted 7 months in 1989–1990. The chapter uses intensive interviews, corporate documents, and media coverage to analyze the question of the paper's demise. It concludes that delivery problems were instrumental in the newspaper's failure.

INTRODUCTION: WHY STUDY THE *SUN*?

Few American cities—about two dozen—have competing daily newspapers, thus, it is generally assumed within the industry that only the largest cities can support two or more dailies. The trend toward one-newspaper cities is so clear that attempts to start new metropolitan dailies are as rare as hand-operated presses.

The last profitable launch of a metropolitan daily was that of New York's *Newsday* in 1940. The *Washington Times* was established in 1982, but industry experts count it as an exception to the trend because of its financial subsidization by the Rev. Sun Myung Moon's Unification Church (Rosenstiel, 1989).

A recent failure that drew national attention was the *St. Louis Sun*, which was founded by Ralph M. Ingersoll II in 1989. It lasted 7 months, but its brief life is worth studying for the lessons it could provide to media managers. One could dismiss the *Sun* as merely a victim of the national trend toward one daily per city, but that would be a mistake. Industry experts gave Ingersoll a realistic chance to succeed in 1989 for several reasons, one of the most important being his proven track record as a newspaper manager. His newspaper empire in 1989 consisted of more than 150 newspapers in the United States and Europe, including a chain of about 40 free-distribution weeklies in the St. Louis area (Sharkey, 1989). Ingersoll was described as "an intellectual" and "no self-deluding newcomer but a crafty revamper of smaller papers" (Henry, 1989, p. 60). *Fortune* selected him as 1 of the 25 most fascinating business people of the year in 1989. Ingersoll said he wanted to use the *Sun* to reinvent the American newspaper with a "post-modern" look—a "laptop" that would attract the video generation (Teinowitz, 1989, p. 82).

Ingersoll's chain of St. Louis suburban weeklies gave him an established advertising base in his target market, which was served by a daily that was vulnerable in several ways. The *Post-Dispatch* was a liberal newspaper in a conservative town and had made its reputation on national and international, rather than local, news. The *Post* was also not as successful financially as one might expect in a monopoly market. The *Post* received only 35% of all local advertising in its market compared with 53% for newspapers nationwide (Heins, 1989).

But if there was an opportunity to establish a new daily in St. Louis in 1989, what happened to the *Sun*? When the *Sun* went out of business in the spring of 1990, the postmortems by academics, journalists, and stock analysts piled up like unsold copies of the paper. The *Sun's* death was blamed on its content (Klotzer, 1990a), its rejection by the St. Louis market, and its lack of financing when Ingersoll's junk bond empire collapsed (Eubanks, 1990). Ingersoll said it was "absolutely clear" that there was no need for another daily in the St. Louis market, which he maintained was "inundated by information" (Coleridge, 1993, pp. 124–125).

All of these factors doubtless played a role in the failure of the *Sun*. The collapse of any enterprise involving hundreds of people and millions of dollars can rarely be tied to one simple cause. However, one overlooked factor that may have doomed the paper before it started publishing was its poorly planned and executed circulation strategy. It is the intent of this chapter to use the case study method to explore how circulation problems contributed to the *Sun's* failure. Data sources for this study included: intensive interviews with some of the key people who worked for the *Sun*, company records on file at the St. Louis Public Library, academic studies, and media coverage of the *Sun*.

The number and variety of sources used should increase the validity of the study by allowing for triangulation of data. An interview subject may have a limited or biased perspective, but comparing his or her story with company documents should aid in coming closer to the truth (Wimmer & Dominick, 1994). The use of multiple data sources also leads to more "thickly described cases" so that the case study can be compared to similar situations (Lindlof, 1995). Thus, such a case study of the *Sun* should provide useful information to media managers, particularly in showing what mistakes to avoid in planning a new enterprise. From a theoretical perspective, this case study should add to the existing work on media management theory as it applies to planning and operating a circulation system.

BACKGROUND

The importance of prompt, efficient service in retaining readers is well documented in newspaper management literature. A guide on improving circulation produced by the American Newspaper Publishers Association (ANPA) and the Newspaper Advertising Bureau (NAB) lists reader "satisfaction with home delivery/single copy service" as one of "ten vital signs" for measuring the health of a newspaper. The report stated that readers must be "serviced with a timely, well-oiled distribution system" (Keating, Topper, Fielder, Foster, Woldl, & Junod, 1990, p. 43). Rankin (1986) pointed out in his text on newspaper management that, "No matter how excellent the editorial product of the newspaper may be, its advertising revenue will be nonexistent if the newspaper is not sold and read" (p. 11). One circulation executive was quoted by Rankin as saying that: "Service and circulation increase are directly correlated over the long run as excellent service makes selling much easier. Retention of the newspaper in the home ultimately depends on the type of service a subscriber receives. Circulation executives must also thoroughly understand the relationship between good delivery service and the image that good service generates in the eyes of an advertiser" (p. 18). Willis (1988) called circulation "a key link in the production chain that leads to fulfillment of the newspaper's overall mission" (p. 94). Thorn and Pfeil (1987), who have written one of the few modern texts specifically on circulation techniques, asserted that dependability is "crucial" for a successful distribution system.

> "Readers whose morning papers frequently are delivered too late to be read before leaving for work quickly lose the habit of newspaper reading. Subscribers have a right to expect that they will receive their newspapers on time. Nonsubscribers wanting to purchase a newspaper on a particular day should find single copies easily accessible. … Erratic production and transportation schedules destroy carrier morale and result in dissatisfied customers" (Thorn & Pfeil, 1987, p. 213).

But perhaps the importance of circulation delivery is best summed up by Fink's (1988) blunt statement: "Be there when readers are—or else" (p. 199).

Research shows that most U.S. daily subscribers are generally satisfied with their delivery service. A 1980 Newspaper Readership Project survey (cited in Thorn & Pfeil, 1987) found that only 5% of respondents expressed any dissatisfaction with their newspapers' delivery. The study found only 22% of nonsubscribers blamed poor service as a reason for not taking the paper. A national study done 10 years later found much the same results:

Only 5% expressed dissatisfaction and 2% either did not respond or said *don't know* (Keating et al., 1990). Because of the scarcity of metropolitan daily startups, previous research that is directly related to establishing new newspapers is limited, or is so old as to be of questionable value.

Perhaps the previous research most related to the death of newspapers is Benjaminson's (1984) study of the problems of metropolitan afternoon newspapers. His book, *Death in the Afternoon*, includes an examination of *Tonight*, the afternoon edition of the *New York News* launched in the early 1980s. Benjaminson essentially used a multiple case study approach to show why some afternoon papers succeeded and other succumbed to what he termed *afternoon newspaper disease*. He recommended several cures, including improving news coverage to attract upscale readers and moving the home-delivery edition to the morning (Benjaminson, 1984).

Many articles about the *Sun* have been published in general circulation magazines or newspapers, but few academic studies have been done on the newspaper. Hellinger (1990) conducted a limited content analysis of the *Sun* and the *Post* during the first months of their competition, and found their content to be similar. This study could indicate that the *Sun* may have suffered because it did not differentiate itself from its competition. A comparison of the content of the *Post*, *Sun*, and *Globe* found evidence that competition increases the diversity of content (Johnson & Wanta, 1993), but none of the content analyses dealt with circulation in more than a tangential manner.

There are also few academic studies on circulation, and most of the studies focus on things like the effect of price on readership or promotion techniques. For example, Lacy and Fico (1991) found a strong relationship between newspaper content quality and circulation. Lewis (1995) found significant negative relations between newspaper price and circulation in her study on newspaper price increases. Picard (1991) studied the effect of price increases on circulation, and found in his case study of a midsize daily that a price increase can be helpful rather than harmful. Niemeier (1988) developed a framework for market evaluation that emphasized identifying opportunities for circulation growth. Gamst (1986) studied retention of youth carriers, and found that nearly half would rather collect fees than have the paper handle collecting because they got tips by collecting in person.

CIRCULATION PROBLEMS OF THE *SUN*

Ingersoll's market research on the new newspaper showed that potential readers were there. In an August 1989 report entitled *New Newspaper in St. Louis*, Kennan Research and Consulting Inc. concluded from focus groups and one-on-one intensive interviews that there was absolutely no doubt that the *St. Louis Sun* had an excellent potential to succeed in the St. Louis market. The report stated that the "main negative" was the tabloid format, but that the negative connotation could be reduced over time as people got used to it. It also recommended that an intensive promotion campaign be conducted to establish the paper's image. The report closed with what would later turn out to be a prophetic comment that it is crucially important to realize that a short period of time (one to three months) after the introduction will determine the future success of the newspaper. A newspaper must focus on its impact; that is, 'hitting hard' during its beginning stages. (Kennan Research and Consulting Inc., 1989).

The man in charge of "hitting hard" was Tom Birkenmeier, the *Sun's* promotions director—a man who had worked in advertising and public relations in St. Louis since 1967. Birkenmeier wrote in a memo to Ingersoll that focus groups showed readers thought the *Sun* was "lively and exciting," but were only lukewarm about the *St. Louis Post-Dispatch* (T. J. Birkenmeier, personal communication, August 5, 1989). "The *Post* has failed to make a positive emotional connection with many readers, and they've had 111 years to do it. It is almost as if they are damned with faint praise" (T. J. Birkenmeier, personal communication, August 5, 1989).

Sun staffers, encouraged by the research and the knowledge they were part of a great challenge, set about lining up subscribers and advertisers. In an interview with the author, Birkenmeier recalled that it was the hardest he had every worked in his life, yet at the same time was very exciting. "My job was to soften up the market, to get ready to receive the new product, to line up as many tryers as we could. We began to do solicitations. We used direct mail, we used a lot of TV and broadcast. We used everything, every known arsenal/weapon/marketing tool to make it happen. That worked pretty well" (T.J. Birkenmeier, personal communication, March 14, 1995).

One of the marketing weapons was Ingersoll himself. The publisher, who had announced earlier that year that he would move to St. Louis to personally run the new newspaper, joined various civic groups. Ingersoll had made himself and the *Sun* logo ubiquitous in St. Louis—Ingersoll through appearances on the civic-lunch circuit, and the *Sun* logo through a $2.5 million promotion campaign, including things like a ski-cap giveaway at a St. Louis Cardinal baseball game (Reilly, 1989).

Birkenmeier said that the promotional campaign worked so well that between 111,000–114,000 people requested trial subscriptions by the launch date, which was Sept. 25, 1989 (T. J. Birkenmeier, personal communication, March 14, 1995). Ingersoll had said he could turn a profit on fewer than 100,000 subscribers (Stroud & Smith, 1989). But what seemed to be an ideal situation for the new paper soon turned into a disaster when the potential subscribers were irritated by poor service.

One of the first mistakes was made in the way the new subscribers were signed up. *Sun* executives decided to try pay-in-advance billing, which, according to Birkenmeier, "does wonders for your cash flow," but was something new to the St. Louis daily market, where most subscribers were used to paying for their newspapers after they were delivered. He said the error was made worse by the design of the bill, which was "unreadable."

It was simply the most confusing thing known to man. The marketing guys were never consulted. Here you get the market all pumped up, you get people to send in their orders, their trial subscriptions. They're pumped; they're ready to go. They get a bill—before the newspaper comes. That in and of itself is not a mortal sin. But when you compound that with the fact that the paper, which is a daily paper, a morning paper, which should be delivered before 7 a.m., doesn't get delivered until 10 and 11 o'clock in the morning, what happens? You have meltdown. (T. J. Birkenmeier, personal communication, March 14, 1995)

The meltdown occurred mainly because of a problem with the *Sun* printing presses. The company planned to print the newspapers on twin presses in a renovated printing plant in the southern part of the metropolitan area. But during a trial run about 3 weeks before the launch date, it was discovered that the two presses in the plant were not twins. Half the papers would thus have to be printed at a Suburban Journals' plant in the northern part of the metropolitan area. "How did this happen? Nobody knows," Birkenmeier said. But the resulting confusion was no secret.

Bear in mind this is all happening with that launch date clicking off every hour. Half your carriers now have to go north instead of south and these guys—right up through this period we are signing people [subscribers] up furiously—we're writing as many orders as we can. So on the day of the launch carriers are coming out with new subscriptions that they just got that day; they've haven't run those routes; they don't know where those people are. The only way I can describe it is it was like watching a thoroughbred racehorse fall down inside the chute when the gates open. The *Sun* never recovered from that problem. (T. J. Birkenmeier, personal communication, March 14, 1995)

Many subscribers got their papers late or not at all. Others could not find them in the vending machines or stores around town. The paper had to install three extra phone lines into its offices to handle about 11,000 phone calls from people who had not gotten their newspapers. Customers who were excited by the publicity campaign became angry at not getting their papers, and became angrier when they could not get a prompt response to their phone calls. "It's a huge, gigantic mess. And what's going on is the customers are getting more and more angry. So then what sets in are cancellations. 'Cancel my subscription! No, don't even call me and talk to me about it because you couldn't get it right!' So you went from orders, orders, orders. … It was like watching a car go off a cliff" (T. J. Birkenmeier, personal communication, March 14, 1995).

By industry standards, the delivery problems were horrendous. Comparing national statistics to a *Sun* market study done a few months after its September launch date suggests the importance of the paper's delivery problems. Recall that the national study mentioned earlier showed only 5% of respondents expressed dissatisfaction with their delivery service (Keating et al., 1990). Ingersoll's readership survey revealed that 15% of single-copy buyers said they had trouble finding copies of the *Sun* (Clark, Martire, & Bartolomeo Inc., 1990). And 67% of former *Sun* subscribers said a delivery problem was the main reason they canceled their subscriptions. One out of two of those who canceled, and said they had called the paper to complain, also said their complaints were not handled well by *Sun* employees.

Yet another way of looking at the *Sun's* problems is counting the number of complaints per 1,000 papers that were home-delivered subscriptions. A ratio of 1 complaint per 1,000 is considered low by industry standards (Keating et al., 1990). Certainly not all of the 11,000 calls a day the *Sun* was receiving were complaints. But even if one is charitable and assumes only half were complaints, at 5,500 complaints per 55,000 home subscribers (the number of subscribers reported by Goodman, 1989), the day the paper was launched yields 100 complaints per 1,000. Put another way, a conservatively estimated complaint ratio for the *Sun* is 10 times what is considered a good figure by industry standards.

The problems were also evident in the newsroom. Kevin Horrigan, the *Sun's* star columnist, told the author in an interview that he did not think the paper's top executives ever "had a handle on the business side" of the *Sun*. "The circulation department was a disaster. They had people begging to subscribe and they couldn't service the accounts. And apparently they didn't know how to get copies of papers to places like 7-11s and Schnucks [a local grocery chain]" (K. Horrigan, personal communication, March 16, 1995).

Sun marketing officials, especially Birkenmeier, wanted to conduct a public relations campaign to explain what had happened to the readers. Birkenmeier wanted to tell St. Louisans that the paper had more subscriptions than it could handle, but that it would correct the problem. But he said the idea was rejected by *Sun* executives. "It was a major mistake. We should have worried about it. It was a classic case of not worrying about the customer. If there was anything we should have done, we should have bent over backward to make those people happy" (T. J. Birkenmeier, personal communication, March 14, 1995).

Sun Publisher Thomas Tallarico said in an interview with the author that a public relations campaign would not have done any good. "We didn't want to acknowledge that we had a problem at that point. We were hopeful we would solve it in short order" (T. Tallarico, personal communication, March 15, 1995). However, Tallarico did say that the plan for establishing the *Sun* was too complex and tried to cover too many facets of the newspaper business. If he were to do it over again, he would not try to deliver papers to the entire metropolitan area, and might let the carriers handle billing. "We were too ambitious in our undertaking. We didn't have the resources for what we were trying to do. I would have started out with a less grandiose scheme" (T. Tallarico, personal communication, March 15, 1995).

One major problem with the plan was that it relied heavily on single-copy sales in a city in which most subscribers wanted home delivery.

Ingersoll said that because the *Post* sold about 120,000 single copies a day, it was reasonable that the *Sun* could sell 75,000 single copies, especially with a colorful tabloid format and more single-copy outlets than the *Post* had (Klotzer, 1990b). But single-copy sales were less than half what had been expected, and were extremely inconsistent from day to day (Klotzer, 1990b).

Ingersoll said the decision to close the paper was based on its failure to increase single-copy sales, despite good weather, the start of the baseball season, and promotions such as bingo games (Gauen & Mannies, 1990). However, both Birkenmeier and Horrigan contended the emphasis on single-copy sales was a flawed concept from the beginning, and that *Sun* executives had research that showed St. Louisans wanted their newspaper home delivered.

> They had all these numbers and all this research ... that said St. Louisans are home-based and interested in family, and I think they were right. But what they failed to recognize was that in this town people wanted a newspaper delivered to their homes because that's where they live their lives. They don't live in fancy restaurants. That was a key piece of information that was there for them that they chose not to see. (K. Horrigan, personal communication, March 16, 1995)

Birkenmeier told the author that it was "absolute, utter stupidity" to emphasize single-copy sales:

> All research in the market showed that St. Louis is a home-delivery market. And there is a very simple reason: We are not a commuter market. We didn't have MetroLink [St. Louis' new light rail system]. Where tabloids do very well is where you have commuter markets, I mean you have lots of densely packed people and single copy is a very big issue. St. Louis is a home-delivery market. Putting boxes on every corner was a huge expense and a huge delivery problem. (T. J. Birkenmeier, personal communication, March 14, 1995)

He concluded that it took resources that might have been devoted to solving the home-delivery problem.

Ingersoll maintained the single-copy emphasis was a reasonable decision in 1989 because there were noncommuter markets like Trenton, New Jersey, where single-copy sales were strong (Klotzer, 1990b). Unfortunately for the *Sun*, St. Louis was not one of those markets. Single-copy sales had settled at about 17,000 a day when Ingersoll pulled the plug on the *Sun* on April 25, 1990 (Coleridge, 1993).

SUMMARY

It is clear from the evidence that circulation problems were a key factor in the death of the *Sun*. The only question that remains is how big a factor circulation problems were compared with other issues, such as quality of content and lack of financing. Two of the three people interviewed for this chapter concluded that the circulation problems were fatal. Birkenmeier contended that the *Sun* never recovered from the mixed up orders when it first began publishing. Horrigan said he agreed "100 percent" with Birkenmeier. "There's no doubt about it. You get people excited about your product and then you can't get your product to them—they're going to give up on you in a hurry. That was certainly something that wasn't thought through" (K. Horrigan, personal communication, March 16, 1995).

The *Sun* research on consumer satisfaction, when compared with industry standards, also indicated a problem of major dimensions. Ingersoll admitted there was "considerable chaos" in the home-delivery system (Klotzer, 1990b). A knowledgeable observer, former *St. Louis Globe-Democrat* publisher G. Duncan Bauman, said the *Sun* had "the most inept circulation department in America" (Kramer, 1990). Even a casual reader blamed delivery problems for the *Sun's* demise. Ritter (1990) wrote in a letter to the editor of the *Post* that he enjoyed both it and the *Sun*, but could rarely find the latter in machines or stores. He added that his mother was an early subscriber, but had to call twice and then wait 2 weeks to get her subscription in order. "These may seem like two small incidents, but if you multiply them by the thousands of city and county residents, it could have made a difference" (p. 2B).

However, Tallarico asserted that the circulation was not a fatal error, and that the main reason the *Sun* failed was that the St. Louis market rejected it: "We got so much excitement and demand that we couldn't cope with it. But one thing you'll never know is how many of those who subscribed did so out of pure curiosity and how many became frustrated because they tried to subscribe and couldn't because of poor service" (T. Tallarico, personal communication, March 15, 1995).

Tallarico is correct in that it is impossible to tell whether the *Sun* would have succeeded had its circulation distribution system worked better. But better planning by management would have given the paper a fighting chance. *Sun* executives should have paid attention to the market research indicating that an emphasis on single-copy sales would not work. They failed to plan for emergencies such as the printing press mixup. Last, their plan was too complex. They tried to serve an area that turned out to be too large for their circulation system to handle. The *Sun* may have died even had circulation worked perfectly, but the poor service doomed it to failure before other factors such as content and advertising sales could even be evaluated.

Ingersoll was often described as a charming, intelligent man who is also very persuasive when describing his ideas. In fact, one St. Louis writer compared him to the Music Man, the movie character who sold an imaginary boys' band to River City (McClellan, 1990). Horrigan agreed with the comparison. "He was a great salesman. He was very persuasive. Instead of us all getting band instruments we were all going to get copies of the *Sun*.

Here's the difference. Professor Harold Hill got the instruments in the hands of the kids, and Ralph never got the paper in anybody's hands" (K. Horrigan, personal communication, March 16, 1995).

Of course research cannot be tied up as neatly as a movie. More research is needed to fully understand what happened to the *Sun*. More of the principals need to be interviewed from Ingersoll on down to someone who was in the trenches, such as a carrier or a vendor. A qualitative analysis of the content, especially when compared with the quantitative content analysis already done on the paper, would be helpful in determining the effect on content on the *Sun's* demise. Last, an examination of the company's finances would shed light on the role the collapse of the junk bond market played in the story.

REFERENCES

Benjaminson, P. (1984). *Death in the afternoon: America's newspaper giants struggle for survival*. Kansas City: Andrews, McMeel and Parker.

Clark, Martire, & Bartolomeo Inc. (1990). *Market study*. St. Louis, MO: Author.

Coleridge, N. (1993). *Paper tigers*. London: Heinemann.

Eubanks, B. (1990, April 30–May 6). Maverick Ingersoll bet against odds and lost. *St. Louis Business Journal*, p. A1.

Fink, C. (1988). *Strategic newspaper management*. Carbondale, IL: Southern Illinois University Press.

Gamst, G. (1986). Carrier turnover correlates. *Newspaper Research Journal, 7*, 1–11.

Gauen, P., & Mannies, J. (1990, April 26). Street sales too weak, editor says. *St. Louis Post-Dispatch*, pp. A1, A13.

Goodman, A. (1989, September 26). St. Louis Sun sells all 200,000 copies. *St. Louis Post-Dispatch*, p. C9.

Heins, J. (1989, July 24). Why Ingersoll picked St. Louis. *Forbes*, p. 52.

Hellinger, D. (1990, March). *Post, Sun* stress public affairs, not sensationalism. *The St. Louis Journalism Review*, p. 5.

Henry, W., III. (1989, September, 25). *Sun*-rise in St. Louis. *Time*, p. 60.

Johnson, T., & Wanta, W. (1993). Newspaper competition and message diversity in an urban market. *Mass Communications Review, 20*, 136–147.

Keating, W. J., Topping, S., Fielder, V., Foster, M., Woldt, H. F., Jr., & Junod, J. (1990). *A way to win: Strategies to evaluate and improve your readership and circulation*. Washington, DC: American Newspaper Publishers Association.

Kennan Research and Consulting Inc. (1989). *New newspaper in St. Louis*. St. Louis, MO: Author.

Klotzer, C. L. (1990a, May). Here. *The St. Louis Journalism Review*, p. 2.

Klotzer, C. L. (1990b, May). Ingersoll explains decision. *The St. Louis Journalism Review*, pp. 1, 10, 11.

Kramer, S. D. (1990, May). Ingersoll praises advertisers; blames consumer resistance. *The St. Louis Journalism Review*, p. 7.

Lacy, S., & Fico, F. (1991). The link between newspaper content quality and circulation. *Newspaper Research Journal, 12*, 53–57.

Lewis, R. (1995). Relation between newspaper subscription price and circulation, 1971–1992. *The Journal of Media Economics, 8*, 25–41.

Lindlof, T. R. (1995). *Qualitative communication research methods*. Thousand Oaks, CA: Sage.

McClellan, B. (1990, October 3). *Sun* veterans recall how it all began. *St. Louis Post-Dispatch*, p. A3.

Niemeier, B. A., Jr. (1988). A multifactor matrix approach to evaluating circulation markets. *Newspaper Research Journal, 9,* 87–99.

Picard, R. G. (1991). The effect of price increases on newspaper circulation. *Newspaper Research Journal, 12,* 64–75.

Rankin, W. P. (1986). *The practice of newspaper management.* New York: Praeger.

Reilly, P. M. (1989, September 21). Ingersoll goes full throttle to promote Monday's launch of St. Louis Daily. *The Wall Street Journal,* p. B8.

Ritter, R. (1990, April 29). Letters from the people. *St. Louis Post-Dispatch,* p. B2.

Rosenstiel, T. B. (1989, March 29). St. Louis may again be a 2-paper town. *Los Angeles Times,* p. (IV)3.

Sharkey, J. (1989, March 31). Ingersoll wants his St. Louis Daily to spur a new era for city papers. *Wall Street Journal,* p. B4.

Stroud, J., & Smith, B. (1989, April 2). First shot sounded in new news war. *St. Louis Post-Dispatch,* p. E5.

Teinowitz, I. (1989, September 25). Ingersoll sees "*Sun*"-ny future. *Advertising Age,* p. 82.

Thorn, W. J., & Pfeil, M. P. (1987). *Newspaper circulation: Marketing the news.* New York: Longman.

Willis, J. (1988). *Surviving in the newspaper business.* New York: Praeger.

Wimmer, R. D., & Dominick, J. R. (1994). *Mass media research: An introduction.* Belmont: Wadsworth.

Chapter 11

The Winner of Air Discontent: Preemption of "NYPD Blue" Amid Economic Risk and Audience Reaction to Gatekeeping

Larry Collette
James D. Kelly
Southern Illinois University at Carbondale

In a climate where broadcast networks mourn the loss of national audiences to competing technologies, it is ironic that one network's actions would be in part responsible for fractionalizing its own audience. The damaging effect a controversial program can have on the affiliate clearance process was made obvious when Steven Bochco's "NYPD Blue" was included in the 1993 fall season lineup and the threads of ABC's patchwork quilt of affiliated stations began to unravel. Beginning with the initial screening of the series pilot at the yearly affiliates meeting in June, it was clear that the program's mix of violence, rough language, and sex would meet with resistance from some station executives (Coe, 1993). The premiere episode of the series did not air in 57 markets where ABC-affiliated stations declined to run the program. As a result, a sizable share of the potential national audience was eliminated in one fell swoop (Mocha, 1993), thus erasing some of the scale economies enjoyed by the network. Rather than a reaction to sagging ratings of an existing program, the local affiliate decisions to preempt arose from concerns surrounding a new program's controversial content.

The tumult and attention generated by "NYPD Blue" prior to its debut exceeded that of any television program in recent memory. Yet the show became the season's highest rated new drama, received a full 22-episode order, and was hailed by *Newsweek* as "simply the best new show on television" ("Blue in the Night," 1993). Eventually the program garnered a record 26 Emmy nominations, rose to sixth place overall in the Nielsen ratings, and became a verified hit (Fretts, 1994).

The Communication Act of 1934 established that the airwaves belong to the people, and a licensed station is required to serve "the public interest, convenience, and necessity." Within this broad mandate, the management of a local affiliate is called on to make programming decisions that anticipate the unique character and composition of the market in which it operates. Yet the lack of perfect knowledge makes this gatekeeping function risky because audience tastes are notoriously fickle, and the assumptions surrounding possible market reaction to a program must often be formed well in advance. Thus, these a priori judgments are guesswork that occurs amid fundamental considerations of retaining a station's network identity and building the prime-time audience needed to maximize an entire evening's schedule ratings. The opportunity costs of making the wrong programming decision are known only *after* the deed, and are evidenced by poor ratings or other audience displeasure.

This chapter examines audience reaction to the preemption of a controversial network offering within a gatekeeping framework applied to entertainment communication. It develops and tests a Gatekeeping Tolerance Index as a measure of audience tolerance of local gatekeeping. In doing so, it measures the extent of audience agreement with a station manager's decision to preempt airing of "NYPD Blue," and examines audience perceptions of the circumstances under which stations are justified in preempting any prime-time program. The utility of the Gatekeeping Tolerance Index is explored within the larger context of the network and affiliate relationship, and the risks associated with programming decisions.

BACKGROUND

Research on audience reaction to controversial television programming has focused primarily on the effects that program messages have on attitudes and opinions (e.g., Lasora, 1989; Walker, 1989). This study differs in that it focuses on the audience reaction to management's decision to preempt programming, thereby precluding any possible effects. A discussion of the industry context in which peremption occurs highlights the dilemma facing station managers in preempting a program. The local station manager's gatekeeping function must be viewed as part of the ongoing dynamic among network, local station, and audience in an era of a shifting market.

Affiliate and Network Programming Relationship Amid Risk

For the local station, the affiliation agreement carries the immediate rewards of a ready supply of high-quality programming, an enhanced advertising environment, and financial compensation for time cleared. From the network's perspective, the primary efficiency is that a single program can be shared across an extensive affiliate system. Competitive advantage results from the network's ability to spread the costs of programming over a wider audience base (Owen, Beebe, & Manning, 1974). At the same time, the marginal costs of adding new audience is deemed to be slight because the first copy costs of a program have already been met.[1]

Despite the efficiencies, the arrangement represents a conundrum for networks that must rely on local affiliates to clear time and air network programming. The harsh implications of widespread preemption of a program are likely to be felt in overall ratings, which in turn affect advertising rates, and ultimately affect the profitability of the network.

At the same time, affiliates remain acutely dependent on network programming, typically relying on the network for roughly 60% of their total schedule lineup (Haldi, 1985). Although local affiliates retain the right to reject network programming by a Federal Communications Commission (FCC) mandate (1941), even the occasional or one-time-only replacement of a network program offering is infrequent. For example, during the 1980s, preemption of network programming accounted for less than a 1.5% loss in national household coverage for the major historic television networks (Owen & Wildman, 1992). The continued or blanket preemption of an entire series is an even more rare occurrence, and has been mostly limited to cases where attractive syndication offerings (e.g., "Star Trek: The Next Generation") and/or declines in local market ratings ("Monday Night Football" in the mid-1980s) provided the primary motivations dictating the preemption.

As network ratings decline, the incentives for affiliates to seek first-run syndicated program replacements can be expected to be greater. Station spending on entertainment programming is expected to increase by 6.8% from 1990 to 1995—a rate faster than the anticipated increase in advertising revenues (Veronis, Suhler, & Associates, 1991). Lin's (1994) census of network affiliate station managers found that running special programs and local programs were the most likely reasons for preemption, and over 80% indicated that poorly rated programs would be an unlikely reason to preempt a network offering. Nevertheless, increased sources of syndicated programs and improved distribution make an array of programming outlets available to affiliates that may indeed represent reasonable substitutes for network fare (Chan-Olmsted, 1991).

Although clearances remain nearly automatic, a degree of uncertainty exists that may ultimately affect the type of programs that networks produce and distribute. Uncertainty reduces the incentive to take risks in offering programs of a type that might jeopardize these clearances. Because

---

[1]Networks also restrain potential program price inflation through standard use of the step process of program acquisition. This practice, which ultimately binds program producers at a fixed price through the life of the contract, has led to deficit production costs to producers and lower costs to the networks. See B. R. Litman (1993).

tastes and standards can be expected to vary by region, the networks may attempt to reduce the risks of nonclearance by commissioning programs that deal to broad, homogeneous tastes in a manner that avoids potentially controversial content. This plain-vanilla approach may be given even greater impetus by regulatory oversight in areas such as indecency. Hence, the number of so-called "breakthrough programs" that challenge conventions has been small as networks seek to engage the widest possible audience (Jencks, 1980; Litman, 1979; Wakslag & Adams, 1985).

Yet the risk of nonclearance exists apart from an even more substantial layer of risk—that associated with audience taste—which will ultimately contribute to a program being a success or a flop. Similar to the consumer goods market, the high risk of introducing new programs (products) makes older, established products or formulae increasingly valuable franchises. Nord's (1983) risk theory of popular arts described a reliance on formula as the compromise struck between producers wishing to sell a single, identical product to an audience and the audience's own desire for suitable entertainment. On the industry side, these formulae have become synonymous with the familiar program types comprising much of the television network's output (e.g., sitcoms, game shows, soap operas, legal dramas). As a result, a frequent complaint is that new programming seasons are troubled by what former network executive Fred Silverman called "a sense of deja vu" (Lack, 1982). Brown (1971) termed this process of repackaging old wine in new bottles the *failsafe system* of programming, where fear of failure, rather than extravagant risk taking, is the norm.

Tannebaum (1980) suggested the network tendency to offer identical new programs resulted from the "uncertainty, competition, and reliable production capability" that make programming decisions based on the best possible model. But increased competition from cable and other technologies has brought a new urgency to the need to innovate, fueling a greater nervousness on the part of broadcast networks (Litman, 1993). The balancing act of making a program ripe for clearance, and at the same time appear fresh and appealing to audiences, must be deftly accomplished each new television season.

Because new programs represent uncertain products, the networks attempt to remove a portion of risk by dealing almost exclusively with producers that have proven track records (Gandy, 1983). The result is a high concentration of creative talent in a limited number of production organizations specializing in specific program formats. Thus, Diane English becomes synonymous with situation comedies, just as Hanna-Barbera is with cartoons.

In discussing the risks associated with media industries, Turow (1992) blamed a general lack of innovation on organizational structures and the fear of a potential chain reaction ignited by unconventionally creative actions. The bureaucratic committee system of programming at the network level comprises such an organizational structure. Turow suggested that breaks from the norm or unconventional television programming are the products of some unexpected tension-inducing changes affecting both the networks and production firms. The eruption of such tension heralds the inception, development, and release of unconventional or riskier program innovations. Similar to the equilibrium upset within a marketplace wrought by a technological "gale of creative destruction," suggested by Schumpeter (1942), competing technologies have rearranged the programming landscape for the broadcast networks. Most dramatically, within households subscribing to pay cable, broadcast network affiliates command a 64% viewing share, as compared with 87% among noncable households (Nielsen Media Research, 1993). This suggests a considerable alteration of the television marketplace once dominated by the broadcast network oligopoly. The future entry of the Regional Bell Operating Companies into video delivery, and the formation of new broadcast networks by motion picture giants, Warner and Paramount, will further heighten competition for TV viewers' attention (Grover & Landler, 1994).

In the face of tension already generated by substantial cable and video cassette inroads into network audiences, ABC called on a producer with a proven track record and a successful formulae to create an innovative and even controversial program for network distribution. Steven Bochco's previous efforts included "Hill Street Blues," "L.A. Law," as well as his innovative, but short-lived, "Cop Rock." With "NYPD Blue," the network used a proven risk-reduction strategy to generate an innovative and even controversial response to the "R-rated" offerings of the new technology that increasingly threatens the networks' audience share.

The Local Programming Decision as Gatekeeping

As made clear by the FCC report (1941), which dealt with radio, but is also applied to television networking, a broadcast station cannot delegate its responsibility for programming functions to the network. Prior to the prerecording of network programs, networks commonly supplied skeletal information to affiliates, including data about the length of the series, length of each program, name of the sponsor, type of program, and, in some cases, the persons appearing on the program. Of course such limited information made any real assessment of a program's content virtually impossible when it came to public interest considerations (Federal Communications Commission, 1941). In the television industry, this situation changed dramatically with the advent of video recording. Affiliates freely previewed program offerings, and exercised increased oversight prior to making clearance decisions. Prerecording removed much of the local affiliates' uncertainty about what they would be airing, but uncertainty about audience reaction still remained.

The program director who exerts a preview-based control and makes in-or-out decisions that influence which programs are available to the public is functioning as a gatekeeper. In its broader sense, gatekeeping occurs when a communication organization or its representatives selects from among a large number of messages a few to be transmitted to receivers (Shoemaker, 1991). The concept of gatekeeping is most often attached to news gathering and decisions regarding news-related information (Berkowitz, 1990), but it is relevant to other forms of communication as well. Here the scope of station management's initial gatekeeping decision is a binary choice of either acceptance or rejection of a network offering—considerably simpler than large volume of continuous messages, as in the case of news. Once a program is rejected, however, the gatekeeping function becomes more similar to the news context.

Gatekeeping is subject to the decision rules that are established both implicitly or explicitly within an organization (Shoemaker, 1991). Although the exact nature of these decision rules varies across differing media organizations, one might fully expect the application of these rules to be guided, to a great extent, by anticipation of the organization's target audience response. For example, one simple (although important) decision rule for station management might be that selected content must be of a reasonable quality so that an audience will be motivated to stay tuned.

Wright and Barbour (1976) detailed a risk model of media decision-making strategies, in which evaluations of potential loss or failure are made by a decision maker who ultimately selects the option entailing the least risk. Translated to the local affiliate, this risk equation needs to consider the effect a controversial program would have on its market. Indeed, Lin (1994) found that 37% of station managers indicated that avoiding offensive programs was a likely or very likely reason to preempt a network show. The actual measurement of risk may be arrived at through the use of relative frequencies, a priori judgments, deduction, or subjective definitions of probability (Hammond, 1968). In this case, the considerations surrounding risk are exemplified by a series of related questions. If a program is aired: How will it be greeted by viewers? Will it attract an audience of sufficient numbers? Will it be offensive to and/or alienate viewers? Will it attract local sponsors?

Often it is the assessment of risk or uncertainty that becomes the pivotal point for decisions in these matters of choice (Slovic, 1968). For any firm whose primary goal is profit maximization, the best that can be done is to estimate the probability of success that may result from its various strategies of a short- or long-term nature (Farrar, 1962; Mansfield, 1992). Paradoxically, in avoiding the risk of offending the local audience, managers who preempt a program that later becomes a commercial success risk losing that program's potential economic rewards in their market.

Audience testing is a standard practice in gauging audience reactions to a program. Testing for "NYPD Blue" included airings on cable-leased access channels, followed by prearranged interviews (Schmuckler, 1993). Still, the degree to which such testing is generalizable to the reactions within a given broadcast market is unknown, and therefore represents an imperfect barometer for programming decisions made in specific broadcast markets. Station managers that lack a sophisticated means to test possible viewer response to a program may make estimates based on personal knowledge of the market and its audience. In a fashion similar to an oil field explorer, they must rely on a subjective probability based on past experience and judgment to make decisions on future events, hoping that not all the wells will turn out to be dry (Megill, 1984). The limited direct feedback in the form of audience letters, threats of boycotts, or protests also play a factor in the decision to run a program (Selnow & Gilbert, 1993). Given the possible fluctuations and uncertainty of audience tastes and tolerance, this task appears most formidable. Himmelweit, Swift, and Jaeger (1980) pointed to the difficulty of such a task: "A combination of high risk and high stakes are the very conditions under which, *in the absence of proper feedback*, the folklore about the audience's tastes and reactions are likely to flourish" (p. 91; italics added).

PURPOSE

This research seeks empirical evidence regarding audience reactions to a television station's decision not to air "NYPD Blue." The situation the authors investigated—a market where local protests, boycott threats, and media attention preceded the show's premiere—was an ideal opportunity to analyze audience perception of gatekeeping, and to measure tolerance levels for the kind of content traditionally not shown on broadcast television.

In the market considered, local media coverage of the decision not to air "NYPD Blue" was extensive. Local newspapers, television and radio stations all devoted coverage to the controversy, and the general manager of the affiliated station appeared nationally on ABC's "Good Morning America" to explain his decision. The station had been picketed by protestors several weeks before the station manager announced his decision. In the announcement, he explained that the decision not to broadcast "NYPD Blue" was not the result of protests or boycott threats, but rather his determination of the inappropriateness of the first three episodes in light of local community standards.

This research measures the extent of audience agreement with a station manager's decision to preempt airing of "NYPD Blue," and examines audience perceptions of the circumstances under which stations are justified in preempting any prime-time program. In addition, the authors investigated the relationship between self-reported gatekeeping tolerance and individual viewer attitudes toward television effects and programming control. The authors wanted to find answers to these research questions:

1. What is the audience reaction to a station manager's gatekeeping decision not to air "NYPD Blue"?
2. What controversial program attributes might an audience perceive as objectionable and as sufficient reason for preempting a program?
3. What is the relationship between gatekeeping tolerance and attitudes toward television programming control and perceptions of television's influence?
4. How well does a measure of gatekeeping tolerance predict reaction to a specific gatekeeping decision when controlling for political orientation, community affiliation, and perceptions of television influence?

METHOD

A telephone survey was conducted over three evenings, October 6–8, 1993—a period following three consecutive weeks in which "NYPD Blue" was preempted in the local market. The broadcast market under study is market ranked in the top 100 Designated Market Area (DMA) and the DMA includes portions of a three-state region, much of it rural. Prior to the premiere, the general manager (who also functions as the program director) of the ABC affiliate had announced his intention to judge the appropriateness of the program on a week-to-week basis, and had rejected the first three episodes.[2] The survey was conducted during the third week of the season, when no area station was broadcasting the program.

To sample local public opinion about the decision, a random list of telephone numbers was computer generated and stratified to include a representative cross-section of the exchanges within the television station's primary coverage area.[3] Interviews were conducted with persons 18 years or older using the last birthday method, and averaged 20 minutes in duration. Four hundred and seven completed surveys were compiled by trained telephone interviewers. The completion rate was 43%.

Measurement

Respondents who indicated they were aware of the affiliate's decision to preempt "NYPD Blue" were asked the extent to which they agreed or disagreed with the decision; responses were scored using a 5-point Likert-

---

[2]On the second day of the survey, the local Fox affiliate announced that it would be the second non-ABC station in the country to carry "NYPD Blue" in the coming weeks.

[3]Because the local dialing exchanges do not perfectly match broadcast market areas, only telephone numbers within a 75-mile radius of the station were sampled. Although this does not include the entire market, it did capture a large proportion excluding those persons who might have been able to receive the signal of a distant affiliate broadcasting the program.

type scale (5=*strongly agree* to 1=*strongly disagree*). Then respondents were asked an open-ended question: What was the main reason the station decided not to show the program?

Next, all respondents, regardless of whether they were aware of the decision, were presented with 14 statements dealing generally with television control and influence. They were asked to respond using the same 5-point scale described. The statements were:

> "I think I am the best judge of what's appropriate for me and my family to watch on TV."
> "Banning TV programs only increases people's interest in them."
> "If a program has high ratings in other areas, the local station has an obligation to show it here too."
> "Media people often create controversies about a program just to increase the size of the audience."
> "Television can have a very powerful effect on the ways in which people behave."
> "People like me are generally unable to influence the decisions made by those who run the media."
> "If people don't like what's on TV, the best thing to do is turn off the set."
> "There is far too much sex and nudity on network television."
> "I would be interested in seeing the show 'NYPD Blue' for myself."
> "TV networks place too many restrictions on program producers."
> "Television is basically entertainment. It has little impact on most people's lives"
> "There is far too much violence and bloodshed on network television."
> "Local television stations should not air any network programs that might offend sensitive people."
> "Generally I am very satisfied with the TV programming available to me."

Each of these statements was used as a variable in the correlational analysis. Two were also used in the regression analysis. "I'm the best judge ... " was used as a measure of respondents' feeling of self-control over television (Self-Control of TV), and "Television can have powerful effects ... " was used as a measure of respondents' beliefs about the power of television (Powerful Effects of TV).

All 407 respondents were asked 12 questions dealing with specific content attributes that were presented as possible reasons for preempting a program during prime time. Each reason for preemption was assigned a value of five if the response was, "Yes, that's an appropriate reason," a value of zero if the response was, "It depends," and a value of negative five if the response was, "No, that's not an appropriate reason." This provided a measure that reacts to both possible polar responses. The sum of all 12 response scores yielded a composite measure labeled the Gatekeeping Tolerance Index (GTI), defined as the degree to which an individual perceives restriction of program content by local affiliates as acceptable. Positive scores indicate higher levels of tolerance for local gatekeeping. Negative scores indicate lower levels of tolerance. This measure was also used in its aggregate form to identify the rank ordering of those program attributes found objectionable by the local market audience. The items comprising the GTI are listed next. In each case, they were followed by this general question: "is that an appropriate reason not to show it locally?"

"If a particular network program shows people being killed, ... ?"
"If a program shows people using illegal drugs, ... ?"
"If a program shows people abusing alcohol, ... ?"
"If a program is racist, ... ?"
"If a program rejects Christian teachings, ... ?"
"If a program advocates extreme right-wing viewpoints, ... ?"
"If a program advocates homosexual lifestyles, ... ?"
"If a program has people using profanity, ... ?"
"If a program shows male nudity, ... ?"
"If a program advocates extreme left-wing viewpoints, ... ?"
"If a program is sexist, ... ?"
"If a program shows female nudity, ... ?"

At the end of the interview, respondents were asked a series of demographic questions. In addition to age, sex, and education level, respondents were asked, "In how many civic, fraternal, religious, or professional organizations are you currently active?" (Organization Membership) and "How often do you attend church per month?" (Church Attendance). As a measure of perceived political orientation, respondents were asked, "On a scale of 1–10, where 1 is *politically very liberal* and 10 is *very conservative*, where would you rank yourself?"

RESULTS

Respondent Profile

The average age of respondents was slightly over 40 years, with a range of 18–78 years of age. From these, 73% were in the key television demographic of 18–49 years of age. Females accounted for 56% and males 44% of the sample.

Six percent had not finished high school, 19% finished high school, 34% had some college, 22% had 4 year college degrees, and 18% had some graduate study. Respondents' average church attendance was 2.3 times per month. Self-reported political orientation averaged 5.48 on a 10-point scale, with the standard deviation of 2.25.

Sixty-seven percent of the respondents knew of the station's decision to preempt "NYPD Blue." In response to the question, "How do you feel about the station's decision not to show "NYPD Blue?", 41% indicated either strong disagreement or disagreement, and outnumbering those who strongly agreed or agreed (38%). The remaining 21% expressed a neutral position. Among the 275 respondents aware of the decision, 32% believed that "local protest and threats of a station boycott" led to the decision not to air the program, 30% thought "local TV standards" were the reason, 21% expressed a variety of other reasons, ranging from "economic" to "a need for more country western music shows," and an additional 17% were "unsure."

Gatekeeping Tolerance Results

The GTI measures a viewer's general tolerance for programming decisions at the local network affiliate gate. The score represents the sum of response values to a 12-item index ranging from -60 (complete objection to any tested program attribute passing through the affiliate gate) to +60 (no objection the local station allowing any tested program attribute pass through the gate).[4] The mean response on the GTI was -18.

Seventy respondents (17.2%) were anchored on the extreme end of the continuum, with a score of -60. For these people, none of the identified reasons was sufficient for a local station to preempt a program. At the other extreme end of the continuum were 14 respondents (3.4%) who identified all 12 reasons for preemption as acceptable. The overall distribution is skewed positively (see Fig. 11.1). Each score is any combination of "yes, reason to preempt" (5) and "not a reason to preempt" (-5) responses. Therefore, 65% of those surveyed expressed low levels of tolerance for gatekeeping activity by the local affiliate.

The means for each of the individual items comprising the GTI also provided method for rank ordering objectionable program attributes deemed so objectionable that they, in many viewers' minds, were enough to justify preemption by the local affiliate. The audience identified scenes of male nudity as the most objectionable program attribute, followed closely by espousal of racist viewpoints, scenes of female nudity, and use of profanity. Extremist political viewpoints were seen as the least objectionable (see Table 11.1).

Correlation of Attitudes with GTI

Correlation statistics were run as an exploratory step to search possible relationships between gatekeeping tolerance (GTI) and the attitudinal measures, as shown in Table 11.2. The correlations also provided a means to test the construct validity of the GTI.

---

[4]Reliability analysis on the GTI produced a Cronbach's alpha = .91.

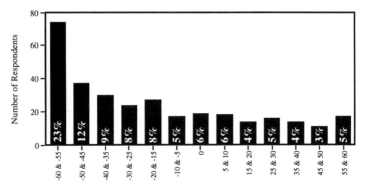

mean scores on the GTI

FIG. 11.1.

TABLE 11.1

Rank Ordering of Individual Items Comprising the Gatekeeping Tolerance Index
(Higher Values Indicate Greater Objection)

Item	Mean score	SD	N
"If a program shows male nudity,...?"	–.10	4.86	398
"If a program is racist,...?"	–.48	4.53	392
"If a program shows female nudity,...?"	–.56	4.85	403
"If a program has people using profanity,...?"	–1.13	4.52	400
"If a program is sexist,..."	–1.33	4.47	391
"If a program advocates homosexual lifestyles,..."	–1.35	4.53	389
"If a program shows people using illegal drugs,...?"	–1.47	4.35	398
"If a program rejects Christian teachings,...?"	–1.65	4.36	390
"If a program shows people abusing alcohol,...?"	–1.93	4.10	391
"If a program shows people being killed,...?"	–1.93	4.10	391
"If a program advocates extreme left-wing viewpoints,...?"	–2.06	4.18	369
"If a program advocates extreme right-wing viewpoints,...?"	–2.10	4.19	367

Note. Statements all followed by: "is that an appropriate reason not to show it locally?"

Analysis of the correlations suggests that those with high tolerance for
gatekeeping think there is too much sex and violence on television already.
The strong positive association between GTI and the statement most directly related to the preemption decision ("local stations should not air")
confirms that the GTI does react in the anticipated manner. Those with high
GTI scores are more likely to see television as powerful, and to see themselves as having too little control over the set. They are more likely willing
to yield outside decision makers, rather than viewing material for themselves. They most likely do not think there are too many restrictions on
program producers. Those more willing to accept preemption decisions are
less likely to say that preemption stimulates interest, or that interest in a
show elsewhere places an obligation on the local station to show it as well.

TABLE 11.2

Correlations of the Gatekeeping Tolerance Index
with Attitudes Toward Television Control and Influence

Statements	Pearson's r
"There is too much sex and nudity on network television."	.456**
"Local stations should not air any programs that might offend sensitive people."	.433**
"There is far too much violence and bloodshed on network television."	.397**
"Television can have a powerful effect on the ways in which people behave."	.267**
"I think I am the best judge of what's appropriate for me and my family to watch on TV."	−.135*
"If people don't like what's on TV the best thing they can do is turn it off."	
"If a program has high ratings in other areas, the local station has an obligation to show it here too."	−.181**
"Television is basically entertainment. It has very little impact on most people's lives."	−.182**
"Banning TV programs only increases people's interest in them."	−.201**
"TV networks place too many restirctions on program producers."	−.224**
"I would be interested in seeing 'NYPD Blues' for myself."	−.372**

Note. Three variables with nonsignificant correlations are not included in the table. $N = 404$.
* $p < .01$.   ** $p < .001$.

Higher tolerance of gatekeeping was also positively associated with age, church attendance, and conservative leanings, and negatively associated with education levels.

GTI as a Predictor of Audience Reaction to Preemption

If GTI is a reasonable measure of audience tolerance of gatekeeping at the local network affiliate level, it should exert considerable influence in predicting an audience's level of agreement with a specific preemption decision.[5] To test its predictive power, GTI and eight other variables were regressed on the response to the question asking how strongly the respondent agreed or disagreed with the preemption decision. A stepwise method was used to enter the variables into the equation, with a probability of F-to-enter of .05.

The resulting equation explained a considerable portion of the total variance in the dependent variable. R square was .51, and the F value was 43.45. GTI was the first variable to enter the equation, and by itself accounted for slightly more than 33% of the variance. Five additional variables also entered the equation: Church Attendance, Political Orientation, Self-Control of TV, Powerful Effects of TV, and Sex. Three variables did not enter the equation as specified: Education, Age, and Organization Membership (see Table 11.3).

---

[5]According to the response filter question, 132 people had no knowledge of the situation surrounding "NYPD Blue," and therefore were excluded from the regression analysis. Additionally, listwise deletion of the cases with missing values was used; this further reduced the number of cases in the analysis to 216.

TABLE 11.3
Regression on Level of Audience Agreement with
Affiliate's Decision to Preempt "NYPD Blue"

R square	.5085		
Standard Error	1.0116		
F	43.454**		

	df	Sum of squares	Mean square
Regression 5	222.349	44.469	—
Residual	210	214.910	1.023

Variable in the equation	b	SE b	Beta	t
Gatekeeping Tolerance Index	.0154	.0002	.3854	6.907**
Self-control of TV	−.3172	0.732	−.2191	−4.331**
Political Orientation	.1352	.0337	.2169	4.006**
Church Attendance	.0788	.0265	.1553	2.072*
Powerful Effects of TV	.2133	.0742	.1477	2.873*
(constant; 2.7029)	.5106			5.293**

Variables not in the equation	Beta if in	Partial	t
Sex	.0921	.1268	1.848
Education (−.0782)	−.1020	−1.483	
Age	.0709	.0968	1.407
Organization membership	−.0165	−.0228	−.330

* $p < .005.$ ** $p < .0001.$

CONCLUSIONS

This chapter examined audience attitudes toward control of television programming and tolerance for gatekeeping in a broadcast market in which a controversial new program, "NYPD Blue," was unavailable due to a management decision to preempt it. Because the preemption decision necessarily precedes viewer examination, the station manager operated based on his best estimate of audience approval and community standards. Clearly, such a decision represents a risk to the station's acceptance and approval by the community. Yet there is also considerable risk associated with the opportunity costs of not airing a program that becomes popular elsewhere. The preemption decision is a difficult one that involves many factors, as shown in the Appendix.

The gatekeeping metaphor provides a solid theoretical base for modeling the decisions involved in local affiliate programming decisions, as well as those that individual television viewers make as they select an evening's entertainment fare.

Audience attitudes about television control were measured, and a 12-item scale was developed to measure audience attitudes toward television programming content. This provided a rank ordering of objectionable content. This scale was summed to create the GTI—a measure of individuals' tolerance of local station gatekeeping. The GTI proved to be a reliable measure of program attributes audiences find so objectionable that they are willing to accede control of the decision gate. It also provides a workable predictor of audience reaction to preemption of particular program offerings. The results confirm the index's reliability as a predictive measure. Therefore, it may offer considerable utility in reducing the inherent uncertainty in deciding whether an audience will tolerate specific controversial programming.

The 12 items that underlie the GTI can indicate what a specific audience finds most objectionable, and therefore what is most likely to evoke support for an affiliate that decides to preempt a specific program. In the case examined here, the audience identified male and female nudity, profanity, and racism as most objectionable. These are the most reactive attributes in the GTI because they violate what is currently accepted as appropriate for broadcast television. "NYPD Blue" was reported to have all of these attributes in quantity. It pushed the traditional boundaries into a content realm formerly reserved for the motion picture theater, but increasingly available in the home as well.

For example, "male nudity" evoked the most objection in this particular market. But male nudity in this society is an infrequent phenomenon generally, aside from museum statues and locker rooms. Perhaps the strength of the objection is a reaction to the seemingly extreme deviation from television conventions and a larger expected societal norm. Interestingly, "NYPD Blue," with its portrayal of a naked Detective Sipowicz in bed with a hooker and a naked Detective John Kelly rolling in bed with an attractive female rookie officer, tests the limits of television's conventions. This is what the press focused its reports on.

The push into new content areas was made by a network addressing a national audience. But the local affiliate must make its decision in light of a smaller, more homogeneous market. In this case, "NYPD Blue" was preempted—it was not passed through the gate because the management guessed that the local audience would object to the program's content.

Although the show contained many of the most objectionable attributes (or at least what people knew of the show's attributes), only 38% agreed with the local station's decision to preempt. This is not counter to what the GTI predicted. Indeed, every one of the items in the index showed a negative score. This means not a single program attribute was so objectionable that a majority of respondents were willing to concede their control over the viewing decision to the local station manager. Even in a conservative, mostly rural market, the audience as a whole was extremely reluctant to allow a local station to deny them their access to a network offering that the rest of the country will see. As is clear in Fig. 11.1, audience preference is that individual members exercise control of programming selection.

Even more revealing is the correlation of gatekeeping tolerance with opinions held about television content and control. Those favoring high levels of gatekeeping perceive less efficacy in their own personalized control of media. For these people, the knowledge that others are willing to adopt the role of arbiter may provide some reassurance in an increasingly violent and hostile world. To them it may seem reasonable and perhaps preferential that forms of entertainment or communication be filtered along the way. A possible verification of this may be seen in the belief by high gatekeeping tolerance types that local stations should not air anything that may offend sensitive people. Clearly, those audience members most likely to be offended are those for whom every programming cloud represents a potential rainstorm—here a minority of the potential audience. Not surprisingly, these people did not wish to even see "NYPD Blue" for themselves. This is in contradiction with the majority view that the best judges of what is appropriate are the people themselves.

In essence, the conflict underlying such decisions is an old and fundamental one that pits the invisible hand of the marketplace against traditional ideas of moral authority. In earlier times, priests decided what the parishioners would know of the Bible. In these modern economic times, market forces are increasingly the final arbitrator; in the long run, Nielsen ratings may prove to be the ultimate indicator of what is acceptable.

Perhaps the most revealing aspects of this study are in the results from the statistical analysis. It is clear that the GTI responded well in terms of the variance explained. What is also worth considering here are the contributions made by the other variables in the final equation. Political Orientation and Church Attendance were powerful predictors as well. Political Orientation has traditionally been one of the stronger predictors of free speech or expressive rights in general (Zaller, 1992). Yet it is difficult to know with any certainty if the audience was responding to the rights of a producer to be heard or their own desire to receive certain content. Future research may help to partial out this subtle, but important, distinction. Church attendance entered the equation because it predicts audience agreement with the affiliate's decision to preempt. This suggests that church-going may be a self-defining public that acts independently within the market audience. That the organization variable did not similarly enter the equation suggests that either the measurement was inadequate or the public measured was uninterested in the preemption decision.

This seems to suggest that audiences are more than just an undifferentiated mass market. Rather, an audience is composed of a collection of previously formed groups that inhabit the geographical area within reach of a broadcast signal. In this vein, McQuail (1987) asserted that an audience "is a collectivity which is formed either in response to media (channels and content) or out of independently existing social forces (when it corresponds to an existing social group or category or the result of activities by a local group to provide itself with its own channels of communication media)" (p. 215). Often it is inextricably both at the same time. The possibility exists that we are dealing with at least two television audiences—each with its own motivations for activity.

McQuail defined a public audience as a preexisting active, interactive, and largely autonomous social group that is served by particular media, but does not depend on the media for its existence. Such public audiences tend to coincide with membership of the most active members in a preexisting community (Stamm, 1985). It is more likely to have interpersonal interaction between its members and a sense of group identity or purpose. It is likely to remain stable over time, and to respond to media actions in public forum. Those who protested the local showing of "NYPD Blue" were perhaps such a public audience.

The *market audience* is defined as a product–consumer relationship, rather than a social or moral one. In this relationship, preemption denies the audience economic opportunity. Loyalty to the network, or more broadly to the media, is actively encouraged for commercial reasons. In this way, the market audience takes on some aspects of the public audience such as long-term stability, boundaries, and awareness of identity. Still, this market audience is much more likely predicated on a self-interest at the individual level, rather than a group-interest motivation at the societal level.

Individuals who express higher levels of self-efficacy are more likely to object to preemption decisions and to reserve control over programming for themselves. Conversely, individuals who view television as having powerful effects are more likely to submit to external control exercised by the local station.

Additional attention from communication scholars into the phenomenon of information access seems warranted by the results of this exploratory investigation. As the sheer volume of content available to the individual increases in the information age, the old public policy idea of the broadcaster as an appropriate controller of a local information gate may seem increasingly antiquated. It may well be that, in an era of abundant information, individuals may see themselves as the only appropriate keepers of the gates.

APPENDIX

A checklist useful to any and all station managers considering preemption decisions is problematic at best. But keeping in mind that the research presented here was limited to a particular market, the authors suggest the following:

- Audiences are generally intolerant of preemption decisions based on program content.
- Some program attributes are more objectionable than others, but none is so obnoxious that it alone is enough for a majority of the audience to desire program preemption.
- Caution should be taken in generalizing from a vocal minority of the audience to the larger market audience.

- Audience members who perceive television as exerting a powerful influence on society are also those most likely to favor greater restrictions on innovative content.
- Audience members less confident of their own judgment in making viewing decisions are more tolerant of control decisions made at the station level.
- Factors such as Church Attendance and Conservative Political Orientation help determine tolerance of gatekeeping by local managers.
- Program attributes that run against the grain of traditional television content (especially nudity and profanity) are more likely perceived as objectionable.
- The GTI can be a useful management tool for gaining a sense of local audience reaction to programming content decisions.

REFERENCES

Berkowitz, D. (1990). Refining the gatekeeping metaphor for local television news. *Journal of Broadcasting and Electronic Media, 34*, 56–68.

Blue in the night (1993, December 13). *Newsweek*, pp. 56–59.

Brown, L. (1971). *Television: The business behind the box*. New York: Harcourt Brace.

Chan-Olmsted, S. (1991). A structural analysis of market competition in the U.S. TV syndication industry, 1981–1990. *Journal of Media Economics, 4*, 49–66.

Coe, S. (1993, June 14). Some ABC affiliates see red over "NYPD Blue." *Broadcasting and Cable*, p.14.

Farrar, D. E. (1962). *The investment decision under uncertainty*. Englewood Cliffs, NJ: Prentice-Hall.

Federal Communications Commission. (1941). *Report on chain broadcasting: Pursuant to commission order no. 37, docket no. 5060*. Washington, DC: Superintendent of Documents.

Fretts, B. (1994, November 11). Copping a new attitude. *Entertainment Weekly*, pp. 22–31.

Gandy, O., Jr. (1983). Television audience size and composition, In B. Devin and M. J. Voigt (Eds.), *Progress in communication sciences* (Vol. V, pp. 219–254). Norwood, NJ: Ablex.

Grover, R., & Landler, M. (1994, December 12). Hollywood scuffle: Demand for product is huge. *Businessweek*, pp. 36–38.

Haldi, J. A. (1985). Affiliated station programming. In S. Eastman, S. Head, and L. Klein (Eds.), *Broadcast/cable programming* (2nd ed., pp. 166–184). Belmont, CA: Wadsworth.

Hammond, J. D. (1968). *Essays in the theory of risk and insurance*. Glenview, IL: Scott, Foresman.

Himmelweit, H. T., Swift, B. & Jaeger, M. E. (1980). The audience as critic: A conceptual analysis of television entertainment. In P. H. Tannebaum (Ed.), *The entertainment functions of television* (pp. 67–108). Hillsdale, NJ: Lawrence Erlbaum Associates.

Jencks, R. W. (1980). How network television program decisions are made. In M. Botein D. M. Rice (Eds.), *Network television and the public interest* (p. 42). Lexington, MA: Lexington.

Lack, A. (Producer). (1982). *Don't touch that dial*. New York: CBS Reports.

Lasorsa, D. L. (1989). Real and perceived effects of "Amerika." *Journalism Quarterly, 66*, 373–378, 529.

Lin, C. (1994). Changing network-affiliate relations amidst a competitive video market. *Journal of Media Economics, 7*, 1994.

Litman, B. R. (1979). The television networks, competition and program diversity. *Journal of Broadcasting, 23*, 393–409.

Litman, B. R. (1993). The changing role of TV networks. In A. Alexander, J. Owers, and R. Carveth (Eds.), *Media economics: Theory and practice* (pp. 225–244). Hillsdale, NJ: Lawrence Erlbaum Associates.

Mansfield, E. (1984). *Principles of microeconomics*. (4th ed.). New York: Norton.

Mansfield, E. (1992). *Principles of microeconomics*. (7th ed.). New York: Norton.

McQuail, D. (1987). *Mass communication theory: An introduction*. Beverly Hills, CA: Sage.

Megill, R. E. (1984). *An introduction to risk analysis.* Tulsa, OK: PennWell.

Mocha, D. J. (1993, September). "NYPD Blue" premiere wins slot despite 57 preemptions. *Electronic Media*, p. 2.

Nielsen Media Research. (1993). *1992–1993 report on television.* New York: Author.

Nord, D. P. (1983). An economic perspective on formula in popular culture. In E. Wartella, D. C. Whitney, and S. Windahl (Eds.), *Mass communication review yearbook* (pp. 287–301). Beverly Hills, CA: Sage.

Owen, B., Beebe, J. H., & Manning, W. G. (1974). *Television economics.* Lexington, MA: Lexington.

Owen, B., & Wildman, S. (1992). *Video economics.* Cambridge, MA: Harvard University Press.

Schmuckler, E. (1993, June 21). Talks between ABC and Bochco continue over "NYPD Blue" as net tests show. *Mediaweek*, p. 3.

Schumpeter, J. (1942). *Capitalism, socialism, and democracy.* (3rd ed.). New York: Harper & Brothers.

Selnow, G., & Gilbert, R. (1993). *Society's impact on television: How the viewing public shapes television programming.* Westport, CT: Praeger.

Shoemaker, P. (1991). *Gatekeeping.* Newbury Park, CA: Sage.

Slovic, P. (1968). Assessment of risk-taking behavior. In J. D. Hammond (Ed.), *Essays in the theory of risk and insurance* (pp. 78–94). Glenview, IL: Scott, Foresman.

Stamm, K. R. (1985). *Newspaper use and community ties: Towards a dynamic theory.* Norwood, NJ: Ablex.

Tannebaum, P. H. (1980). Entertainment as vicarious emotional experience. In P. H. Tannebaum (Ed.), *The entertainment functions of television* (pp. 107–129). Hillsdale, NJ: Lawrence Erlbaum Associates.

Turow, J. (1992). *Media systems in society.* New York: Longman.

Veronis, Suhler, & Associates. (1991). *The Veronis, Suhler & Associates communications industry forecast.* New York: Author.

Wakslag, J., & Adams, W. J. (1985). Trends in program variety and the prime time access rule. *Journal of Broadcasting, 29,* 22–34.

Walker, J. R. (1989). The impact of a mini-series: A quasi-experimental study of "Amerika." *Journalism Quarterly, 66,* 897–901.

Wright, P., & Barbour, F. (1976). The relevance of decision process models in structuring persuasive messages. In M. Ray & S. Ward (Eds.), *Communicating with consumers* (pp. 32–45). Beverly Hills, CA: Sage.

Zaller, J. R. (1992). *The nature and origins of public opinion.* Cambridge, England: Cambridge University Press.

Chapter 12

Pathway to the Top: How the Top Newspaper Chains Train and Promote Publishers

Martha N. Matthews
University of Washington, Seattle

In the early part of this century, when newspapers were still a growing industry, most newspaper publishers owned the papers they managed. An entrepreneurial individual would start a newspaper, generally in the town in which he or she resided, as a means to earn a living and often to promote a particular political point of view. Dramatic increases in chain ownership in the 1970s and 1980s changed that model of ownership in the majority of American newspapers. Today, three-quarters of all newspapers are owned by chains (Newspaper Association of America, 1996), and most newspaper publishers are employees of larger media organizations. As employees, their power is limited to what their employer (the chain) will allow, and their decision making is influenced by what the chain demands.

Chain ownership, and its impact on the management of newspapers, has been criticized on a number of levels. In particular, chains have been accused of placing too much emphasis on generating a profit, and not enough emphasis on producing quality newspapers. Chains have also been accused of managing their individual newspapers by "formula," leaving publishers and editors little room for individuality. It has been argued that survival in some corporate newspapers has become a function of how well an individual learns and adapts to the parent company's values.

Publishers—who hold the top-ranking position in a newspaper, and usually serve as the person to whom the editor reports—are responsible for ensuring their newspaper earns an acceptable profit for the parent company. As the top-ranking persons on a newspaper, publishers have the power to set budgets, make employment decisions, and occasionally make journalistic decisions that reflect the concerns of the parent company. Given the enormous pressure they are under to generate revenue, there is a strong concern among practicing journalists that today's corporate publishers are managing with less concern for news quality than ever before.

So what do the newspaper chains look for when they seek out individuals to serve as publishers of their newspapers? Are the chains all looking for the same set of skills and professional experience? Or do they vary according to individual value systems? The focus of this chapter is to determine how the largest newspaper chains in the country compare to one another in terms of the selection and training of their publishers.

BACKGROUND

There are many studies that have investigated the impact of chain ownership on newspapers. Among those studies, evidence suggests chain-owned newspapers are more profit-oriented than independently owned newspapers (Busterna, 1989; Demers & Wackman, 1988). In addition, a 1990 survey of editors by the American Society of Newspaper Editors found that 91% of editors at chain-owned newspapers claimed that chains are more concerned with profits than with individual papers or communities.

Investigations into the effects of chain ownership on the editorial quality of newspapers, however, have yielded mixed findings. The research has yet to find a consistent link between chain ownership and a decrease in quality. In one of the first published studies investigating the impact of chain ownership on the quality of news coverage, Grotta (1971) found no differences in quality between newspapers that became chain owned in the 1950s and newspapers that remained independently owned through 1968. He measured quality by comparing the number of editorial employees, the size of the newshole, the proportion of local—total news, the size of the editorial page newshole, and the proportion of local—total editorial content.

However, in the 1970s, Wackman, Gillmor, Gaziano, and Dennis (1975) observed that chain-owned newspapers have a tendency to be homogeneous in their endorsement of presidential candidates. Wackman et al. warned that this finding could be indicative of other areas of homogeneity in chain-owned newspapers, such as hiring practices, management procedures, and peer pressure to push chain newspapers toward editorial uniformity. Similarly, Thrift (1977) tested the hypothesis that, after they have been purchased by chains, newspapers that had been independently owned will have a smaller proportion of argumentative editorials on controversial topics. His study found a significant decrease in editorial "vigor" in the newspapers that became chain owned.

The criticism of homogeneity within the chains is not limited to academic scholars. David Burgin, former editor-in-chief of *The Daily Review* in Hayward, California, described the corporate environment in modern newspapers as "the homogenization of American newspapers." According to Burgin, "They look alike. They feel alike. It's me-too journalism all over the country" (cited in Underwood, 1988).

Chain ownership of newspapers is also criticized for sacrificing local news coverage. Olien, Tichenor, and Donohue (1988) argued that corporate ownership of daily newspapers may lead to a more "cosmopolitan than localite orientation." However, Grotta (1971) found no difference between chain and independent newspapers in their coverage of local news.

Bagdikian (1990), one of the most ardent critics of chain ownership, claimed that, under chain ownership, the coverage of news gradually becomes skewed in favor of corporate interests. He argued that editors engage in self-censorship to avoid conflict with their corporate owners. According to Bagdikian, this type of impact is difficult to document because many editors may be unaware or unwilling to admit that they are subtly censoring the news.

Other studies have yielded mixed conclusions regarding whether chain- or independently owned newspapers have larger staffs, different workloads, and subscribe to more or fewer wire services (Lacy, Fico, & Simon, 1989; Litman & Bridges, 1986). Hale (1980) found no difference in readers' perceptions of quality in independently and chain-owned newspapers, but did find that the majority of readers would prefer to have their newspaper locally owned.

Although many lament the rise in chain ownership of newspapers, some experts argue the transition to corporate ownership has brought about more neutral coverage and balanced editorial pages in American newspapers. As Henry (1986) wrote, "No one is potentially more recklessly unfair than a family patriarch, or matriarch, with no outsiders to answer to" (p. 16).

Similarly, Compaine (1985) argued that locally owned, small-town news-papers "were never very good." He claimed "the typical chain-owned paper today is probably much better than the locally owned paper of 50 years ago" (p. 88).

When it comes to career opportunities, editors working for chain-owned newspapers admit that chain ownership definitely has its advantages. Most notably, editors of both chain- and independently owned newspapers say chain-owned newspapers offer greater opportunity for advancement, more sharing of ideas, less pressure from advertisers and special interests, greater overall financial backing, and better access to outside experts (American Society of Newspaper Editors, 1990).

But the path to the top in a newspaper chain may require a rising newspaper executive to place the chain's financial goals ahead of the community a particular newspaper serves in order to get ahead. As Soloski (1979) observed, the publisher of a chain-owned newspaper may see his or her position as merely a stepping stone to a better position within the chain—either at a larger, more prestigious newspaper, or in the corporate office. This can breed a type of publisher with little long-term interest in the community he or she serves. According to Soloski,

The publisher of a group newspaper does not own the paper; he or she is an employee of the group. At a group paper, the publisher's primary responsibilities are to the group and not to the community in which the paper is published. ... To keep his or her job or to increase the chances for advancement, the group publisher may be under pressure to meet or exceed business goals set for his or her paper by the group. (pp. 22, 24)

Soloski's findings suggest that the ability to generate strong profits may be the most desirable trait in a prospective publisher. Thus, revenue-generating departments of the newspaper, such as advertising and circulation, seem a likely training ground for future chain publishers.

WHO ARE THE PUBLISHERS?

Who are the people who run chain-owned newspapers? To answer this question, data were taken from a 1992 survey of newspaper publishers working for the five largest publicly owned newspaper chains and the five largest privately owned newspaper chains in the United States, ranked by circulation. The chains in the study include the following: Cox Enterprises, Donrey Media, Gannett Company, Hearst, Knight-Ridder, Media News, Newhouse, New York Times Group, Thomson Newspapers, and Times Mirror.[1]

Surveys were mailed to publishers from each of these chains, asking questions regarding managerial practice and professional experience. Newspapers located in the same city of the home office of the parent company were excluded from the sample, as were newspapers that were part of a joint operating agreement or where the group had less than a 50% interest in the newspaper. This excluded a number of major newspapers from the sample, such as *The New York Times*, the *Atlanta Journal and Constitution*, and the *Seattle Post-Intelligencer*. Out of 183 surveys mailed, 130 were returned, yielding a response rate of 71%. Response rates from the individual chains ranged from 56% to 100% of the sample.

A review of the mean responses to the survey questions yielded the following publisher profile: The average respondent was a 47-year-old White male with a bachelor's degree who has been in the newspaper business for 26 years and has served as publisher in his current position for a little more than 5 years. He talks on the phone with someone from his home office at least twice a month, and he personally visits the home office once or twice per year.

He agrees with the statement, "As long as profit quotas are being met, a publisher has complete autonomy over how his or her newspaper is run."

---

[1]Rankings of the chains by size were obtained form the 1992 "Facts About Newspapers," which is published by the Newspaper Association of America (NAA). Although Dow Jones & Co. was technically the fourth largest publicly owned chain in terms of circulation that year according to the NAA, it was not included in this study because more than three quarters of its circulation is derived from the *Wall Street Journal*, which is not typical of a local, community-oriented daily newspaper.

He can spend up to $5,000 without first seeking corporate approval (this was the most frequently cited budget limit among the survey respondents); he is required to submit an operating plan to his home office on a yearly basis; and about 20% of his annual income is tied to his newspaper's profit performance. He belongs to an average of seven local organizations and serves on an additional five boards.

THE BEST ROUTE TO THE TOP IS ... ADVERTISING

Publishers responding to the survey cited advertising most often as the department where they worked immediately prior to being named publisher, followed by administration, news, served as a publisher elsewhere (tied with news), finance, circulation and marketing (see Table 12.1). However, although advertising was the most common route to the top overall, each chain had its own distinct pattern of advancement, suggesting that there is not one "typical" path to the top for publishers of all chain-owned newspapers. Rather, the route to the top is highly dependent on the chain in which the publisher works.

For example, Donrey Media and the New York Times Group tended to promote their publishers from the advertising department. Donrey Media also had the greatest percentage of publishers who were promoted from the finance department. Within the Cox chain, however, the most common path to the top was through the news division.

Most chains try to promote publishers with diverse backgrounds. More than half of all publishers responding to the survey reported they had worked in the advertising department at one time in their career, and nearly

TABLE 12.1
Department Publisher Worked in Immediately Prior to Being Named Publisher

	Department						
Chain %	News %	Advertising %	Circulation %	Marketing %	Finance %	Publishing elsewhere %	Administration %
Cox	45	11	—	—	—	11	33
Donrey	—	55	10	—	20	10	5
Gannett	27	27	13	7	7	13	6
Hearst	—	13	—	—	13	50	24
Knight-Ridder	6	6	—	—	6	18	64
Media News	—	33	—	—	—	17	50
Newhouse	42	17	—	8	8	8	17
New York Times	7	40	—	—	13	13	27
Thomson	21	35	—	7	—	21	14
Times Mirror	20	—	—	—	—	20	60
Overall	16	28	4	2	8	16	26

one half reported they had worked in the news department at some time. Publishers from the Gannett, Knight-Ridder, Media News, Newhouse, New York Times Group, Thomson, and Times Mirror chains reported they had worked in a diverse group of departments. Publishers from the Cox chain largely spent their careers in the news department exclusively, whereas publishers from the Donrey Media and Hearst chains were more likely to have spent the majority of their careers in revenue-producing departments, such as advertising or circulation (see Table 12.2).

Although publishers for most of the chains responding to the survey indicated they had spent at least some time working on the news side of the newspaper, the length of their tenure varied considerably. Of those who indicated they had worked on the news side at some point in their career, the Newhouse publishers reported the longest tenure—an average of 15.7 years—whereas the Donrey publishers had put in the least amount of time on the news side—5 years (see Table 12.3).

Overall, the publishers were most likely to say they believe the advertising department provides the best training ground for a publisher (see Table 12.4). However, the notable exception to this belief was the group of publishers who had been promoted from the news department; they said they believe the news division provides a better training ground.

ARE PUBLISHERS WITH A NEWS BACKGROUND ON THE DECLINE?

Although the data collected for this study clearly show an overall tendency on the part of newspaper chains to promote individuals to the position of

TABLE 12.2
Departments Publishers Have Worked in at Some Time in Their Career

Chain %	News %	Advertising %	Circulation %	Marketing %	Finance %	Admin-istration %
Cox	78	22	11	22	11	22
Donrey	33	76	43	5	52	14
Gannett	53	40	27	20	13	53
Hearst	—	89	44	33	22	44
Knight-Ridder	56	44	44	22	17	50
Media News	50	67	67	33	33	33
Newhouse	58	50	42	42	25	33
New York Times Group	44	80	44	27	27	53
Thomson	71	64	36	36	21	36
Times Mirror	50	50	20	25	—	50
Overall	49	59	39	24	25	38
Public	54	57	36	25	18	48
Private	43	61	41	23	33	28

TABLE 12.3
Average Number of Years Publisher Worked in News by Chain

Chain	Number of Years in News
Newhouse	16
Knight-Ridder	15
Cox	14
Times Mirror	13
Gannett	12
Thomson	10
New York Times Group	9
Media News	8
Donrey Media	5
Hearst	NA

TABLE 12.4
Department Publishers Believe Provides the Best Training

Chain %	News %	Advertising %	Circulation %	Marketing %	Finance %	Admin-istration %
Cox	78	11	—	—	—	11
Donrey	—	75	15	—	5	5
Gannett	46	27	9	18	—	—
Hearst	—	88	—	12	—	—
Knight-Ridder	41	23	6	18	6	6
Media News	17	33	33	17	—	—
Newhouse	36	36	—	—	19	9
New York Times Group	19	56	—	6	13	6
Thomson	31	54	15	—	—	—
Times Mirror	20	20	20	20	—	20
Overall	29	46	8	7	5	5
Public	32	39	8	11	5	5
Private	26	52	9	3	5	5

Note. — signifies a zero response rate.

publisher from the advertising division, is there evidence to suggest that publishers coming from the news side are on the decline?

About 10 years before the present study, Meyer (1983) found that 61% of publishers of chain-owned newspapers responding to his survey of ethics for the American Society of Newspaper Editors had experience working on the news side of a newspaper, and had spent an average of 15 years there. However, this study found that only 47% of chain publishers indicated that they had worked on the news side of a newspaper at some point in their career—a 14% decline. Those who reported having news experience had spent an average of 12 years on the news side—a 20% decrease from Meyer's finding.

These findings are especially significant given that there is no statistically significant difference in the average age of the publishers in the Meyer study and the present study. Thus, all things being equal, it appears that, overall, newspaper chains are more likely than ever to promote individuals to the position of publisher from a revenue-producing department, such as advertising, and less inclined to promote from the news side. Of course, the exception to this would be chains such as Cox Enterprises, where a conscious effort is made to promote from the news division.

IMPLICATIONS FOR THE FUTURE

In today's corporate journalistic culture, it is a fact of life that a publisher must be able to generate an acceptable profit margin and speak the language of the financial analysts. The data generated by this study seem to indicate that, although most chains value a diverse professional background in their prospective publishers, with few exceptions, there is clearly a strong emphasis on revenue-generating skills and less of an emphasis on journalistic training.

To get to the top in the newspaper business, an individual is well advised to learn his or her chain's culture and pattern of progression, and either adapt to that culture or seek employment in a chain that is more compatible with his or her skill and background. For nearly all of the chains, business training is a must. Although each of the chains studied in this analysis has its own distinct pattern to the top, the advertising department appears to be the most popular place to recruit future publishers among the chains overall. The chains seem to be much more comfortable with recruiting their top executives from revenue-generating departments and then sending them to work in the news department for a while than they are with recruiting from the news department and providing business training later.

Although newspaper publishers have always been responsible for looking out for the business side of the newspaper, the finding that publishers with news experience appears to be on the decline may be an indication of a shift in priorities in the major chains. If there is a new breed of corporate publishers emerging, who are becoming increasingly detached from the news side of the business, the implications of this trend may be reflected in the editorial quality of chain-owned newspapers in years to come. Newspaper chains should be strongly encouraged to continue to promote cross-training in their rising executives—for more than just a couple of years—so that future publishers will continue to have experience in, and an appreciation of, the news side of the business.

Although the verdict is still out on whether chain ownership results in better newspapers than independent ownership, it is clear that chain ownership is here to stay, and with each passing year the industry seems to become more and more numb to the corporate style of management. In the

1990s, news of major chain acquisitions, such as the Gannett Company's recent purchase of Multimedia Inc., provoke little controversy. Instead of there being 82 Gannett newspapers, there were 93. Big deal. Similarly, when the Daniels family of Raleigh, North Carolina sold *The News & Observer* to the McClatchy chain, after getting over the initial shock, most people simply said, "At least they sold to a good chain."

In the future, one is likely to see newspaper chains carving out even stronger identities for themselves, and newspapers differentiating themselves from one another along chain lines. Instead of the old press barons of the penny press era, there will be a variety of newspaper groups, each with its own personality and varying concern for news quality, but all with an eye on the bottom line.

REFERENCES

American Society of Newspaper Editors. (1990). *Ownership survey.*

Bagdikian, B. H. (1990). *The Media Monopoly* (3rd ed.). Boston: Beacon Press.

Busterna, J.C. (1989). How managerial ownership affects profit maximization in newspaper firms. *Journalism Quarterly, 66,* 302–307, 358.

Compaine, B. M. (1985). The expanding base of media competition. *Journal of Communication, 35*:3, 81–96.

Demers, D. P., and Wackman, D. B. (1988). Effect of chain ownership on newspaper management goals. *Newspaper Research Journal, 9,* 59–68.

Grotta, G. L. (1971). Consolidation of newspapers: What happens to the consumer? *Journalism Quarterly, 48,* 245–250.

Hale, F. D. (1980). What subscribers think of group ownership of newspapers. *Journalism Quarterly, 57,* 314–316.

Henry, W. A. III. (1986, September). Learning to love the chains. *Washington Journalism Review,* pp. 15–17.

Lacy, S., Fico, F., & Simon, T. (1989). Relationships among economic, newsroom and content variables: A path model. *Journal of Media Economics, 2*(2), 51–67.

Litman, B., & Bridges, J. (1986). An economic analysis of daily newspaper performance. *Newspaper Research Journal, 7,* 9–26.

Meyer, P. (1983). *Editors, publishers, and newspaper ethics.* Reston, VA: American Society of Newspaper Editors.

Newspaper Association of America (1996). *Facts about newspapers.*

Olien, C. N., Tichenor, P. J., & Donohue, G. A. (1988). Relation between corporate ownership and editor attitudes about business. *Journalism Quarterly, 65,* 259–266.

Soloski, J. (1979). Economics and management: The real influence on newspaper groups. *Newspaper Research Journal, 1,* 19–27.

Thrift, R. J. Jr. (1977). How chain ownership affects editorial vigor of newspapers. *Journalism Quarterly, 54,* 327–331.

Wackman, D., Gillmor, D., Gaziano, C., & Dennis, E. (1975). Chain newspaper autonomy as reflected in presidential campaign endorsements. *Journalism Quarterly, 52,* 411–420.

Chapter 13

Compensating Broadcast Salespeople: Some Recommendations

Charles Warner
University of Missouri, Columbia

There has been a move in recent years by many companies to incorporate into their compensation systems rewards for (a) achieving company goals rather than individual goals, and (b) teamwork and cooperation (Cespedes, Doyle, & Freedman, 1989). This trend was confirmed by an article reporting on a sales compensation survey conducted in 1995 ("What Salespeople Are Paid," 1995). The survey showed that fewer than one% of U.S. salespeople were paid on a straight commission basis, the dominant system in broadcasting.

In a major reorganization of the Digital Equipment Corporation's (DEC) sales force in 1993, the compensation system was changed radically to reflect new corporate strategy. The new sales incentives were based, in part, on: (a) measuring customer satisfaction more accurately via surveys, and (b) factoring these customer survey results into compensation plans (McWilliams, 1993). At the beginning of 1994, IBM restructured its compensation system to reward profitability and customer satisfaction. In the new system, 60% of sales commissions (about 35% of a salesperson's total remuneration) are based on the profitability of an order, not on overall revenue, and 40% are based on customer satisfaction, based on buyer surveys (Sager, 1994). Customer satisfaction surveys are growing in popularity as a management tool, and, according to a 1994 survey by Bain & Co., are the second most widely used management tool in business (Graves, 1994).

Schuster and Zingheim (1986) compared the sales compensation plans of the best performing companies with those of the worst performing companies in their sample across several industries. The best performing companies always integrated their sales compensation plan with corporate goals, and did not follow industry practices in designing and implementing their sales compensation plans. Also, the best performing companies gave rewards that were primarily based on performance on desired sales activities, rather than just on volume or total revenues.

Cespedes (1990) reported that approximately two thirds of U.S. companies use a combination of salary and incentive compensation. The reasons companies give for using salary-plus-incentive systems is that it (a) helps them keep compensation costs flexible, (b) is helpful in setting performance standards that achieve desired company objectives, and (c) allows management to maintain greater supervision and control over selling efforts.

OBJECTIVES OF A COMPENSATION SYSTEM

A well-designed compensation system in broadcasting should accomplish as many of the following objectives as possible, as suggested by Lawler (1981, 1990), Henderson (1979), and Nash and Carroll (1975):

1. Aid in meeting an organization's strategic objectives.
2. Aid in communicating corporate goals, performance standards, and expectations.
3. Tie compensation directly to current sales performance.
4. Attract and hold good people.
5. Keep salespeople's motivation high.
6. Help in analyzing sales potential, planning account coverage, and allocating selling time.
7. Be understood by salespeople.
8. Be fair to employees.
9. Be fair to the organization.
10. Provide management control.
11. Enhance teamwork and cooperative effort.

GUIDELINES FOR A SOUND COMPENSATION SYSTEM

Some of the guidelines for designing a sound plan are:

1. The variable portion (bonus or incentive) must be large enough to justify a salesperson's extra effort. An incentive that is given over and above a salary should be over 15% of the total compensation (in the period the incentive or bonus covers) to be effective. Incentives under 15% of total compensation are not effective, and provide little additional motivation or incentive.
2. There should be a good balance between security and incentive.
3. Rewards should be based primarily on an individual's performance and effort, and directly commensurate with desired sales behaviors, activities, and results.
4. The plan should be competitive in the industry and the area (market or region).
5. The plan should reflect the strategy and objectives of the organization.
6. The difference between the compensation of high and low performers must be significant: The highest paid salesperson should earn a minimum of 40% more than the lowest paid salesperson.
7. There should be rewards for both hard (quantitative) and soft (qualitative, behavior-based) performance criteria.

8. There should be no perceived ceiling on earnings.
9. Opportunity for reward must be equal among all salespeople.
10. There is management control over what is sold.
11. There are some rewards for nonselling duties.
12. Incentive payments should generally be prompt and frequent while remaining large enough to be sufficiently motivating.

MAJOR PROBLEMS WITH COMPENSATION SYSTEMS

The biggest problem with most sales compensation systems is that they violate Objectives number 1 and 2: Aiding an organization in achieving its strategic objectives, and communicating corporate goals, performance standards, and expectations. These problems occur for two reasons: (a) Sales management has not thought of linking sales compensation directly to strategic objectives, and (b) most sales departments have no clear idea of what their long-term goals, standards, and expectations are, other than "go out and get an order" or "bring in enough billing to make budget."

DEFINITION OF SALES PERFORMANCE

Drucker (1954) wrote that there is only one valid definition of business purpose: to create a customer. Drucker understood that it is the customer who determines what a business is, because the customer is the foundation of a business and keeps it in existence. Thus, the purpose of a sales department and of every salesperson, is to create customers and, as Harvard Business School Professor Theodore Levitt (1983) added, to keep them. Therefore, the proper objectives of salespeople are to (a) continually develop new business, (b) maximize revenue, and (c) retain and increase current business. These are the three objectives that should be rewarded, not merely "getting orders" or "making budget."

To meet these objectives, salespeople have three overall strategies: (a) sell solutions to advertising problems, (b) create added value, and (c) help competitors get rich (which means to continually develop new business to increase the size of the advertising dollar pie and constantly push rates up by generally selling for rate rather than for share; Warner, 1992. To carry out these strategies, salespeople have three primary functions: (a) position their station to have a differential competitive advantage, (b) manage relationships with their customers, and (c) solve problems. Keeping these objectives, strategies, and functions in mind, Table 13.1 is a comparison of the positive and negative features of the three basic compensation methods commonly used by American businesses, reprinted from Wyatt Data Services' (1994) *Manual of Sales Incentive Plans, Volume II*. The following are the types of commission systems commonly used in the broadcasting industry.

TABLE 13.1
FEATURES OF SALES COMPENSATION METHODS

Feature	Salary Only	Salary Plus Incentive	Commission Only
Sales representative income	Highest income security with lowest degree of income at risk.	Balances income security and income at risk.	Lowest income security
Sales behavior	Easily used to encourage customer service and nonsales work.	Flexibility to tailor compensation mix to varied sales situations.	Tends to encourage aggressive sales at the expense of customer service and nonsales work.
Reward flexibility	Lowest degree of flexibility to reward high producers.	Flexible reward mechanism through variable incentive component.	Highest degree of flexibility to reward high producers.
Design flexibility	Relatively easy to change goals, territories, and accounts.	May be difficult to change goals, territories, and accounts.	Difficult to change goals, territories, and accounts.
Administration/ communication	Easy to administer, understand, and communicate.	May be costly to administer, complex, and not easily understood by the sales force.	Easy to administer, understand and communicate.
Cost of sales	Predictable selling costs with tendency to high fixed selling costs during business downturns.	Decrease in sales expenses during business downturns depends on variable portion of salary/incentive mix.	Tends to increase cost of sales by automatically raising commissions paid without extra effort.

From *Manual of Sales Incentive Plans–Book II* (p. 9) by Wyatt Data Services, 1994, Rochelle Park, NJ: Author. Copyright 1994 by Wyatt Data Services. Reprinted by permission.

Straight Commission or Commission Only

A commission-only system typically pays a 15% (or another appropriate percentage) commission on sales.

Billing Versus Collection.   Commissions can be paid on the basis of billing or collections. If commissions are paid on collections, the station is taking the precaution that salespeople do not sell schedules to advertisers who cannot or will not pay their bills.

Many stations, particularly those in smaller markets where cash flow is often critical, use the paying-on-collections approach in these days when few accounts pay their bills on a current basis. Many small accounts stay 60–90 days behind, and many smaller advertising agencies do not pay the media until their clients pay them, which usually means stations wait a minimum of 45 days for payment. Many larger agencies do not pay their bills for 60–90 days to use the float to their advantage.

Although it may help cash flow and keep salespeople from selling to too many deadbeat accounts, paying on collections is hard on salespeople, and is not recommended by experts ("You Said It," 1991). They often do not see the commissions on a sale for months after they have made it. Even worse, many organizations make salespeople collect from past-due accounts, which is a further demoralizing element (the business manager should be primarily responsible for collecting past-due accounts in a nice, gracious manner, and in consultation with salespeople). If salespeople are responsible for collections, they can "get carried away, push too hard, and lose all sense of ethics" ("You Said It," 1991, p. 20).

It is usually better to pay on billings than on collections. If stations pay on billing, there must be an accounting system in place that keeps track of collections so that salespeople can be charged back for billing on which they have been paid commissions, but that is not subsequently collected in 90 or 120 days. This charge-back system must be rigidly enforced in order to discourage salespeople from selling to accounts that are not creditworthy, or, worse, from placing phantom orders. Phantom orders are placed by unscrupulous salespeople for accounts that they know have no intention of paying their bills, or who were not even solicited.

Many organizations add commissions back to a salesperson's paycheck if an account subsequently pays after the 120 days. However, most of these stations deduct from these repaid commissions any costs that they might have incurred in collecting the past-due money. This deduction of collection expenses is a good idea because it reinforces to salespeople the importance of selling to accounts who can and will pay their bills on a timely basis.

Draw Versus Guarantee. Salespeople on commission usually receive a draw or guarantee at the beginning of each month against anticipated commissions. This draw or guarantee is meant to tide them over until they get paid their commission on advertising schedules that are run.

One major problem with a draw is that it is difficult for beginning salespeople to get started and see commissions begin to come in. It is not unusual for starting salespeople to have to live on a relatively small draw for several months and then see their first commission check disappear as the draws are subtracted from it. It is not a particularly good idea to have a compensation system that discourages new salespeople.

To overcome this problem, many stations give new salespeople a guarantee instead of a draw. A *guarantee* is a payment given at the beginning of a month that the organization promises will be the minimum compensation that salespeople will be paid.

Some stations give beginning salespeople a guarantee for 3 or 6 months, and then change them over to a draw. This system might be workable in a situation where there is absolutely no chance of money being taken back, even in a slack month. However, in smaller markets, where there is a possibility the salespeople might not earn enough commissions to cover a draw, this system is not a good idea. People are apt to take the guarantee for the protected period while they desperately seek another job that gives them a more secure feeling of a steady income. Some stations offer new salespeople a reasonable guarantee (say $1,500 per month), and then reduce it by one-twelfth each month for a year—in the hopes that a salesperson will have established a viable account list by the end of a year.

If compensation is based on commissions only, the guarantee system is better. The draw system does not build trust or a feeling of loyalty or security. If salespeople cannot bring in enough billing after a few months to cover a reasonable guarantee, then sales managers have probably hired the wrong salespeople, trained them poorly, or have too many salespeople on the staff.

Commission Only Is Not the Most Effective System

A commission-only compensation system is not the most effective way to pay salespeople. Kiechel (1988) wrote:

> Yes, you can pay ... on a commission-only basis, particularly if you just want them to ring as many doorbells as possible. But don't expect much managerial leverage that way. The sales staff will simply sell the products they have always had the most success with. What they probably won't do: push new offerings that, while important to the company, are hard to sell; spend a lot of time providing follow-up service to customers; spend time to cultivate new prospects. If you hope to have some say in what your salespeople do, you will have to treat them, in this one respect, like other employees: You may have to pay them a salary, which you then can supplement with commissions or a bonus. (p. 180)

One of the reasons that commission-only systems are used is that they meet several management administrative (as opposed to strategic) goals: (a) They are easy to administer, and (b) their costs are in direct proportion to revenue. However, in other industries that sell services, sales compensation systems are typically more complicated because of the complex role of the salesperson (Keenan, 1990).

Some stations are following the trend in other industries and using salary-plus-incentive arrangements. There are several reasons that the commission-only system is being discarded:

1. A commission-only system does not aid in meeting strategic objectives. In fact, it often impedes objective setting. Because commission-only systems place emphasis solely on short-term billing, other vital sales objectives—such as developing new business, effective use of inventory, selling for high rates, selling specials, and maximizing revenue—are often given short shrift by salespeople.

2. It does not aid in communicating corporate goals or performance standards because remuneration is based strictly on billing, which is measured quantitatively. There is no weight given to qualitative factors, such as work habits, effort, cooperation, using written presentations, top-level client prospecting, or ethical selling.

3. A commission-only system often creates intradepartmental competitiveness and conflict because billing is based, to a large degree, on two variables: the quality

of a salesperson's account list, and the amount of inventory available to sell. Under a commission-only system, destructive internal warfare often develops over who gets the best account list, with no thought given to who can best sell a particular account. Secrecy and selfishness are usually the result.

4. Maximizing revenue is forgotten as salespeople try to maximize their own billing, often by selling as much inventory as possible for whatever price they can get so they can sell it before someone else does.

5. It does not give management much control over inventory, and it makes account-change decisions difficult. People get extremely possessive about accounts, thus limiting management flexibility.

6. It creates short-term thinking to the detriment of developing long-term relationships.

7. The assumption underlying the commission-only system is that people are motivated only by money. This assumption was probably never valid, and is even less so in the more quality-of-life-conscious generation of the 1990s. People are turned on by friendly, cooperative coworkers, challenges, interesting work, security, caring and supportive management, and growth-oriented situations, not just money. People in broadcasting today have a number of interesting and exciting alternatives for making money, and what they are looking for is satisfying, interesting work (Warner & Spencer, 1991).

Super sports agent Mark McCormack wrote an article in *Sales & Marketing Management* entitled "The Case Against Commissions" (McCormack, 1994). He wrote:

> ... I made up my mind a long time ago that the best way to keep our company going was to encourage teamwork, communication, and cooperation. That's why I choose to compensate my salespeople on a salary plus a bonus plan. When the company gains, so do the salespeople. A commission structure, which tends to pit a salesperson's self-interest against the company's best interests, doesn't seem to fit this scenario.

Commission-Only Variations

There are two variations on the commission-only method that are occasionally used: graduated commissions and variable commissions. In general, both should be avoided. Graduated commission plans go two ways: up or down. The systems either pay progressively higher commission rates as billing goes up, or they pay progressively lower commission rates as billing goes up. Progressive and retrogressive commission systems tend not to work in practice. The progressive system can quickly get out of hand and cost a company too much. The system also fosters internecine warfare among the salespeople for accounts. The retrogressive scale punishes people for selling more, which is counterproductive. It is simply a way for a company to save money and reduce a salesperson's level of opportunity—a condition that salespeople recognize immediately and dislike intensely.

Most variable commission systems tend not work either, except under certain conditions. A typical variable system might pay a different commission rate for new business, another rate for particular day parts, or another rate for special packages or promotions.

If a higher commission is given for new business, it must be for developed new business—business that a salesperson can prove that he or she made an effort to develop by showing presentations, letters, and so on. It is counterproductive to give a higher commission for "new" business that has not been on the air for 12 or 13 months, and that a salesperson cannot prove he or she has made a tangible effort to develop.

Also, for a higher new business commission to provide extra motivation, it must be substantially higher than the regular commission. A new business commission must be at least 100% greater than the regular commission to have any hope of succeeding (otherwise the majority of salespeople will not bother).

The basic problem with most variable commission rates are the underlying assumptions that (a) a relatively small differential amount of money will influence salespeople's behavior, and (b) salespeople will have a significant degree of control over what clients buy.

For example, if a company paid a 10% commission on regular business and a 15% commission on new business (a 50% premium), the assumption would be that the higher commission would motivate salespeople to concentrate on developing new business. Here is an example: If a salesperson could expect monthly billing of $30,000 from regular business, he or she could earn $3,000. In assessing billing potential, the salesperson would estimate how much new business could be developed. Next, the salesperson would estimate how much effort would have to be expended to develop new business. Then, the salesperson would make a comparison between how much new business could be developed with the extra effort versus how much additional regular business could be developed with the same effort.

Continuing the example, assume that a salesperson estimated that the extra effort could bring in 25% more business in the average month (or an additional $7,500 new business on an average monthly billing of $30,000), or $1,125 in additional commissions at the 15% new business rate. However, the same amount of additional effort might bring in the same 25% increase in regular business, or an additional $750 in commissions at 10%. The difference is only $375 in income for going after the more difficult to sell, long-term new business. Salespeople will usually stay within their comfort zone and settle for the lesser amount, assuming they decide that any extra effort is worth the additional money, which, of course, they may not.

A television station in Los Angeles tried a system of paying approximately 1% commission on regular business and 6% on new business—a whopping 500% bonus for developed new business. After several years, the station abandoned the system because it did not motivate any of its entrenched agency salespeople to bring in new business, whereas some of the retail-oriented salespeople (those who preferred to call on direct business) were compensated at such high levels that corporate headquarters questioned management's sanity. The motivation to develop new accounts is more a function of a salesperson's basic personality and selling preferences than it is of the amount of new-business commission premium.

Salespeople who view themselves as primarily agency service people (farmers) often cannot change their personalities overnight to become missionary salespeople (hunters). If a station wants to emphasize new business development, it should change its commission structure and see if it motivates people to get on board with the station's sales strategy, and then replace people who cannot adjust. In the new, tough, competitive business environment of the 1990s, the majority of people on a sales staff need to be hunters to some degree.

Many stations are dividing their sales staffs into two separate teams—a developmental or marketing team, and an agency or transactional team—and paying them differently. The agency team is often on a lower salary and a higher incentive, and the developmental team is on a higher salary and lower incentive to encourage long-term thinking and reduce the pressure of closing business.

Salary-Plus-Bonus Based on Quota or Budget Achievement

Some stations use a system of paying salespeople a salary plus a bonus based on achieving individual monthly or quarterly sales billing quotas or budgets. For example, a company might pay a salesperson a $750 monthly salary plus a bonus (often a stated dollar amount) of $1,500, for achieving a predetermined billing quota, budget, or target.

The problems with salary-plus-bonus systems is that they take a great deal of time to administer, because the manager must have monthly discussions with all the salespeople to set quotas, budgets, or targets. These discussions are often prolonged and heated because sales managers usually try to set quotas that have stretch in them, and salespeople want low quotas to ensure that they get their bonuses. In these situations, the highest rewards often go to salespeople who are best at negotiating quotas or budgets, and who have the best account lists, not necessarily best at selling. Also, it is extremely difficult to set quotas that are perceived to be fair by all salespeople (Sibson, 1981).

Furthermore, quotas are often based on the previous year's billing level, which tends to focus on past performance success, rather than on a realistic assessment of future opportunities and current performance in turning prospects into customers. Also, accurately forecasting or projecting future billing is quite difficult in the volatile media marketplace today. Making an estimate of future business and demand for planing purposes is one thing, but it becomes more difficult when compensation is based on budget setting; lowballing by salespeople becomes common practice. Rewarding

salespeople for reaching a predetermined budget or goal works much better
when advertising revenues are rising from year to year than when advertising revenues are declining. In the latter case, salespeople often have to
work harder than ever and are still not able to meet last year's numbers (on
which goals are typically based), and thus have virtually no chance of
reaching the goals or getting a bonus.

By far the worst outcome to tying compensation to making budgets is
that the system absolutely guarantees that salespeople will stop working
as soon as they make the budget. They know that going over budget means
that their budgets will subsequently be raised accordingly next year and in
subsequent years, making it virtually impossible to make a budget in the
long term.

Also, paying based on making budget emphasizes billing, which means
that whoever has the best list has the best chance of making budget.
Therefore, compensating based on hitting a budget number causes salespeople to behave the same way they do under a commission-only system.

Thus, the purpose of setting demanding, but achievable individual sales
budgets or goals to help a company achieve its overall objectives is usually
defeated under a salary-plus-bonus system. Additionally, under a salary-
plus-bonus system, maximizing revenue is not a goal—making budget is.
A sales department can make or miss a budget in any month or quarter
depending on luck (e.g., ratings decline, market economy declines, etc.), but
luck plays no part in maximizing revenue—a concept based on demonstrat-
ing an intelligent effort regardless of ratings, forecasts, budgets, economic
conditions, or account movement in or out of the market or medium.

Salary-Plus-Commission System

Some companies use a salary-plus-commission arrangement. The advantage of this type of commission system is that it provides some security for
salespeople, tends to even out income over a year, and gives stations a
method of rewarding nonselling activities, such as involvement in company promotions and presentations. The salary-plus-commission system,
depending on the size of the salary, tends to put a higher floor and a lower
ceiling on salespeople's earnings than does a commission-only system.

The disadvantage of this system is that salespeople continue to behave
as if they were being paid under a commission-only system. It has all of the
disadvantages of a commission-only system and none of the advantages of
cooperation and teamwork of other systems, especially a pool system.

Salary-Plus-Incentive Pool

More and more stations are using a salary-plus-incentive pool compensation system of one type or another. The typical salary-plus-pool system pays
salespeople a base salary, then gives them a percentage of a commission

pool. Salaries can vary among salespeople based on a variety of variables, such as seniority, ability, past performance, and so on. Table 13.2 is an example of how one station structures the salary portion of its compensation plan.

The previous system uses a wide variety of measurement and performance tracking criteria to determine salespeople's salary level and bonuses. It recognizes and rewards improved skill development and increased job responsibility. Increases in the base salary are only provided on the basis of demonstrated merit, not for the cost of living or length of time with the station.

Bonuses are based on attainment of a billing quota (negotiated with and accepted by each salesperson) and multiple other performance measurements (time management, use of sales tools, prospecting, written presentations, etc.). Promotion to the next title/pay level is based on demonstrated skill and performance improvement.

Implementation of a Pool System

The amount of money that goes into a pool can be based on several factors, such as a percentage of a station's local or total billing. If a percentage of total billing (local and national) goes into the commission pool, it tends to encourage salespeople to work on national accounts.

The percentage of the pool that a salesperson receives at some stations is based on the percent of the station's billing that the salesperson did the year before. Thus, if a salesperson did 29% of the local billing the previous year, he or she would receive 29% of the pool. These systems are not effective in achieving corporate goals because they have many characteristics of a commission-only system, in which billing—thus account lists—are the most important factor.

Most stations that use a pool system base a salesperson's share of the commission pool on factors other than billing—sales effort and selling behavior are the key factors. Sales managers describe the behaviors for which they want to reward all members of the sales staff, and then they award pool shares based on performance on the listed behaviors, effort, and activities. For example, a sales manager may want to reward salespeople for developing new business, getting high rates, and using qualitative

TABLE 13.2

SALESPERSON SALARY & COMPENSATION LEVELS

Title	Salary		
	Monthly ($)	Annual ($)	Annual with Bonus ($)
Sales Representative	1,200–1,400	14,400–21,600	18,720–28,080
Marketing Consultant	1,750–2,350	21,600–28,800	28,080–37,440
Senior Marketing Consultant	2,400–4,500	28,800–54,000	37,440–70,200

Provided by Lou Vito, President, WPKO/WBLL, Bellefontaine, OH.

research in written presentations. At the end of the month or quarter, the sales manager evaluates each salesperson's performance on the desired behaviors, and gives the salesperson an appropriate share of the pool. The behaviors and activities are determined in advance for all salespeople, not for individual salespeople, so that everyone can be evaluated on an equal, fair basis.

Thus, the salesperson who did 29% of the company's billing the previous year might have done so because of a good list of accounts, and might not have developed new business or done well on other performance criteria. The sales manager might reduce that salesperson's share to, say, 15% of the pool while raising another lower billing salesperson's share to reward him or her for making an extra effort on the desired, predetermined behaviors and activities, such as getting high rates or developing new business.

This type of pool system is better than a commission-only system or a pool system, which rewards people based on their current or past billing; the former rewards salespeople for selling the way the company wants them to sell, and for helping the company reach its strategic sales objectives. This type of pool system allows sales managers to reward people according to effort and cooperative, team-oriented behavior, not according to billing, which is determined, in large part, by a salesperson's acquired (usually through attrition of other salespeople) account list. A flexible management-discretion pool system also helps salespeople focus on how well the entire sales department and their fellow salespeople are doing.

The biggest benefit of a salary-plus-pool system is that it aids in building teamwork and cooperation. It can help stations get their salespeople to think of what is best for the organization, not just for themselves. For example, salespeople are much more willing to trade accounts in a pool system—they want the salesperson with the best personality fit with a customer to call on that customer, regardless of previous account assignments. The goal in a pool system is for the station's billing to increase.

Also, money from the pool can be used for special recognition awards, such as a $1,000 surprise award for landing a large new account, or money can be used to reward a salesperson for getting a major renewal, stressing the importance of relationships and long-term business. Furthermore, a small percentage of the pool can be given to sales support and traffic personnel if desired. Such a small percentage given to the usually under-paid support staff is invariably supported enthusiastically by salespeople.

The drawbacks of a salary-plus-pool system are: (a) pool systems are often erroneously perceived as group rewards and not as individual re-wards; (b) salespeople can consider the system to be unfair and inequitable if they perceive that there is a great deal of disparity in ability and expended effort among the staff, especially if a few strong salespeople feel they are carrying several weaker ones; and (c) if shares of the pool are based on past performance, such as last year's billing, it tends to unfairly favor people with seniority and larger account lists, regardless of current performance and effort. Pool shares must be based on current performance and effort, with higher pool shares going to salespeople who make an extra selling effort and have the desired sales behavior.

Fairness is the critical element in a pool system. In every sales department, the salespeople know who the best salesperson is. The salespeople see who works the hardest, who makes the most calls, who develops the most new business, who has the best relationships with clients, and who gets the highest rates. As long as the salesperson who others perceive to be the best earns the most money, and the second best earns the second most money, and so on, the majority of the salespeople will perceive the compensation system to be fair.

A good rule of thumb is that salary should not be more than approximately 66% of a salesperson's total compensation. If salary exceeds 66% of the average salesperson's compensation, complacency could develop. However, one of the best performing sales staffs in broadcasting (according to an agency survey) is paid a salary that is 70% of their total compensation. Relatively high salary levels tend to have the same effect that pool systems do: They give management more control, they foster cooperation and account switching among a staff, they give salespeople a sense of security (especially in difficult rating or economic downturns), and they tend to reduce staff turnover.

A COMBINATION OF SYSTEMS IS BEST

The most effective type of compensation system for today's media salespeople is a combination of systems. Using the monthly billing levels in the prior examples, this section shows how a combination system might look if an organization compensated six salespeople by giving them a monthly salary of $750, plus a share of a pool that is based on 12% of total local billing. Shares of the pool are paid quarterly (or monthly, if preferred) based on the sales manager's evaluation of performance on several important, predetermined, specific, and communicated behaviors and activities. If pool shares are paid quarterly, salespeople can be given a monthly draw against expected pool shares. Pool share percentages in the following example vary substantially, depending on the sales manager's evaluation of a salesperson's performance.

Billing (% Total)	Salary	12% Pool	Total Compensation
#1 5,000 (3.6%)	750	840 (5%)	1,590
#2 10,000 (7.1%)	750	2,520 (15%)	3,270
#3 20,000 (14.3%)	750	1,680 (10%)	2,430
#4 25,000 (17.9%)	750	4,200 (25%)	4,950
#5 30,000 (21.4%)	750	1,750 (25%)	4,950
#6 50,000 (35.7%)	750	1,400 (20%)	4,110
140,000	4,500	16,800	21,300 (15.2% of 140,000)

In this example, each salesperson has been given a share of the commission pool based on the sales manager's evaluation of the salesperson's performance based on several criteria that the sales manager communicated to everyone beforehand (a list of performance criteria is given later in this chapter). The sales manager has given Salesperson 1 a slightly higher percent of the pool than the person's billing might indicate, perhaps because that ranked higher on desired performance criteria than others did. Salesperson 2 has had his or her pool percentage more than doubled, compared with the percentage of local billing, indicating a superior effort in achieving performance criteria. Salesperson 6 billed 35.7% of the local total, but is given only 20% of the pool, because the salesperson ranked low on the desired performance criteria for the period (month or quarter). The effort was below what was expected, and the effort and subsequent rankings were not as good as the efforts of Salespeople 4 and 5. As discussed previously, salaries do not all have to be equal for all salespeople, although they are in the previous example.

The salary-plus-pool system is a powerful one that allows management to reward salespeople for activity- and effort-based performance (a quantitative element), and for qualitative, behavior-oriented elements. The salary-plus-pool system also allows compensation to be tied to sales performance on desired sales dimensions, Warner (1994).

IMPLEMENTING A COMBINATION OF SYSTEMS

The combination of systems described earlier comes close to satisfying more of the objectives and guidelines for a sound compensation system, given at the beginning of this chapter than any other compensation system does. When designing a system using this model, managers generally should keep the total incentive portion above 33% of a salesperson's total annual remuneration.

Also, when a system includes a percentage of a pool based on qualitative, behavior, and activity elements, it is imperative that the elements be clearly communicated to the sales staff before each evaluation period, and that each salesperson be given candid, specific feedback immediately at the end of an evaluation period (monthly or quarterly, but no longer than quarterly). When salespeople are told why they were awarded their pool percentage, desired behavior and activities are being reinforced, and they are being given specific feedback on what is expected of them to fit in with the station's selling strategy.

None of the evaluative elements can be either billing or achieving an individual sales budget. If billing or making a budget are included as one of the factors evaluated, salespeople will behave as if they were working under a commission-only system—account lists become of utmost importance, they will not trade accounts, and they will work for themselves and not the station.

Furthermore, there should be a significant difference between the lowest and highest pool payment. If salespeople perceive that the payments are relatively equal, the payments lose all of their reinforcing power, and salespeople come to expect an average payment as part of their overall compensation system. They do not view pool payments as rewards for good sales behavior or consequences for poor sales behavior.

When salespeople are informed about their pool share, they should also be told the range of all the other salespeople's pool shares in dollars and in percentages (top amount and share and bottom amount and share), and they should be told what their rank position is compared with other salespeople so they clearly know where they stand in relation to the others. It is also a good idea to post a list of the ranks of the top half of the sales department where everyone can see it (e.g., Charlie #1 pool share for first quarter, Sandy #2 pool share, and Jane #3 pool share). The purpose of publishing only the top half of the ranks is to reward those who do well and avoid embarrassing those who are at or near the bottom.

The following list includes the behaviors and activities on which pool-share payments might be made (i.e., evaluation elements). It is best to choose just four or five elements (no more than six) to use as a basis for periodic evaluations, and to change these elements from time to time based on a station's strategic selling needs.

1. Performance on sales dimensions
2. Customer satisfaction
3. Developing new business
4. Individual goal achievement
5. High rates
6. Selling specials and sports
7. Closing target accounts
8. Creating added value
9. Cooperative attitude
10. Use of qualitative research
11. Depth of account knowledge
12. Selling ideas, spec spots
13. Creative packaging
14. Vertical agency selling
15. Amount of long-term business
16. Co-op dollar development
17. Vendor dollar development
18. Collections
19. Percentage of renewals
20. Knowledge of competition
21. Knowledge of market
22. Knowledge of competitive rates

23. Seeking management help
24. Meeting deadlines
25. Positive attitude about station, management, coworkers, etc.
26. Support of other salespeople
27. Accurate paperwork
28. Observing policies
29. Effective time management
30. Active participation in sales meetings
31. Effective prospecting
32. Effective category development
33. Taking personal responsibility for getting results (for clients)

THE FLOATING SALARY-PLUS-POOL SYSTEM

Some stations allow both their salary and pool levels to go up or down in proportion to revenue. In other words, as revenue goes up, the amount of money in the pool goes up, as in previously described systems; as revenue goes up, salaries also go up. This system is based on the principle that a fixed percentage of revenue is put into the salary pool, rather than a fixed amount of money. Management can distribute increases (or decreases) in the salary pool evenly among salespeople or according to performance. This system makes salespeople very happy when billing goes up because they share in the increases both with higher salaries and with more in the pool to distribute. The system provides less of a safety net for salespeople when revenue falls, but it does provide management with a lower potential floor on salaries. It is recommended that the salary pool increases, but never decreases with billing.

WARNING ABOUT IMPLEMENTING A NEW SYSTEM

Many radio and television stations have implemented a salary-plus-incen-tive pool system and found them highly successful. However, when switch-ing from a commission-only system, one or two of the salespeople with the best account lists often quit. These salespeople are typically list jockeys whose account lists have grown because of attrition of other salespeople, and who have top billings because of their lists, not because of their efforts. Stations are usually glad to see these entrenched list jockeys leave. Typically, billing, new business, and rates go up after a commission-only system is dropped and the list jockeys leave. Therefore, when switching to a new system, expect to lose a few list jockeys, or at least for the top billing salespeople to be unhappy initially.

CONFIDENTIALITY VERSUS OPEN SYSTEMS

If there are different salary and compensation levels among salespeople, as is inevitably the case, sales managers have to decide whether to let everyone know what everyone else is making or to keep compensation information confidential.

The arguments for confidentiality are: Salespeople do not necessarily know the details about other salespeople's performance (e.g., degree of difficulty of account list, amount of new business, creativity, initiative, average rates, etc.), and thus it is sometimes difficult for them to evaluate each other objectively. In an open compensation system, if one employee complains about his or her remuneration level compared with someone else's, the sales manager has to give an elaborate explanation that might violate another salesperson's privacy. In an open compensation system, where everyone knows what everyone else is making, some managers avoid the potential for conflict and give everyone close to the same amount, as pointed out by Mills (1985). A general rule of thumb is that openness about salaries often causes the difference in pay between top performers and average performers to drop in half (Mills, 1985).

In open systems, where sales compensation is regularly posted (e.g., monthly), salespeople do not have to guess who is making the most money—they can see it. An open system tells salespeople where they stand—it is clear, measurable feedback. If, and it is a big if, a compensation system is fairly administered by sales management, an open system is an excellent way to demonstrate management fairness and how management rewards activities, effort, and strategic selling. An open system can generate a high degree of trust in management (O'Brien, 1993).

If management has something to hide (e.g., unfair account list distribution, playing favorites, rewarding seniority rather than performance), confidentiality is probably better. If management has nothing to hide and wants to gain the trust of its salespeople, an open system is best. Some stations communicate the pool shares, but keep salaries confidential. This system seems to be a good compromise. In either case, a 40% spread between top and average salespeople's compensation levels is desirable.

BONUS BASED ON EXCEEDING REVENUE
OBJECTIVES OR BUDGETS

To make the salary-plus-pool system even more effective, a bonus can be added based on the sales department exceeding its overall yearly or bi-yearly local or total revenue objectives, budget, quota, or target. For example, if a station's total sales budget is $2,000,000, all salespeople might be offered a bonus of 15% of their total remuneration as soon as they go 5%

over the yearly budget. Thus, when total billing reaches $2,100,000 (105% of budget) at the end of October or November, a salesperson who has made a total of $45,000 so far that year would receive a bonus of $6,750. Do not give bonuses for hitting revenue objectives or a budget, which should be expected, but give one for exceeding revenue objectives or budget by several percentage points (105% is a good number). In this manner, bonus money does not have to be paid if a station goes over a budget by a small amount (e.g., just $10).

Bonus arrangements can vary a great deal. They might be based on a percent of compensation to date, a flat amount given to all salespeople, or as a higher percent of billing going into a pool on all subsequent business (but make it high enough to make a real difference). Whichever method is selected, the bonus should be a minimum of 15% of a salesperson's renumeration. This 15% rule holds true for contests or any incentive award. It takes at least 15% to get salespeople's attention. Paying salespeople a large bonus based on exceeding a budget is also an excellent way to create strong peer pressure on underperformers.

One of the big problems with paying bonuses based on making budgets is that making a company's budget is often not a function of sales performance, but of other factors, such as ratings or market growth, or the needs of ownership to pay bankers. Hence, it is possible to reward a sales staff for a below average sales performance in a year of unexpected market revenue growth (which makes top management angry) or, even worse, fail to reward salespeople for a spectacular performance in an off year when ratings drop significantly or market revenue declines substantially. In the latter case, it is easy for management to make salespeople feel like losers because they did not meet an unrealistic budget. Making people feel like losers is a poor way to motivate and retain them.

WORD OF CAUTION

One of the common errors that sales managers make is to believe that money motivates most salespeople most of the time (the "money-moti-vates-me-so-it-must-motivate-everyone-else-syndrome"). Research indicates that motivating salespeople with money is like trying to fool people. It works with some people all of the time and with all of the people some

Examples of a salary-plus-pool-plus-bonus system:

$60,000 Remuneration Level		$45,000 Level	
$36,000 Salary (60%)		$27,000 Salary (60%)	
24,000 Pool (40%)		18,000 Pool (40%)	
$60,000		$45,000	
9,000 Bonus (15%) for exceeding total local budget		6,750 Bonus (15%)	
$69,000 Total		$53,750 Total	

of the time, but it cannot be used with all of the people all of the time (Warner & Spencer, 1991).

In addition to money, other rewards—such as recognition, career opportunities, security, independence, sense of accomplishment, autonomy, client satisfaction, and friendly coworkers—motivate salespeople (Warner & Spencer, 1991). Different types of people give different levels of importance, or valance, to these rewards. In general: (a) increased financial rewards are most highly valued by experienced salespeople and by those with large families, and (b) other rewards, particularly promotion and opportunities for accomplishment and growth, are most valued by less experienced salespeople, those who are unmarried, and those who have relatively high levels of formal education.

FLEXIBILITY IS VITAL

The fact that different people are motivated by a fairly wide range of different elements is a good argument for having a flexible compensation system that allows management to tailor compensation packages to suit the needs of individual salespeople and encourage them to be as productive as they can be. In the media business today, selling is too complex to rely on ineffective, inflexible compensation systems that were designed decades ago for a simpler age of selling.

THE NEW REALITIES

Lawler (1990) wrote: "The world of business has changed dramatically in the last several decades, yet pay practices of most organizations have not. Fundamentally, they differ little from the practices of the 1950s, when American companies dominated the world's economy" (p. 3). Lawler went on to say that he believes many organizations are more concerned with doing the wrong things right than with searching for the right pay practices. "They have pay systems that are driven more by history and what other organizations do than by strategic analysis of organizational needs" (p. 3). He indicated that, "instead of trying to gain competitive advantage by doing different things, most companies seem happy to copy what other companies do and thereby avoid being at a competitive disadvantage" (p. 3).

Research over the last 20 years has made great strides in establishing the effectiveness of various new pay practices. The experience of companies such as Toyota, Honda, Herman Miller, Procter & Gamble, and Lincoln Electric can also serve as models of how innovative pay-for-performance systems can increase productivity. It is time for those in the media industries to look for new compensation systems.

SUMMARY

The ideal compensation system is one that (a) rewards salespeople for achieving a company's strategic selling objectives, (b) is flexible and takes into account individual differences, and (c) is perceived to be fair by the salespeople. The compensation systems discussed in this chapter are ranked from least effective to most effective:

- Salary-plus bonus (typically based on making budget)
- Draw against commission
- Guarantee against commissions
- Salary-plus commission
- Fixed salary-plus pool
- Relatively high flexible salary-plus-pool-plus-bonus combination (salary paid monthly, pool paid quarterly, bonus paid on achievement of station revenue objectives)

REFERENCES

Cespedes, F. V. (1990). A preface to payment: Designing a sales compensation plan. *Sloan Management Review, 38*, 59–69.

Cespedes, F. V., Doyle, S. X., & Freedman, R. J. (1989). Teamwork in today's selling. *Harvard Business Review, 67*, 44–58.

Drucker, P. (1954). *The practice of management.* New York: Harper & Row.

Graves, J. M. (1994, May 30). Management tools that work. *Fortune,* p. 15.

Henderson, R. I. (1979). *Compensation management: Rewarding performance.* Reston, VA: Reston.

Keenan, W. (1990, March). The difference in selling services. *Sales & Marketing Management,* pp. 48–52.

Kiechel, W. III. (1988, March 14). How to manage salespeople. *Fortune,* pp. 179–180.

Lawler, E. E. (1981). *Pay and organization development.* Reading, MA: Addison-Wesley.

Lawler, E. E. (1990). *Strategic pay: Aligning organizational strategies and pay systems.* San Francisco: Jossey-Bass.

Levitt, T. (1983). *The marketing imagination.* New York: The Free Press.

McCormack, M. (1994, February). The case against commissions. *Sales & Marketing Management,* pp. 47–48.

McWilliams, G. (August 30, 1993). *BusinessWeek,* p. 74.

Mills, D. Q. (1985). *The new competitors.* New York: Wiley & Sons.

Nash, A. N., & Carroll, S. J. (1975). *The management of compensation.* Belmont, CA: Wadsworth.

O'Brien, T. (1993, December 20). Company wins worker's loyalty by opening its books. *Wall Street Journal,* B2, B6.

Sager, I. (1994, February 7). *BusinessWeek,* p. 110.

Schuster, J. R., & Zingheim, P. (1986). Sales compensation strategies at the most successful companies. *Personnel Journal, 65*, 112–116.

Sibson, R. E. (1981). *Compensation.* New York: AMACOM.

Warner, C. (1992). *Selling for survival.* Washington, DC: National Association of Broadcasters.

Warner, C. (1994). *Performance coaching for broadcast salespeople.* Columbia, MO: University of Missouri.

Warner, C., & Spencer, J. (1991). *Radio and television sales staff profiles, compensation, practices, and motivation.* Columbia, MO: School of Journalism, University of Missouri.

What salespeople are paid. (1995, February). *Sales & Marketing Management,* pp. 31–33.

Wyatt Data Services. (1994). *Manual of Sales Incentive Plans—Volume II,* Rochelle Park, NJ: Author.

You said it. (1991, March). *Sales & Marketing Management,* pp. 16–20.

Chapter 14

The Domain of Inquiry for Media Management Researchers

Douglas A. Ferguson
Bowling Green State University, Bowling Green, OH

At a meeting of the Management and Sales division of the Broadcast Educa-tion Association (BEA), James Webster (1990) responded to a group of papers on media management with a probing question: How does the study of media management differ from research done by departments of economics or by schools of business administration? Webster stated that there probably was no separate domain for the study of media management. A lively discussion ensued, without much consensus among the participants.

Just as scholars in the interpersonal communication field have wrestled with the questions of domain of inquiry, so too have mass communication re-searchers. The problem of staking out a separate domain for a specialty area such as media management presents an even greater struggle. This chapter is a first step toward a conceptual domain for the study of media management.

Every field of exploration has three components: a set of scholars, a domain of inquiry, and a methodology (Reinharz, 1982). This chapter focuses on the second component: What is it that makes media management research distinct from the domains of inquiry found in other academic units, such as economics and business administration? What is it that media management researchers do? This task is marked with difficulty. Capella (1987) warned: "Attempts to define whole domains of inquiry are usually doomed to be inaccurate or incomplete. No sooner has the pen been lifted from paper but an uncooperative researcher will have published a new line of inquiry that seems not to fit the newly penned definition" (p. 185). He allowed that the definition of domains of inquiry functions as both detecting and making trends.

COMMUNICATION ANALOGY

Defining the domain of media management is analogous to the larger problem of separating the study of communication into a separate domain of inquiry. As for almost any specialty area of media research, part of the difficulty for communication in particular lies in the relative youth of the field. Schramm (1963) noted a generation ago that communication was not a discipline like mathematics, but "an academic crossroad where many have passed, but few have tarried" (p. 2). Since then, however, communication has acquired "the trappings of a discipline" (Berger & Chaffee, 1987, p. 15). As the study of the communication has grown—most noticeably in its diversity of journals and institutions—the domain has widened considerably. Qualitative methodologies first developed in Europe are probably responsible for the broadening of the communication discipline (Brown, 1970; Gerbner, 1983; Merton, 1957; Tan, 1986).

Assuming that defining communication is possible, such an activity has been the most common first step toward delineating its domain of inquiry. Krippendorf (1969) defined *communication* as "a process of transmission of structure among the parts of a system which are identifiable in time and space" (p. 107). This accounts for a wide range of emphases: communication as messages, communication as process, and communication as technical facilities. Krippendorf was concerned with what distinguishes inquiries into processes of communication from other fields. He rejected the usual disciplinary differentiations: unique method, specific subject, and narrow purpose. Instead, he emphasized "the *theoretical commitment*" (p. 111, italics in original) to the objects observed.

Definitions are somewhat less complex for a field such as interpersonal communication or mass communication. For one thing, the scope is limited to human communication. Capella (1987) stated that the essential feature of interpersonal communication "is that persons influence one another's behavior over and above that attributed to normal baselines of actions" (p. 228). Mass communication is similar, but with the additional filter of the gatekeeper (Westley & MacLean, 1957; White, 1950). More than any area of mass communication theory, the idea of the gatekeeper is best suited to research on media managers.

Some writers have indicated that the quest for a domain of inquiry for communication research is independent of a given definition of communication. Sayre (1948) asserted that communication is not definable. Fisher (1978) guessed that if one visited any International Communication Association (ICA) or Speech Communication Association (SCA) convention, tripped 10 members at random in the hall, and asked for a definition of *communication*, there would be 10 differing answers. Fisher summarized a diverse range of definitions, including the transmission of symbols model (Shannon & Weaver, 1949) and the idea of "shared meaning" (Gode, 1959). The common property is that communication is a process based on social integration. He concluded that defining communication is "incredibly simple. ... But understanding communication is considerably more complex" (p. 10). Hence, a definition of *communication* ensues from the perspective employed to understand it, not the other way around.

THE NARROW FOCUS ON MEDIA MANAGEMENT

This distinction between knowledge and understanding is important to the domain of media management. Researchers in other disciplines have studied media management as both the dependent and the independent variable, usually the latter. But media management has not been their focus for long. Sociologists and organization communication researchers are more interested in how people behave in groups or cultures. Psychologists study individual behavior. Researchers in business schools seek to understand the managerial process. To do this, some develop models that define the process. Others compile lists of functions that describe the process. The most dedicated find ways to explain the process.

Because of the recent institutionalizing of electronic media study, some researchers feel ill at ease borrowing from economics and business. However, they may be falsely basing the precedence of other fields on ivy-covered buildings. Just as the philosophy of science precedes discipline-specific discussions of theory and methodology, the broader study of communication precedes other fields of human science (Schramm, 1971; Thayer, 1968). Does historical precedence give a given social field squatter's rights to a domain of inquiry? Rather than a media management researcher being concerned with *doing* economics, the economist might just as well be worried about *doing* media management.

This *doing* is the essence of any specialty area's domain of inquiry. The underlying assumption that particular problems must be unique to a field is not new. Devons and Gluckman (1964) proposed that researchers have a duty to follow "a rule of disciplined refusal to trespass on the field of others" (p. 168). However, strict adherence to the rule would have prevented Watzlawick, Beavin, and Jackson (1967) from crossing over from the psychology department into the domain of communication, with their pragmatic perspective and modified general systems theory. The general systems approach has been adopted recently by media management theorists (Covington, 1994; Sherman, 1987).

Unique theory and a corresponding set of problems present one way to delineate a unique domain for communication research. Despite the withering of effects-oriented domains, such as cognitive dissonance (Festinger, 1962) and persuasion (Hovland, Janis, & Kelley, 1953), there are several enduring theoretical perspectives under which mass communication researchers labor. The uses and gratifications paradigm (Blumler & Katz, 1974), the agenda-setting function of the media (McCombs & Shaw, 1972), and knowledge gap studies (Tichenor, Donohue, & Olien, 1970) are three examples of domains of inquiry unique to mass communication research.

Media scholars should not suffer the criticisms of older fields of science, such as economics and business. The media industries are too ubiquitous to be unimportant. Neither should researchers in the social science disciplines envy scholars in the hard sciences. Chemistry squandered centuries of research on alchemy. Medicine was practiced by barbers not so long ago. Even today, physicists cannot decide whether light is a particle or a wave. Indeed, light is a wave *and* a particle, depending on the type of experiment and methodology.

Krippendorf (1969) said, "problems are the sole motivation for inquiries" (p. 112). Regardless of the inquiry, methods are only tools to solve problems. Maslow (1946) argued against means centering, believing that it leads to a hierarchy of sciences and a reification of methodology. The kinds of problems—the domain of inquiry—change over the years, but the development of theory and explanations is constant. Capella (1987) could just as well have been speaking of mass media management when he summed it up this way:

> The most accurate and least explicit definition of interpersonal communication as a field of study would be what researchers do and what they allow other researchers to publish under the title of interpersonal communications. On this view, a definition of interpersonal communication will always be incapable of capturing the history and dynamic current affairs that characterize an active and lively scholarly community bridging several disciplines. (p. 185)

WHAT MAKES MEDIA INDUSTRIES DIFFERENT?

The first step in staking out a specialty area such as media management is to enumerate ways in which that area is special to media studies. Lavine and Wackman (1988) identified five factors that differentiate media industries from most manufacturing concerns: (a) the "perishable commodity" nature of the product, (b) the type of employees (e.g., being highly creative and perceiving themselves as members of a profession), (c) the type of organization structure ("flexible, horizontal structure"), (d) the societal role of the media (e.g., high visibility and large influence), and (e) the blurring of lines among the traditional media. The first and third factors are probably the least useful distinctions because other nonmedia businesses deal in perishable commodities and operate with a horizontal structure.

Sherman (1987) linked 10 major components of systems theory to media management. In particular, he noted, "the media are characterized by a high degree of interrelationship and interdependence with other economic, social, political and cultural systems" (p. 41). Based on a careful reading of the few media management textbooks that address theoretical issues, the following list suggests how media industries are different from other kinds of industries.

1. *Media industries are often larger than life.* On the surface, studying media industries is merely analyzing business and finance. Some would argue that one business is much the same as another, with minor differences. Yet Irving Berlin would have had us believe that "there's no business like show business" (*Annie Get*

Your Gun, 1947). Is this necessarily an exaggeration? Is there another area of management and finance connected to as much larger-than-life excitement than that of media industries?

2. *Media industries operate in a fishbowl.* Marcus (1986) postulated an ego variable among media managers that is unmatched in other industries. Most certainly, the decisions (and subsequent successes and failures) of media managers frequently receive greater attention than other types of business, with the possible exception of sports franchises. Media managers are closely identified with a highly visible industry, such that they often become a public extension of that industry. Because the media are continually visible, almost by definition, their managers are closely linked to the media by a wide segment of the public. For example, it is not unusual for the manager of a broadcast station, to take personal any criticism of station policy. In essence, such managers become their own stations.

3. *Media industries lack unique expertise in the eyes of consumers.* Few ordinary citizens pretend to know much about banking, manufacturing, or providing complex services. Yet many who own a television set or read a magazine seem to be experts on the media. This is the price the media pays for being ubiquitous. There is no shortage of people who think they understand the intricacies of the media, and therefore wonder why media managers are sometimes ineffectual. Unless there is a 265-million-barrel oil spill off the coast of Alaska, there are few who would dare to question the management of a company like Exxon. Nevertheless, almost anyone can offer an opinion on the running of mass entertainment companies, such as television networks and motion picture studios.

4. *Media industries manage creativity.* With rare exceptions, mass media managers deal with an unusually free-spirited band of practitioners. Of course, the intangible qualities of a business can haunt managers in any area of endeavor. It is in the mass media industries, however, that nearly all of the employees are producing an intangible product held loosely together by something as nebulous as human creativity. For example, as salespeople, mass media managers are selling the sizzle more often than the steak. Ettema and Whitney (1982) provided many directions for studying the role of creativity in mass media organizations.

5. *Media industries are webs of gatekeeping.* Although the concept of gatekeeping originally described the activities of wire copy editors in the newspaper industry (White, 1950), high-level media managers today are frequently involved with news decisions. Moreover, it is no exaggeration that the media act as a giant filter for all public discourse. Some would argue (e.g., Postman, 1985) that the media even prevent public discourse. As gatekeepers, the media industries are responsible for agenda-managing the public's access to information. Dimmick and Coit (1982) suggested that media decisions are made on many levels, such that the organization acts as a gatekeeper. Whitney (1982) summarized studies in which gatekeeping varied with the different levels of analysis, from individual to institutional.

Such an approach to gatekeeping suggests many research questions for those who would claim the domain of media industry studies. If media systems are hierarchical, then who are the real gatekeepers? How often do the media managers, from the top level, exert control on the free flow of information? This list is far from comprehensive. A few points are certainly debatable. At the very least, most of these alleged differences make interesting research questions. At the most, however, they may point to a theoretical framework for media management.

AREAS FOR FURTHER RESEARCH

Starting with the idea of gatekeeping, there is a need for a comprehensive model of media management. Such a conceptual framework should embody one or more of the differences exhibited by media industries, as listed earlier. Webster (personal communication, November 29, 1990) suggested that such a framework should include "managing creativity on one hand and managing the audience's consumption of that creative output on the other."

The call to theoretical commitment by Krippendorf (1969) suggests that research into media management should spend more effort on building theory. For example, there is a need for an examination of the exact role of the media manager, beyond that of a gatekeeper. Does the influence of management operate at different levels (e.g., economic, political, social) of the organization?

Future studies of media industries could focus on more critical, and less administrative, aspects of sales and management. Webster (1989) mapped the study of media management under the realm of administrative studies, but called for a commitment to disciplined pluralism of both realms. A robust investigation of the forces at work in media ownership may serve to enhance understanding of media management. Students of media studies would benefit from more attention to broader issues, although not necessarily at the expense of a practical education.

Critical examination of management issues need not be polemic. One approach involves calling into question the various assumptions about how popular media operate. For example, the continued importance of schedule versus menu-based programming should be explored. Jankowski and Fuchs (1995) defended the status quo, but scholars have been slow to weigh in. The opposing viewpoints (e.g., Gilder, 1994) need to be tested by media management researchers.

Another approach is the reexamination of ownership issues. For example, a careful analysis of the underlying issues of merger mania in 1995 and 1996, beyond simple description, is needed. Although there seems to be no shortage of opinion, empirical evidence may be able to shed some light on whether media industries can continue to grow bigger when computer technologies are making independent production more feasible in terms of production and distribution.

Certainly, public policy is one area that has received scant attention from media management scholars. Is the private enterprise model that helped forge powerful American media industries still valid in an international market? Perhaps it is even more valid, but the assumptions about privatization could stand a thorough exploration with regard to different levels of government support for the media. For example, a research study could contrast the paths of foreign countries' forays into government-blessed private enterprise against recent domestic attempts to auction off additional digital channels to broadcasters for high-definition television.

Finally, more attention to the economics of new media technologies will likely foster media management research in the future. Willis and Willis (1993) commented on the challenges of technology, pointing out future directions for research. If management is dealing with people and money, the challenge may lie in effectively working with smaller staffs and more substantial capital outlays. The case study approach, as applied to media industries outside the United States (e.g., Akhavan-Majid, 1992), should be pursued with American media.

The common attribute shared by all of these approaches is a basic questioning of the way media managers think. The answer to where media management is headed does not necessarily lie in case-specific analysis (e.g., price-fixing at Los Angeles television stations). Researchers can contribute more by looking ahead than by reexamining where management has been in the past or near present.

An important step toward staking out a separate domain of inquiry for media management researchers will be to construct and follow a distinct theoretical framework. The key components of such a framework must address a broad range of perspectives, not just media economics and applied management strategy. Until the scope of research is widened, outside observers may continue to wonder if media management is a sovereign area of study.

REFERENCES

Akhavan-Majid, R. (1992). Public service broadcasting and the challenge of new technology: A case study of Japan's NHK. *Gazette, 50*(1), 21–36.

Berger, C. R., & Chaffee, S. H. (Eds.). (1987). The study of communication as a science. In C. R. Berger & S. H. Chaffee, *Handbook of communication science* (pp. 15–19). Newbury Park, CA: Sage.

Berlin, I. (1947). *Annie get your gun.* [Piano-vocal score]. New York: Berlin Music Co.

Brown, R. L. (1970). Approaches to the historical development of mass media studies. In J. Tunstall (Ed.), *Media sociology: A reader* (pp. 41–57). Urbana: University of Illinois Press.

Capella, J. N. (1987). Interpersonal communication: Definitions and fundamental questions. In C. R. Berger & S. H. Chaffee (Eds.), *Handbook of communication science* (pp. 184–238). Beverly Hills, CA: Sage.

Covington, W. C. (1994). *Systems theory applied to the management of television stations in the midst of a multichannel marketplace.* Unpublished dissertation, Bowling Green State University.

Devons, E., & Gluckman, M. (1964). Conclusion: Modes and consequences of limiting a field of study. In M. Gluckman (Ed.), *Closed systems and open minds: The limits of naivete in social anthropology* (pp. 158–262). Chicago: Aldine.

Dimmick, J., & Coit, P. (1982). Levels of analysis in mass media decision making: A taxonomy, research strategy, and illustrative data analysis. *Communication Research, 9*, 3–32.

Ettema, J. S., & Whitney, D. C. (Eds.). (1982). *Individuals in mass media organizations: Creativity and constraint.* Beverly Hills, CA: Sage.

Festinger, L. (1962). *A theory of cognitive dissonance.* Palo Alto, CA: Stanford University Press.

Fisher, B. A. (1978). *Perspectives on human communication.* New York: Macmillan.

Gerbner, G. (1983). Ferment in the field [Special issue]. *Journal of Communication, 33*(3).

Gilder, G. F. (1994). *Life after television* (Rev. ed.). New York: Norton.

Gode, A. (1959). What is communication? *Journal of Communication, 9*, 5.

Hovland, C. I., Janis, I. L., & Kelley, H. H. (1953). *Communication and persuasion.* New Haven, CT: Yale University Press.

Jankowski, G. F., & Fuchs, D. C. (1995). *Television today and tomorrow.* New York: Oxford University Press.

Krippendorf, K. (1969). Values, modes, and domains of inquiry into communication. *Journal of Communication, 19*(2), 105–133.

Lavine, J. M., & Wackman, D. B. (1988). *Managing media organizations.* White Plains, NY: Longman.

Marcus, N. (1986). *Broadcast and cable management.* Englewood Cliffs, NJ: Prentice-Hall.

Maslow, A. H. (1946). Problem-centering vs. means-centering in science. *Philosophy of Science, 13*, 326–331.

McCombs, M., & Shaw, D. (1972). The agenda-setting function of mass media. *Public Opinion Quarterly, 36*, 176–187.

Merton, R. K. (Ed.). (1957). The sociology of knowledge and mass communications. In R. K. Merton (Ed.), *Social theory and social structure* (Rev. ed., pp. 439–455). Glencoe, IL: The Free Press.

Postman, N. (1985). *Amusing ourselves to death: Public discourse in the age of show business.* New York: Viking.

Reinharz, S. (1982, August). *The future of feminist psychology.* Paper presented at the annual convention of the American Psychological Association, Washington, DC.

Sayre, W. W. (1948). Communication as a first principle in philosophy. *Quarterly Journal of Speech, 34*, 128–136.

Schramm, W. L. (1963). *The science of human communication.* New York: Basic Books.

Schramm, W. L. (1971). Nature of communication between humans. In W. L. Schramm & D. F. Roberts (Eds.), *The process and effects of mass communication* (pp. 3–53). Urbana: University of Illinois Press.

Shannon, C. E., & Weaver, W. (1949). *The mathematical theory of communication.* Urbana: University of Illinois Press.

Sherman, B. L. (1987). *Telecommunications management: The broadcast & cable industries.* New York: McGraw-Hill.

Tan, C. Z. (1986, August). *Ferment in the field revisited: Its basis and future.* Paper presented at the annual meeting of the Association for Education in Journalism and Mass Communication, Norman, OK.

Thayer, L. (1968). Communication: *Sine qua non* of the behavioral sciences. In D. L. Arm (Ed.), *Journeys in science; single steps, great strides* (pp. 48–77). Albuquerque, NM: University of New Mexico Press.

Tichenor, P. J., Donohue, G. A., & Olien, C. N. (1970). Mass media flow and differential growth in knowledge. *Public Opinion Quarterly, 34*, 159–170.

Watzlawick, P., Beavin, J. H., & Jackson, D. D. (1967). *Pragmatics of human communication.* New York: Norton.

Webster, J. (1989). Media study in a time of technological change. *Feedback, 30*(3), 20–24.

Webster, J. (1990, February). *Response to papers.* Remarks presented at the meeting of the Broadcast Association, Las Vegas.

Westley, B. H., & MacLean, M. (1957). A conceptual model for communication research. *Journalism Quarterly, 34*, 31–38.

White, D. (1950). The "gate keeper": A case study in the selection of news. *Journalism Quarterly, 27*, 283–290.

Whitney, D. C. (1982). Mass communicator studies: Similarity, difference, and level of analysis. In J. S. Ettema & D. C. Whitney (Eds.), *Individuals in mass media organizations: Creativity and constraint* (pp. 241–254). Beverly Hills, CA: Sage.

Willis, J., & Willis, D. B. (1993). *New directions in media management.* Boston: Allyn & Bacon.

Author Index

Subject Index

191